S0-ALL-390

Leadership and Management
of Quality in Higher Education

Leadership and Management of Quality in Higher Education

EDITED BY
CHENICHERI SID NAIR,
LEONARD WEBSTER
AND PATRICIE MERTOVA

Chandos Publishing
Oxford • Cambridge • New Delhi

Chandos Publishing
TBAC Business Centre
Avenue 4
Station Lane
Witney
Oxford OX28 4BN
UK
Tel: +44 (0) 1993 848726
Email: info@chandospublishing.com
www.chandospublishing.com

Chandos Publishing is an imprint of Woodhead Publishing Limited

Woodhead Publishing Limited
Abington Hall
Granta Park
Great Abington
Cambridge CB21 6AH
UK
www.woodheadpublishing.com

First published in 2010

ISBN:
978 1 84334 576 3

© The editors and the contributors, 2010

British Library Cataloguing-in-Publication Data.
A catalogue record for this book is available from the British Library.

All rights reserved. No part of this publication may be reproduced, stored in or introduced into a retrieval system, or transmitted, in any form, or by any means (electronic, mechanical, photocopying, recording or otherwise) without the prior written permission of the Publishers. This publication may not be lent, resold, hired out or otherwise disposed of by way of trade in any form of binding or cover other than that in which it is published without the prior consent of the Publishers. Any person who does any unauthorised act in relation to this publication may be liable to criminal prosecution and civil claims for damages.

The Publishers make no representation, express or implied, with regard to the accuracy of the information contained in this publication and cannot accept any legal responsibility or liability for any errors or omissions.

The material contained in this publication constitutes general guidelines only and does not represent to be advice on any particular matter. No reader or purchaser should act on the basis of material contained in this publication without first taking professional advice appropriate to their particular circumstances. Any screenshots in this publication are the copyright of the website owner(s), unless indicated otherwise.

Typeset by RefineCatch Limited, Bungay, Suffolk
Printed in the UK and USA

Printed in the UK by 4edge Limited - www.4edge.co.uk

Contents

List of figures and tables

Figures

Tables

About the authors

Thuwayba Al Barwani (EdD) is a member of the State Council (Upper Chamber of the Omani Parliament), Associate Professor of Curriculum and Instruction and the Dean of the College of Education at the Sultan Qaboos University. She is also a member of the Council for Higher Education which is the highest policy making body in higher education in Oman and a member of the Founding Committee and a member of the Board of Trustees of Al Sharqiya Private University. She served as the Undersecretary of Social Affairs and Undersecretary of Social Development in the Government of Oman, and has presented extensively on issues related to social development. She has researched and published in areas of quality in higher education, teaching English as a foreign language, education and empowerment of Omani women, gender issues in education and family studies.

Dr Lorraine Bennett is the Associate Director of the Centre for the Advancement of Teaching and Learning at Monash University, Australia. She has extensive experience in senior leadership, having held a large number of roles in higher education and local and state government. The main focus of her work is in the scholarship of learning and teaching and covers staff development, teaching, research and national teaching excellence projects. Her special areas of interest include leadership capacity building, organisational reform, change management, strategic planning, policy development, quality improvement and internationalisation.

Associate Professor Martin Carroll is a Pro Vice-Chancellor and the Director, Teaching & Learning at Charles Darwin University in Australia. He was previously an international higher education consultant based in the Sultanate of Oman. He specialises in assisting governments with the establishment or refinement of higher education systems. Previously, Martin has served as Consulting Director for the Oman Accreditation Council, Audit Director for the Australian Universities Quality Agency, and in senior quality management roles at Victoria University of Wellington and Massey University (both in New Zealand). He is a founding member of the Universities Quality Assurance International Board in Dubai, and is an external reviewer for numerous external quality agencies worldwide.

Dr Hamish Coates leads higher education research at the Australian Council for Educational Research. Over the last decade he has designed and led numerous projects that have influenced international, national and institutional research, policy and practice. Dr Coates' research and publications focus on the definition, measurement and evaluation of educational processes, contexts and outcomes. His active interests include large-scale educational evaluation, tertiary education policy, learner engagement, institutional leadership, quality assurance, and assessment methodology. He teaches research methods at all levels, works routinely with national and institutional advisory groups, publishes and presents widely. He has worked with all Australian universities and numerous training organisations, serves on a number of editorial boards, has been a consultant to the World Bank and OECD, and has held visiting fellowships at the University of Michigan and UNESCO's International Institute for Educational Planning.

Dr Anci Du Toit joined Monash South Africa in 2009 as Programme Accreditation and Review Manager. From 2005, she was the Coordinator: Quality Promotion of the Support Services at the University of Johannesburg, South Africa. She presented papers and workshops in the field of Quality Management at various national and international conferences. Previously (since 2002), she was a researcher in the Quality Care Unit at the Rand Afrikaans University. In this capacity, she was responsible for coordinating, advising on and supporting the self-evaluation and peer review processes of academic departments and service units. She also conducted surveys on student experience at the institution. Before that, she lectured in Zulu Linguistics for more than 20 years.

Robyn Harris is Director – Governance, Policy and Planning Services at Victoria University in Australia. She is responsible for leadership and management of the Division which incorporates the Quality, Information and Planning Branch and Governance and Policy Branch. Prior to joining VU in 2008, Robyn was Director of the Centre for Higher Education Quality at Monash University, Australia. She was an Audit Director for the Australian Universities Quality Agency (AUQA) from 2002–5, where she was involved in the development of AUQA systems and policies and in eight Cycle 1 university audits. Before joining AUQA, Robyn was Acting Director of the New Zealand Universities Academic Audit Unit

(Te Wāhanga Tātari). She has extensive experience of undertaking quality audits internationally including in Singapore, Hong Kong, Malaysia, Vietnam and the People's Republic of China, and has led consultancies on the development of institutional quality systems and external quality audit in Fiji, New Zealand and Hong Kong. She holds the qualifications of BA and MA (First Class Honours).

Lee Harvey is Professor at Copenhagen Business School. Prior to that he established and was Director of both the Centre for Research into Quality at University of Central England in Birmingham and the Centre for Research and Evaluation at Sheffield Hallam University. He was also Director of Research at the Higher Education Academy. Lee has wide experience of social research as a research methodologist and social philosopher. He has a teaching qualification alongside his Master's in Information Technology and Doctorate in Sociology. His areas are higher education policy, on issues of quality, employability and student feedback. He is widely published with over 35 books and research monographs and over 120 articles in international journals, books and compendiums. He has been a quality adviser to institutions across the world. He is regularly invited as a keynote speaker at major international conferences.

Associate Professor Jan Holzer lectures in Political Science at the Faculty of Social Studies at Masaryk University (Czech Republic). He is also an Associate Dean for Teaching and Learning in the Faculty of Social Studies, Editor of the *Central European Political Science* journal and a Deputy Chair of the Czech Political Science Society. He is the author and co-author of a number of academic publications, such as: *Communism in the Czech Republic* (1999); *The Russian Political System: In Search of the State* (2001); *The Russian Political Parties: In Search of the Identity* (2004); and *Post-Communist Undemocratic Regimes* (2009). He has also published numerous academic journal papers in Czech, Polish and English. He specialises in the theory of undemocratic and 'hybrid' regimes; the phenomenon of transformation of the post-communist regimes (with particular focus on Russia and the Post-Soviet republics); the position of political science as an academic discipline; and modern Czech politics. His involvement in the field of quality and evaluation includes: membership in a disciplinal panel for Political Science and Law of the Czech Research Council and the faculty co-ordinator of a large project entitled 'Implementation of a national system of tertiary qualifications'.

Professor Bente Kristensen is the former Deputy President at the Copenhagen Business School (CBS) (1994–2006), where she (among other duties) had the overall responsibility for quality at CBS. She has a Master's degree in German Language for Special Purposes and Law. She is now a quality adviser at the CBS Learning Lab. She is the former chair of the European Higher Education Society and the European Centre for Strategic Management of Universities Benchmarking Programme. She was co-founder of the Danish Evaluation Agency and was its first Chair of the Board. Further, she was previously a member of the Board of the Norwegian Agency for Quality Assurance in Education and member of an international advisory committee to the Swedish National Agency for Higher Education. She is a member of the pool of evaluators of the European University Association Institutional Evaluation Programme. She has been a member of numerous evaluation and accreditation teams across Europe.

Dr Laurie Lomas was until very recently Assistant Director (Programmes) of the King's Learning Institute at King's College London. Since his semi-retirement he has been Senior Lecturer in Higher Education at the Institute and now works on a Higher Education Funding Council for England funded Leadership Development project and supervises international PhD students. While at King's College London and his previous institution, Canterbury Christ Church University Business School, his major research interest and many of his publications have been related to higher education quality management. For the last few years, Laurie has been a regular contributor at the annual European Conference on Educational Research.

Ranald Macdonald is Emeritus Professor in Academic Development at Sheffield Hallam University in the UK, following early retirement in 2009, and is a freelance higher education consultant. A former Co-Chair of the UK's Staff and Educational Development Association, he was also founder and Chair of its Research Committee until 2008, is a SEDA Fellowship holder and a current member of its Executive Committee. Ranald was awarded a UK National Teaching Fellowship in 2005, the Williams Evans Visiting Fellowship to the University of Otago, Dunedin, New Zealand in 2007 and is a Fellow of the UK's Higher Education Academy. His main research and scholarly interests are in the areas of academic development; assessment and plagiarism; problem and enquiry-based learning; enhancing links between research, learning and teaching; and professional development for the leadership and management of educational change. He was Co-Director of Sheffield Hallam's Centre for Promoting Learner Autonomy from 2005–7 and has extensive experience of academic development activity throughout the UK and internationally.

Dr Patricie Mertova is currently a Research Fellow in the Department of Education, University of Oxford, England. She was previously a Research Officer at the University of Queensland, and, prior to that, a Research Fellow in the Centre for the Advancement of Learning and Teaching (CALT) and the Centre for Higher Education Quality (CHEQ), Monash University, Australia. She has recently completed her PhD focusing on the academic voice in higher education quality. She has research expertise in the areas of higher education and higher education quality. Her background is also in the areas of linguistics, translation, cross-cultural communication and foreign languages.

Nicolene Murdoch is the Director of Institutional Planning and Quality Assurance at Monash South Africa. In her current role, she has a broad portfolio, which includes: strategic planning, institutional governance, institutional audit, programme accreditation, coordination of institutional surveys and evaluation, and enhancement of quality. Previously (until 2006), she was the Quality Assurance Manager at the Monash South Africa campus. Ms Murdoch also lectures on a part-time basis in the Faculty of Education at the University of Johannesburg, and does higher education and industry consultancy work in the field of quality assurance. Further, she regularly presents at conferences and has authored a number of journal papers in the field of quality assurance.

Dr Sid Nair is Professor of the Higher Education Department at the Centre for Advancement of Teaching and Learning, University of Western Australia (UWA), Perth. Prior to his appointment to UWA, he was Quality Adviser (Research and Evaluation) in the Centre for Higher Education Quality at Monash University, Australia. He has an extensive expertise in the area of quality development and evaluation, and he also has considerable editorial experience. Currently, he is Associate Editor of the *International Journal of Quality Assurance in Engineering and Technology Education*. Prior to this he was also a Managing Editor of the *Electronic Journal of Science Education*. Professor Nair is also an international consultant in a number of countries in quality and evaluations: Oman, Saudi and India. He is also involved in a project to implement effective student evaluations across Indian universities.

Mohamed Eltahir Osman (PhD) is the Assistant Dean for Postgraduate Studies and Research, College of Education at Sultan Qaboos University and Assistant Professor of Instructional Systems Technology. He teaches postgraduate and undergraduate courses in the areas of instructional systems design, information and communication technologies, and research in educational technology. He was previously a Senior Instructional Designer responsible for management training and human resource development at FedEx Corp, Memphis, Tennessee. He has presented and researched extensively on issues related to quality assurance, web-based learning environments, e-portals, student empowerment and improving academic performance. He has also been a reviewer of a number of journals, including the *American Journal of Educational Technology Research and Development*.

Dr Fernando F. Padró is Associate Professor in the EdD Programme in Educational Leadership at Cambridge College, Cambridge, Massachusetts, USA. He has been actively involved in researching the impact of the field of quality on school and university organisational behaviour and policy for more than 25 years. He has written a number of articles pertinent to issues of quality, quality assurance and accreditation in higher education. He has also presented on these subjects at over 50 conferences and similar forums in Australia, Europe and the USA. He has been a Malcolm Baldrige National Quality Award Examiner in the USA as well as a Peer Reviewer with the Academic Quality Improvement Programme project and is currently responsible for his college's School of Education Teacher Education Accreditation Council accreditation process. At present, he is the Chair of the American Society for Quality's (ASQ) Higher Education Advisory Committee and ASQ's Education Division Vice-Chair for International Activities.

Dr Christine Teelken is an Associate Professor at the VU University, Amsterdam, while previously she was at the Radboud University Nijmegen, Netherlands. Her research interests involve higher education, managerialism, new public management and diversity. She has published nationally and internationally in this field (e.g. in journals such as *Research in Higher Education* and *Higher Education Policy*) and is currently preparing an edited volume for Routledge on 'Leadership, Management and the Professions in the Public Sector' (to be published in 2010). She has initiated the European Group for Organizational Studies (EGOS), a scholarly association which aims to further the theoretical and/or empirical advancement of knowledge about organisations, and is currently on the EGOS board. She is also a co-convenor for the European Conference for Educational Research, recently, for example, featuring a critique of the Bologna Process. She is also a member of the editorial board of the *Journal of Change Management*.

Dr Jani Ursin is a Senior Researcher at the Finnish Institute for Educational Research of the University of Jyväskylä, Finland. His research focuses on quality assurance in higher education and more recently on the mergers of Finnish universities. He is also a national project manager of the Organization for European Cooperation and Development Feasibility Study for the International Assessment of Higher Education Learning Outcomes. Jani is a link convenor of the European Educational Research Association's Network 22: Research in Higher Education, and also the Chair of the Consortium of Higher Education Researchers in Finland.

Professor Graham Webb is the Deputy Vice-Chancellor of the University of New England in Australia. His previous career includes eleven years at Monash University in Australia where he was Pro Vice-Chancellor (Quality) and for a period, CEO of Monash College Pty Ltd (a wholly owned company of Monash University comprising six educational businesses); eleven years at the University of Otago in New Zealand; six years at the University of the West Indies in Jamaica; and seven years at the University of Ulster in Ireland. He holds the qualifications of BA Honours, MSc, PhD with distinction and PGCE. Graham is author or editor of nine academic books and numerous book chapters and journal articles concerning the theory and practice of teaching and learning in higher education and staff development. He is an Editorial Advisory Board member for five international journals and has played an active role internationally in quality assurance and improvement. He chaired the first and subsequent audits for the Australian Universities Quality Agency and is a trainer, auditor or consultant for national academic audit agencies in six countries. In 2008, he received the Australian National Quality Award.

Associate Professor Len Webster has expertise in educational policy, educational development, quality development and flexible learning. Currently he is an Educational Adviser in the Centre for the Advancement of Learning and Teaching at Monash University, Australia, with specific expertise in digital learning research, academic development, open and distance learning. His previous book on narrative inquiry provided insight in the use of alternative methods of researching complex learning environments. Dr Webster is also an editorial reviewer for a number of educational journals. Previously, he was the director of an educational development unit in the Faculty of Law, Monash University (where he was the Faculty Quality Development Coordinator), was the inaugural chair of the Monash University Quality Network and a reviewer of the Australian University Quality Agency conference proceedings.

Preface

Quality development may be an agent of improving learning and teaching or at risk of becoming another bureaucratic exercise attempting to quantify the complexities and variables within education. Currently, quality development is a part of the higher education rhetoric both nationally and internationally, and it is a topical yet often misunderstood term in the higher education sector. Is it driven by the voice of those who teach or by governing and political forces with different agendas?

This book provides informed commentary on the concept and practice of higher education quality by both developed and developing nations in an increasingly complex world. There are 13 chapters in total giving an outline of not only the growth of the quality movement but also perspectives of the state of play at various institutions. According to the chapter focus, the book is divided into the following six sections: Overview, Leadership of quality in higher education, Approaches of managers to quality in higher education, Auditing quality in higher education, Academic development and quality in higher education, and Resources and trends in higher education quality.

The contributions in this book capture the experiences of senior leaders, managers and practitioners from around the world. In this publication, we also draw attention to the human-centred approach to quality, as we argue that in any activity there is a need to take account of human values and attitudes.

In brief the parts and chapters are:

Part 1: Overview

Chapter 1   Growth of the quality movement in higher education

This chapter is written by Dr Patricie Mertova of the University of Oxford, UK and Associate Professor Len Webster from Monash University, Melbourne, Australia with Professor Sid Nair from the University of Western Australia, Perth, Australia. It portrays the landscape of complex factors impacting the notion of higher education quality. In particular, the chapter highlights the need for the higher education sector to inculcate quality as a culture with the aim to improve the educational experiences of stakeholders.

Part 2: Leadership of quality in higher education

Chapter 2   Initiative-based quality development and the role of distributed leadership

This chapter is written by Professor Bente Kristensen and Professor Lee Harvey from the Copenhagen Business School in Denmark. It describes a distributed leadership-based approach to a quality culture and highlights the role of human-centred approach in quality, specifically the role of leadership to engage all levels of the university.

Chapter 3   A leadership model for higher education quality

This chapter is written by Associate Professor Fernando Padró from Cambridge College, USA. In it he provides a model for senior university leaders who are faced with the challenges of meeting the quality demands of modern higher education. He particularly argues that leadership in higher education is complex and a quality model provides an approach to successfully and proactively lead universities in the current times.

Chapter 4   A framework for engaging leadership in higher education quality systems

This chapter is written by Dr Lorraine Bennett from Monash University, Melbourne, Australia, and provides a framework to engaging leadership. In particular, it outlines a practical or 'hands-on' approach to leading improvement with the capacity to be applied across not only the higher education sector but also to other organisational structures.

Part 3: Approaches of managers to quality in higher education

Chapter 5   Quality management in higher education: a comparative study of the United Kingdom, the Netherlands and Finland

This chapter is written by Dr Laurie Lomas from King's College London (UK), Associate Professor Christine Teelken from VU University Amsterdam (Netherlands) and Dr Jani Ursin from the Finnish Institute for Educational Research, University of Jyväskylä, Finland. The chapter is a case study of lecturers' perceptions of quality assurance and enhancement in three European countries: the United Kingdom, the Netherlands and Finland. In particular, it highlights the value of the 'academic voice' in achieving quality outcomes.

Chapter 6   Towards a culture of quality in South African higher education

This chapter is written by Nicolene Murdoch and Dr Anci Du Toit from Monash South Africa, South Africa. The uniqueness of this chapter is that it provides an overview of quality in a developing nation, South Africa. It also highlights the role that an institution has in advancing the quality movement within the complexities of a developing nation.

Part 4: Auditing quality in higher education

Chapter 7   Auditors' perspectives on quality in higher education

This chapter is written by Robyn Harris of Victoria University, Australia and Professor Graham Webb, University of New England, Australia. It provides a conceptual framework for External Quality Assurance (EQA) and proposes ways in which the EQA can evolve to better suit the needs of higher education. In particular, it addresses the perception that EQA is a value-adding exercise rather than a bureaucratic one.

Part 5: Academic development and quality in higher education

Chapter 8   Academic development as change leadership in higher education

This chapter is written by Emeritus Professor Ranald Macdonald from Sheffield Hallam University, UK. It highlights the strategic role of academic developers in drawing on ideas for institutional development and quality, and also provides an approach for change management.

Chapter 9   Quality in the transitional process of establishing political science as a new discipline in Czech higher education (post 1989)

This chapter is written by Associate Professor Jan Holzer of Masaryk University, Czech Republic. It provides a transformative picture of how quality has evolved since the re-establishment of academic freedom in the Czech Republic. In particular, it gives an insight into quality from a discipline-specific angle.

Chapter 10   Academic development and quality in Oman: mapping the terrain

This chapter is written by Associate Professor Thuwayba Al Barwani and Assistant Professor Mohamed Eltahir Osman of Sultan Qaboos University, Sultanate of Oman. It draws on case studies to illustrate the strengths and pitfalls of a diversified quality system within an institution. Specifically, it shows the necessity of a uniform approach to quality for quality outcomes.

Part 6: Resources and trends in higher education quality

Chapter 11   New directions in quality management

This chapter is written by Dr Hamish Coates, Australian Council for Educational Research, Melbourne, Australia. It is the first in the section on resources and trends in higher education quality, and specifically reviews the use of feedback instruments and makes predictive comments on how these instruments for measuring quality may change in the future.

Chapter 12   Dubai's Free Zone model for leadership in the external quality assurance of higher education

This chapter is written by Associate Professor Martin Carroll of Charles Darwin University, Australia, Higher Education Consultant in the Sultanate of Oman. It considers the importance of contextualised quality assurance and situates this in the developing higher education system of Dubai. Most significantly, this chapter describes how one nation, Dubai, is satisfying the demands of a local context while retaining the international nature and quality of imported programmes using a flexible and pluralistic quality framework.

Chapter 13   Trends in quality development

This chapter is written by Robyn Harris of Victoria University, Australia and Professor Graham Webb of the University of New England, Australia, and provides a systematic approach to quality development of teaching and learning. Specifically, it suggests that new data capacities lead to a changed emphasis for management. It also provides a closing summary to this book by pointing to the future of higher education quality.

Part 1
Overview

Growth of the quality movement in higher education

Patricie Mertova, Len Webster and Sid Nair

Abstract

This chapter aims to provide background to quality in higher education in order to situate the subsequent chapters in a particular context. The chapter describes the development of the quality movement, including its origins and how it was introduced into higher education. It outlines the understandings of the notion of quality in higher education and gives an overview of critique of quality in the higher education context.

Key words: development of the quality movement; higher education; quality enhancement; quality assurance.

Introduction

The subject of quality has been a global issue in higher education for nearly two decades, during which time quality has developed from a marginal to a central concern. The greater focus on quality in higher education has resulted from a range of competing factors, the most prominent being: political control over higher education, growth in the number and changes in the expectations of students, and financial control on the part of national governments. Quality monitoring has become a mechanism for governments worldwide to tackle these competing factors. At the same time, it can be argued that it has been frequently employed to disguise the dominant focus on accountability, rather than enhancement, in higher education (Barnett, 1992; Harvey and Green, 1993; Morley, 1997; Lomas, 2000; Harvey, 2004, 2005).

It can be further argued that the significant changes in approaches to quality in higher education have been management-driven, underpinned by a desire to develop a range of mechanisms of control (Lomas, 2000; Jones, 2003). However, human-centred aspects, which play a crucial role in higher education, have been largely missing in quality mechanisms. Furthermore, the management-driven mechanisms and systems have frequently been found unsuitable or only partly suitable for the higher education sector, due to their disregard for the nature of higher education and its employees, in particular the academics (Birnbaum, 2000; Green, 1994). In response, this book focuses on the human-centred aspects and related issues regarding higher education quality. The book represents the international perspectives of a number of higher education leaders, managers and auditors, including academics and academic developers.

Where did quality come from?

Quality control as a practice has been around in some form since at least the Middle Ages, when individual guilds took up the responsibility for overseeing the quality of products. More formal quality control, focused on inspection, measurement and testing, came to the fore of professional practice only at the beginning of the twentieth century, accompanying the increase in mass production. Systematic quality management originated in the manufacturing sector in the 1900s with a rapid growth of standardisation. Until 1915, Great Britain was the only country in the world with some type of national standardisation, and then the number of standardisation organisations throughout the world increased dramatically, particularly between 1916 and 1932. The United States joined the movement around 1917 (Voehl, 1994).

After the Second World War, Japan became the main driver of the efficiency/quality movement. In 1946, US General MacArthur was assigned to oversee the re-building of Japan, particularly through creating quality control tools and techniques to improve efficiency of Japanese industries. General MacArthur invited W. E. Deming and J. M. Juran, two key individuals involved in the development of modern quality concepts in the USA at that time, to lead the quality drive. Deming and Juran promoted collaborative quality concepts to Japanese businesses, and within twenty years, quality became a worldwide movement. Beginning with Deming and Juran in the late 1940s/early 1950s, the movement was eventually reinvigorated in the United States by Feigenbaum in the 1960s. Feigenbaum introduced and coined the concept of Total Quality Control (TQC).

In the 1980s, Britain took the lead in the quality movement with the introduction of BS 5750 as an international quality standard. Britain first introduced it as a quality standard for the European Commission, and later it was accepted as an international standard known as ISO 9000 (Voehl, 1994).

The concept of quality has undergone a number of changes in focus. Quality control dominated manufacturing and engineering from the 1940s to the 1980s. The 1990s saw the emergence of quality as a profession with a focus on quality systems when, not only in Britain but also in many other Western European countries, quality spread from industry and business into the public sector, including healthcare and higher education (Westerheijden et al., 1994; Woodhouse, 2004).

Quality development in higher education

The origins of accreditation systems as a form of quality assurance in US higher education date back to the late nineteenth and early twentieth centuries (Woodhouse, 2004). The British system of external examiners assuring standards in universities can be traced back to the mid-nineteenth century (DETYA, 2000). Another form of official quality assurance was introduced into a part of the British higher education sector (the former polytechnics) in the mid-1960s. However, external quality assurance, as 'a world-wide phenomenon', began only in the 1980s and grew rapidly in the 1990s (Woodhouse, 2004).

Higher education systems of the former Soviet satellite countries in Central and Eastern Europe (such as Czechoslovakia, Poland and others) were virtually unaffected by the quality phenomenon in Western Europe in the 1980s. This was due to the Communist rule in these countries. Quality of higher education was claimed by the individual Communist states, however it was rarely examined. Quality monitoring in the form of state-controlled accreditation was introduced shortly after the fall of the Communist regimes when the Czech Republic became the first to establish a higher education accreditation agency in 1990. This was largely an attempt of the newly established state to hold some form of control over higher education institutions which had gained extensive academic freedom. The approaches in other post-Communist countries of Central and Eastern Europe were similar (CHES, 2001; Van der Wende and Westerheijden, 2003).

In the 1990s, a range of quality management systems was introduced into Western European higher education from the business sector.

Western European higher education institutions, particularly in Britain, started adopting these quality management systems in the hope of increasing the efficiency and effectiveness of the higher education sector (Lomas, 2000).

Management systems were first introduced into higher education in the USA in the early 1960s (Birnbaum, 2000). Birnbaum argued that management systems ('management fads') were usually introduced first into the business or government sectors and were subsequently adapted by higher education. Common to such systems was their fairly quick succession: attention to one approach was generally soon replaced by another. The Planning Programming Budgeting System (PPBS) was one of the first management systems initially introduced to the US Defense Department which then migrated into the higher education sector. Recent similar examples include Business Process Reengineering (BPR) and Benchmarking (Birnbaum, 2000).

Benchmarking and Total Quality Management (TQM)/Continuous Quality Improvement (CQI) belong to the better known management techniques adopted within the context of higher education (Birnbaum, 2000).

Benchmarking was introduced to US higher education in the 1980s. It required 'an institution to study the processes of others and then use these understandings to set future goals or benchmarks for itself' (Birnbaum, 2000, p. 81). Performance indicators form a part of the process of benchmarking. Birnbaum pointed out that, as it proved difficult to measure productivity in the service sector in general (and in higher education in particular), the most problematic aspect of benchmarking and performance indicators has been that they were, to a large extent, based on the assumption that only what is measurable is worthwhile.

TQM was introduced by Deming, who developed statistical control and sampling processes for a telephone company in the USA in the late 1940s. It was increasingly applied in US higher education in the 1980s and 1990s, latterly being renamed CQI (Birnbaum, 2000). As Birnbaum noted (p. 107): 'TQM/CQI was perhaps the first management fad in higher education that provoked a serious discussion not only of its technical merits, but also of its educational and social implications.'

Birnbaum also highlighted that no management technique could perfectly suit all requirements of a higher education institution, suggesting that it was operating 'effectively and efficiently'. He argued that 'different systems serve different purposes', and that there are always political as well as technical aspects involved when choosing a management technique.

What is quality?

According to Newton (2002), quality is a 'contested' issue. There are a number of both complementary and contradictory interpretations of quality. For instance, Lomas (2000) argued that there are two major approaches to quality improvement: 'quality assurance and quality enhancement'. In his view, quality assurance is oriented mainly towards the product or service being of good standard. It is a 'preventative' measure, which is 'regarded as a means of improving overall quality' and it relates to the notion of 'fitness for purpose'. Quality enhancement, on the other hand, is 'directly concerned with adding value, improving quality ... and implementing transformational change'. In relation to an individual academic, this concept is 'based on the premise that they want their students to do well' (p. 158).

Adding to Lomas's argument, Jones outlined several dichotomies when approaching higher education quality:

> One views quality improvement at the macro or university level, another focuses at the micro or educational-delivery level. One sees quality assessment as an administrative 'check-off', the other sees quality as a continuous improvement in educational delivery. One values quantitative measures to demonstrate quality, the other values qualitative measures. (Jones, 2003, p. 223)

Jones argued that there is a need for integration of these dichotomies, so that quality improvements at the educational-delivery level would complement and be reflected at the university level.

Kogan and Hanney (2000, p. 240) referred to quality as 'the most potent of the change agents [in higher education]'. In that context, Watty (2003) investigated change as a result of quality initiatives. She revealed 'two schools of thought', one relating to context and the other relating to stakeholders. 'The first attaches quality to a context and as a consequence quality becomes meaningful ... For example, [this might be] references to the quality of assessment, student intake, academic programmes, teaching and learning ...' (p. 213). From the second perspective, quality acquires 'a stakeholder-specific meaning' (p. 213). Quality is considered in relation to a variety of stakeholders with an interest in higher education, and each of these stakeholders may potentially perceive quality differently.

Westerheijden et al. (1994) argued that quality is multi-dimensional, referring to Brennan et al. (1992) who suggested that: 'there are (at least) as many definitions of quality in higher education as there are categories of stakeholders ... times the number of purposes, or dimensions, these stakeholders distinguish' (p. 17).

Within the British higher education system, Harvey (2005, p. 263) outlined the range of quality monitoring mechanisms which have been historically employed in the UK:

> The UK has had several processes for monitoring the quality of higher education. These include the external examiner system, professional accreditation of programmes, inspection of provision, quality audit of institutional processes, assessment of programmes, and research assessment. The first three predate the relatively recent concern with quality assessment and assurance ... [However] the long-running external examiner system has been the mainstay of standards in the ever-expanding university system in the UK.

Since the 1980s there has been a gradual emergence of what Westerheijden et al. (1994) referred to as 'new' approaches to quality assessment 'as a result of the expansion of higher education systems in combination with limited budgets, of internationalisation of higher education and of economic competition, of more openness of governments in general and ... of ideologies of neo-liberalism and deregulation ...' (p. 19).

Scott (1994) further developed this argument concerning the multiplicity of factors which impact on quality, pointing out that the very factors that made quality a key political concern in higher education, have also made it almost impossible to agree on a common definition. Attempting a broad approach, Scott outlined the following five concepts of quality.

- *Quality as 'excellence'.* This is a perspective of quality through a relatively fixed hierarchy of academic merits. This perspective is the most common in higher education, according to Scott, who highlighted a number of its drawbacks. First, it regards the definition of quality as unproblematic, and this 'assumption [is] difficult to sustain in a mass system' (p. 64). Secondly, 'its delivery mechanism, peer review, assumes a professional collegiality as well as shared intellectual values, [however] neither of [them] ... can be taken for granted in an increasingly competitive and market-oriented system' (p. 64).

- *Quality as 'audit'.* This approach to quality focuses on 'the procedures used by universities to safeguard and maintain quality' (p. 64). The approach is modelled on the 'closed' analytical style employed in the corporate world, and it 'has proved to be difficult to reconcile with the open interpretative ethos of universities' (p. 65).

- *Quality as 'outcomes'*. Scott pointed out that a focus on outcomes fails to relate outputs to inputs, and thus 'neglects issues of "value added", [which are] an important measure of higher education's effectiveness' (p. 65). According to Scott, what is also important to consider is that some outcomes, particularly in the case of higher education, 'only become clear long after graduates have left higher education, which undermines the usefulness of this approach in policy and managerial terms' (p. 65).

- *Quality as 'mission'*. This interpretation of quality emphasises the need to judge quality in the context of mission. For example, 'a small college should not be judged by the same standards as a large comprehensive university or a research university' (p. 65). This approach to quality has been referred to as 'fitness for purpose', and it was first employed around the mid-1980s, to discourage 'policy makers from judging the former polytechnics by inappropriate criteria designed with traditional universities in mind' (pp. 65–6).

- *Quality as 'culture'*. Another approach to quality emphasises 'the need to build a "quality culture" that permeates the whole institution rather than devising discrete standards to judge the quality of each individual operation' (p. 66).

Scott further suggested that there are a number of other different models of quality, which can be described in terms of a series of spectra, between:

> ... informal and formal modes ... professionally-oriented (top-down) and those that are market driven (bottom-up), between systems designed to monitor process and those that measure substantial outcomes, between threshold setting (or benchmarking) and ranking, between holistic systems that assess entire institutions and reductionist systems that examine operating units within them. (p. 67)

He also highlighted that these various models are not 'mutually exclusive' and that they can be 'mixed-and-matched'.

Green (1994) also noted that concern for quality and standards was not new in the British higher education context. The debate has become more 'visible' since the 1980s, because it became more externalised and has grown in intensity. Green also highlighted the multi-dimensionality of quality. She further suggested that quality is an elusive term, and that, 'we all have an instinctive understanding of what it means but it is difficult to articulate' (p. 12). She also argued that quality is 'a value-laden term: it is subjectively associated with what is good and worthwhile' (p. 12).

Further, on defining the concept of quality, Harvey, Green and Burrows (1993) indicated that there are a number of ways of viewing quality. They outlined six different notions of quality. The first notion relates to what they called the *traditional* concept of quality. The concept associates quality with an idea of exceptionally high standards. The second notion perceives quality in terms of *consistency* 'it focuses on process and sets specification that it aims to meet' (p. 144). It relates to the concept of *zero defects*. Their third approach to quality is that of *fitness for purpose*, where quality is judged 'in terms of the extent to which a product or service meets its stated purpose' (p. 144). The fourth concept of quality is that of *value for money*, and thus concerns accountability. It relates to the increasing pressures in the British public service, including education, to be accountable to the public, funders and others. They acknowledged that this trend is spreading all over Europe. The fifth notion of quality perceives it as a *transformative process*, an ongoing transformation of the participants. Another concept of quality is a *pragmatic* approach, where it is defined in terms of a range of qualities. This concept recognises the fact that an institution may be of high quality in relation to one factor but of low quality in relation to another aspect.

Harvey, Green and Burrows (1993) further highlighted that quality is 'stakeholder' relative, and the best that can be achieved in that sense 'is to define, as clearly as possible, the criteria used by each interest group when judging quality ...' (p. 144).

To sum up, the number of diverse definitions of quality point to the conclusion that, particularly in the field of higher education, quality has been a 'contested' concept and issue. This has been largely due to its multi-dimensionality and complexity.

Critique of current higher education quality models

Stoddart (2004) argued that, as in other spheres that demand a significant amount of public funding, in recent decades there has been a shift in emphasis from a focus on the individual, and the traditional form of peer review, 'to the systematic application of external judgments that aim to satisfy the need for accountability' (in Brown, 2004, p. x). He explained that the criteria for judgement changed from being internal, tacit and informal to broader ones, accounting for wider socio-economic parameters, because 'higher education institutions have grown more complex and managerially more sophisticated' (in Brown, 2004, p. x).

The critics of many current higher education quality models realised that the socio-economic changes in higher education around the world had to bring with them changes to the traditional perspectives on quality. One of these, at times negatively perceived, was a change in focus to the predominantly quantitative, objective and measurable aspects of higher education quality. The aspects of quality that really matter to academics on a more individual, personal level have increasingly been judged as unimportant. For instance, Jones (2003, pp. 223–4) pointed out that:

> In an age in which more attention is being placed on developing objective measurements of quality in educational delivery, it is both surprising and alarming that the very purpose of a university, that of educating students, should be apparently overshadowed by concern about administrative measurement issues …

> Numerous measures by which to judge quality of educational delivery are being developed, with a particular focus on objectives measured by central administration, and statistical comparison. What is receiving less attention, and stands to be eclipsed as a means of measuring quality, are traditional quality assurance measures, administered by academics at the micro (delivery) level [to assist continuous improvement] …

Jones also highlighted that administering student surveys centrally with a focus on quantitative measures has the potential of giving a very inaccurate picture, and thus it is important to link the centrally collected quantitative data with the collection of qualitative student and teacher feedback to help to create a more holistic picture.

Concerning the balance in focus on improvement as opposed to accountability, Harvey (1998, p. 237) emphasised that: 'Despite good intentions, quality monitoring has become over-bureaucratic and the potential for significant change has been hampered by a focus on accountability rather than improvement … By focusing on accountability, the transformative potential of quality monitoring is not fulfilled …'

Harvey (1998) further pointed out that quality has become associated with control and that the term 'quality' at present is too often used 'as a shorthand for the bureaucratic procedures than for the concept of quality itself …' (p. 246). He further pointed out that this should not come as a surprise,

> … as behind nearly all external quality monitoring is a political motive designed to ensure two basic things: that higher education is

still delivering despite the cut in resources and increase in student numbers; and that higher education is accountable for public money. (pp. 246–7)

Brown (2004) further emphasised that the focus on auditing is particularly dangerous for higher education, and that, ironically, such an approach in fact threatens real quality in the educational process through its focus on documentation.

Focusing on the British higher education system, Watson (1995) outlined the main arguments against the approaches to higher education quality:

- excessive demands on institutions;
- violation of academic autonomy and freedom, linked to the fostering of a 'compliance culture';
- creation of 'hard managerialism' and managerial intrusion in academic matters;
- damage to Britain's hard-won reputation for quality. (in Brown, 2004, p. 80)

Further, Harvey (2005) was rather sceptical about the current quality monitoring processes in UK higher education. He perceived quality monitoring as being 'beset by overlapping and burdensome processes, competing notions of quality, a failure to engage learning and transformation, and a focus on accountability and compliance' (p. 271). According to Harvey, it is unfortunate that instead of undertaking a more holistic review of quality issues enabling a reflection, the process was taken over by the Government and its agencies which 'piled one initiative on another to create the "British quality juggernaut", as it is referred to in parts of Europe' (p. 271).

Harvey also argued that: 'Quality evaluations involve game playing to cast the evaluated programme or institution in the best possible light' (p. 272). Thus he believed that quality evaluations are more aimed at compliance, and there is little space for any 'constructive dialogue to aid real improvement' (p. 272). He pointed out that real quality improvement of the student experience happens mostly as a result of internal review and monitoring processes, and that these rely on 'student feedback, examiners' reports, and internal improvement audits' which are far more effective than external reviews, 'which do little more than result in a flurry of centrally-controlled and produced documentation and evoke a performance and game-playing culture' (pp. 273–4).

Reflecting on the decade or more of external quality assessment (with particular focus on the UK), Harvey (2005) highlighted that despite the fact that academic staff complied with external quality monitoring requirements and learnt to 'play the game', most of them did not perceive that these external quality monitoring processes would result in any 'significant and long-lasting changes in the student experience' (p. 274). He also remarked on some more cynical views which argued that the external quality monitoring mechanisms were devised to hide 'a worsening academic base' (p. 274).

Harvey was of the view that evaluations which rely on 'fitness for purpose' generally tend to be reductionist and result in fragmenting the concept of quality rather than assisting in further exploring the complex interrelated aspects of quality. His concern was that the 'bureaucratic and burdensome paraphernalia of quality' would even increase with the process of internationalisation, and that in such circumstances it is unlikely that the real quality of the student experience would improve.

Further to the concerns expressed by Harvey, Mathias (2004) pointed out that quality assurance favours formal, bureaucratic procedures which are totally disconnected from real teaching issues. According to Mathias, quality enhancement (QE) has become 'a missing "E" in the quality movement' (p. 1). He also underlined the fact that quality assurance (QA) seemed to have brought on 'worrying trends towards teaching staff disengagement' (p. 1), and explained that the reasons for this were related to the fact that there was hardly any recognition or reward for quality enhancement, and that personal engagement and satisfaction were overshadowed by excessive demands of quality assurance.

Mathias emphasised that there were, for instance, departmental or institutional rewards (in the form of favourable ratings in league tables) connected to compliance with quality assurance. However, to him, the rewards or drivers towards quality enhancement were 'difficult to locate' (p. 1). He believed that there were some personal gains of professional satisfaction related to QE, nevertheless there were 'few career and status rewards' (p. 1) connected to it. This, to Mathias, reflected the reality that institutional learning and teaching policies were increasingly prepared by professional administrators without consulting academic practitioners.

Mathias further argued (2004, p. 2) that: 'In the politicised environment in which universities now operate, the rhetoric of goals, targets and strategies often gives way to the quick fix.' He went on to say that this was understandable, given the changing external demands. However, this, according to him, significantly undermined reflection which is essential in the educational process.

Brown (2004, p. 162) summarised the key assumptions for an effective quality assurance system as the following:

- The underlying purpose must be improvement, not accountability.
- The regime must focus on what is necessary for quality improvement.
- The regime must bolster, not undermine, self-regulation.
- The arrangements must be meaningful to, and engage, all those involved.
- The arrangements must promote diversity and innovation.
- There must be adequate quality control.
- There must be clear accountability of the agency.
- There must be proper coordination with other regulators or would be regulators.

Birnbaum (2000) highlighted some positive potential of introducing new management techniques of quality assurance into higher education in that they may play a crucial part in an organisation's renewal. They might emphasise alternative values or introduce variety in an otherwise conservative organisation.

However, taking UK higher education as an example, Brown argued that, despite an enormous amount of effort invested into the UK higher education quality assurance, particularly after 1992, the procedures told very little about the actual quality of the UK higher education. According to Brown (2004), this was because the effort has 'been focused on the wrong targets (comparative judgements of performance) when ... [it should have been targeted] at what it is that assists quality improvement' (p. 163).

Brown also expressed a concern that there was a 'danger that institutions will come to see periodic external regulation as all the regulation that is needed, and/or that their internal procedures will simply mimic those of the external agency' (p. 163). He emphasised that rather than inventing new quality systems, there was a need to map the quality systems onto the existing academic structures and that activities ought to be better coordinated to prevent duplication. In summary, Brown challenges the notion of quality assurance arguing that it may actually be detrimental to quality.

Summary

The concept of quality originated around a century ago, arising within British manufacturing industry, in response to the need for standardisation.

In the 1980s and early 1990s, quality in Britain spread from industry and business into the public sector, including healthcare and higher education. Many Western European countries soon followed the British example. The former Soviet bloc countries of Central and Eastern Europe introduced quality assurance in the form of a state-monitored system of accreditation of higher education in the 1990s.

Quality is a complex, multi-dimensional issue and its meaning is often difficult to articulate. Quality is defined in terms of: *'value for money'*, *'fitness for purpose'*, *'zero defects'*, *'consistency'*, *'transformative process'* and other concepts. The approaches to higher education quality mandated through political agendas of governments have been critiqued as being one-dimensional, schematic and simplistic, and thus overlooking the issues of complexity, multi-dimensionality and also personal views of academics on quality. Despite differing views on the meaning of quality, the higher education sector has moved to inculcate quality as a culture with the aim to improve the educational experiences of stakeholders. While the higher education sector in general has embraced the quality concept, it is difficult to render an overall verdict with respect to effectiveness, as with all quality systems it is what is done within the 'walls' of these institutions to improve that really counts.

References

Barnett, R. (1992) *Improving Higher Education: Total Quality Care*. Buckingham, UK: SRHE/Open University Press.

Birnbaum, R. (2000) *Management Fads in Higher Education*. San Francisco, CA: Jossey-Bass.

Brennan, J., Goedegebuure, L., Shah, T., Westerheijden, D., Weusthof, P., Anderson, D., Johnson, R. and Milligan, B. (1992) *Towards a Methodology for Comparative Quality Assessment in European Higher Education*. London: CNAA.

Brown, R. (2004) *Quality Assurance in Higher Education: The UK Experience since 1992*. London: RoutledgeFalmer.

Centre for Higher Education Studies (CHES) (2001) *Tertiary Education in the Czech Republic*. Report for Department of Education, Youth and Sports, by J. Benes, H. Sebkova, January 2001. Prague, Czech Republic. Online, available at: *http://www.csvs.cz/_en/documents/Tertiary%20Education%20in%20the% 20CR,%202001.rtf* (accessed April 2009).

Department of Education, Training and Youth Affairs (DETYA) (2000) *Quality Assurance and Accreditation in Australian Higher Education: An assessment of Australian and international practice*. Report prepared by D. Anderson, R. Johnson and B. Milligan (Centre for Continuing Education, Australian National University). Commonwealth of Australia.

Green, D. (ed.) (1994) *What is Quality in Higher Education?* Buckingham, UK: SRHE/Open University Press.

Harvey, H. and Green, D. (1993) 'Defining quality', *Assessment and Evaluation in Higher Education*, 18(1): 9–34.

Harvey, L. (1998) 'An assessment of past and current approaches to quality in higher education', *Australian Journal of Education*, 42(3): 237–55.

Harvey, L. (2004) 'War of worlds: who wins in the battle for quality supremacy?', *Quality in Higher Education*, 10(1): 65–71.

Harvey, L. (2005). 'A history and critique of quality evaluation in the UK', *Quality Assurance in Education*, 13(4): 263–76.

Harvey, L., Green, D and Burrows, A. (1993) 'Assessing Quality in Higher Education: a transbinary research project', *Assessment and Evaluation in Higher Education*, 18(2): 143–8.

Jones, S. (2003) 'Measuring the quality of higher education: linking teaching quality measures at the delivery level to administrative measures at the university level', *Quality in Higher Education*, 9(3): 223–9.

Kogan, M. and Hanney, S. (2000) *Reforming Higher Education* (Higher Education Policy Series 50). London: Jessica Kingsley.

Lomas, L. (2000) *Senior Staff Member Perception of Organisational Culture and Quality in Higher Education Institutions in England.* Unpublished PhD thesis, University of Kent, UK.

Mathias, H. (2004) 'The missing "E" factor in "QA" ', *Learning Matters*, Newsletter No 14, April 2004. Institute of Education, University of London, UK, pp. 1–2.

Morley, L. (1997) 'Change and equity in higher education', *British Journal of Sociology of Education*, 18(2): 231–42.

Newton, J. (2002) 'Views from below: academics coping with quality', *Quality in Higher Education*, 8(1): 39–62.

Scott, P. (1994) 'Recent Developments in Quality Assessment in Great Britain', in D.F. Westerheijden et al. (eds) *Changing Contexts of Quality Assessment: Recent Trends in West European Higher Education* pp. 51–73, Utrecht, Netherlands: Uitgeverij Lemma B.V.

Stoddart, J. (2004) 'Foreword', in R. Brown, *Quality Assurance in Higher Education: The UK Experience since 1992.* London, UK: RoutledgeFalmer, pp. x–xiii.

Van der Wende, M. and Westerheijden, D. (2003) 'Degrees of Trust or Trust of Degrees? Quality assurance and recognition', in J. File and L. Goedegebuure (eds) *Real-Time Systems: Reflections on Higher Education in the Czech Republic, Hungary, Poland and Slovenia*, Brno, Czech Republic: Vutium.

Voehl, F. (1994) 'Overview of total quality', in R.G. Lewis and D.H. Smith (eds) *Total Quality in Higher Education*, pp. 27–62. Delray Beach, Florida: St Lucie Press.

Watson, D. (1995) 'Quality assessment and "self-regulation": the English experience, 1992–94', *Higher Education Quarterly*, 49(4): 326–40.

Watty, K. (2003) 'When will Academics Learn about Quality?', *Quality in Higher Education*, 9(3): 213–21.

Westerheijden, D., Brennan, J. and Maassen, P. (eds) (1994) *Changing Contexts of Quality Assessment: Recent Trends in West European Higher Education.* Utrecht, Netherlands: Uitgeverij Lemma B.V.

Woodhouse, D. (2004) 'The Quality of Quality Assurance Agencies', *Quality in Higher Education*, 10(2): 77–87.

Part 2
Leadership of quality in higher education

Initiative-based quality development and the role of distributed leadership

Bente Kristensen and Lee Harvey

Abstract

The Copenhagen Business School (CBS) views quality as an ongoing process of change and has engaged in comprehensive and continuous quality work since the beginning of the 1990s. The university has developed a distributed leadership-based approach to the development of a quality culture, with major emphasis on reflective and responsive leadership at all levels. Quality is a consequence of, as well as a contributor to, a process of continuous change. The evolution of CBS has involved a systematic shift from teaching to learning, which has been a core element of the development of CBS as a 'learning university'. In this respect CBS has taken advantage of external international and national evaluations and has adopted a multi-faceted approach to quality. The key has been the primacy of leadership of quality not the management of quality. Although the vision of the leadership and the enthusiasm and encouragement of the senior team are important, the transformation of CBS could not have been achieved without significant leaders at all levels of the organisation, including department heads, innovative lecturers and committed students. Rather than impose a set of bureaucratic quality procedures, CBS has adopted an initiative-led approach, encouraging academics, administrators and students at all levels to get involved in a variety of quality-related projects.

Key words: leadership-based approach to quality; multi-faceted approach to quality; quality culture; Danish higher education; Copenhagen Business School.

Introduction

The Copenhagen Business School (CBS) has developed a leadership-based approach to the development of a quality culture. CBS has been fortunate in having a stable senior management team for over a decade, with a long-serving President who has facilitated a dynamic and evolving approach to quality assurance and improvement. Quality has been seen as an ongoing process of change at CBS, not a once-and-for-all event. It has increasingly been a focal point of activity since 1994 and its position as a strategic focal point has been reinforced in the latest strategy document adopted by the Board of Directors in December 2008.

CBS has undertaken a flexible and multi-faceted approach to quality, with major emphasis on reflective and responsive leadership. The key has been to see quality as a consequence of, as well as a contributor to, a process of continuous change.

The establishment of a quality culture and a comprehensive and operational quality system need leaders who care for quality, have an international orientation regarding quality, embed the quality aims in the vision, mission and strategic goals of the university, who are able to motivate and inspire people in the organisation to create a balanced top-down/bottom-up approach to quality and who base the institutional quality assurance and quality enhancement on the values and the culture of the institution.

Quality in a wider context

As a university, the CBS places itself in the international, academic community of research and education. However, university leaders must be able to operate both in a national, regional, European and global context. Developments at national level are primarily determined by the political system, whereas developments at regional, European and global level are driven both by the political system and by changing opportunities in the market. Thus national, regional, European and global contexts are related to the academic system, the political system and the market which has an important impact on quality practices.

In 1992, a national evaluation agency for higher education was set up by the Danish Ministry of Education with the aim of evaluating programmes nationwide over a seven-year cycle. The Vice-President at CBS from 1994 to 2008, with the overall responsibility for quality, was one of the founders of the agency in her capacity as Chair of the National Educational Advisory Board for the Humanities and Theology. According to the new University Act of July 2003, Danish universities are still obliged to conduct subject and programme evaluations but are free to use the Danish agency or any other recognised international agency. Although the aim of the 2003 University Act, which replaces all elected leaders with appointed leaders and the former Senate with a Board of Directors having an external majority and an external chair, was to give more autonomy to the universities, all degree programmes offered by the university were subject to the approval of the now Ministry of Science, Technology and Innovation. This continued until autumn 2007 when the Danish Accreditation Institute was established, an independent agency with the aim to assure and prove quality and relevance of disciplines and programmes at Danish higher education institutions. The academic system 3+2+3, the so-called Bologna Process, had already been introduced in Denmark with the 1992 law.

As one of the signatories of the Bologna Declaration 1999, Denmark has been active in implementing the aims of the Bologna Process. However, with the strong focus on external quality assurance of the subject and programme level, most Danish universities have not had strong external motivation to put emphasis on quality at the institutional level. After the Berlin Communiqué 2003, where the ministers responsible for higher education in the EHEA stressed 'that consistent with the principle of institutional autonomy, the primary responsibility for quality assurance in higher education lies with each institution itself and this provides the basis for real accountability of the academic system with the national quality framework', and after the Bologna signatories at their meeting in Bergen 2005 adopted the standards and guidelines for quality assurance in the European Higher Education Area as proposed by ENQA, this might have led to a focus on the institutional level when the Danish Accreditation Institute was established in 2007. This, however, did not happen.

CBS, like other Danish universities, is faced with a situation of stronger cooperation but also stronger competition. There is increased competition for funding for research and a global market for students. To be prepared for these global challenges, quality plays a crucial role. With comprehensive and continuous quality work since the beginning of the 1990s, CBS has tried to prepare itself to meet these challenges at different levels.

Events crucial for the internal quality development at CBS

CBS began its long journey of development as a 'learning university' in the mid-1990s. In the early 1990s one might characterise it as a teacher-led, didactic institution in which students had a very high number of lectures a week with little in the way of interactive sessions; student-centred learning was not a significant part of the learning process. The institution was also scattered around the city in buildings many of which were not originally designed as learning environments, and there was no noticeable student learning community: students tended to turn up to lectures and then dissipate without much intra-student interaction. Over the last 15 years this has completely changed, yet there is no intention for the university to consider the 'job done'. Continuous improvement is still at the core of university strategy for the future. CBS has learned and continues to learn from experience.

The following events have been crucial for the leaders and the quality work at CBS.

1. The development of CBS as a 'learning university'.

2. The CRE-Audit in 1996 and the Follow-Up Visit in 1998.[1]

3. The adaptation of the stakeholder-related concept and definition of 'quality', by Harvey and Green (1993).

4. The involvement of external expertise.

The 'learning university'

In the self-evaluation report for the CRE-Audit 1996, CBS sets out that one of its strategic goals is to develop as a 'learning university'. According to the self-evaluation report CBS was aware that:

> the image of CBS as a 'learning university' requires a more specific definition of this concept, not the least of which is a clarification of how a number of basic and necessary prerequisites can come about: How is the type of recruitment and ongoing competency development controlled? How is organizational innovation developed so that CBS acquires the ability to 'think the unthinkable'? How are reward systems and structures for incentives built in to support the strategic development at CBS? These are all issues to be confronted. Universities

must deliver an effective and attractive framework within which researchers, students, and the environment can be brought together and inspire one another. The demand for evaluation, systematic analysis, and coordination must be balanced with the need for experimentation, creative culture, room for impulsive action, and non-traditional ideas to provide the student-of-today with the ballast needed to be an employee and manager in the corporation-of-tomorrow. In the future, CBS will hopefully be a creative and innovative university with carefully selected information systems, with an understanding of its purpose that enables effective follow-up processes initiated at all levels by the people in the organization.

The CRE-Audit of 1996 and the Follow-Up Visit of 1998

No doubt the very supportive CRE-Audit and the Follow-Up Visit two years later stimulated and influenced the strategic process at CBS significantly. The self-evaluation, the site visits and the dialogue with the evaluation team were a turning point for the university. It allowed CBS, at all levels, to start thinking collectively about the way forward for developing an internal quality culture. The Follow-Up Visit was not a mechanistic 'tick the box' exercise, but the experts (the same as for the first visit) gave CBS ideas to help the university move to the next stage of its development as a 'learning university'.

According to the CBS Strategic Update from 1998 the term, in the CBS context, originates from the combination of the classic notion of the university as a forum for learning and knowledge and the modern concept of 'the learning organisation'. CBS strives to develop a learning environment based on learning rather than teaching and individual talent support rather than mass education. It intends to develop an ongoing system of quality development featuring flexibility, innovative capacity, a balanced mix of systematic analysis and experiments and external and internal peer reviews, which would transform CBS into a learning organisation. CBS views the capacity for continuous organisational renewal as a key requirement for building an innovative learning environment for students and researchers.

However, the strategy depends on development of new pedagogical methods, ability to combine research-based teaching and experience-based learning, increasing use of multimedia-aided learning, focus on mobilising the students' resources for the learning process, project-based courses with interdisciplinary groups and action-learning programmes.

For the organisation as a whole, the strategy depends on commitment to continued quality development and competence enhancement, building external and internal networks, creating an innovative organisational culture for all staff groups, encouraging venture spirit and testing new organisation principles.

A stakeholder-related concept of quality

Another turning point was the introduction in 1994 of a quality system based on the stakeholder-related concept of quality as defined by Harvey and Green (1993). According to this definition, quality means different things to different people and is relative to processes or outcomes. The widely varying conceptualisations of quality are grouped into five discrete but interrelated categories. Quality can be viewed as exceptional, as perfection, as fitness for purpose, as value for money and as transformation.

From 1994 onwards, CBS has launched projects and quality activities within all five categories as part of its continuous quality improvement process.

Use of external expertise

Since 1994 CBS has gained valuable feedback for the further development of the internal quality assurance and quality development from peers on the site visit teams of various external evaluations. The leaders themselves have participated as peers on evaluation teams with the opportunity to share knowledge about quality improvement with colleagues throughout Europe.

The second author has been involved with CBS as an external expert since 1994. He has significantly contributed to a continuous exchange of ideas and input within the organisation. He has visited CBS regularly and interviewed a wide range of internal stakeholders (such as students, faculty, decision makers, directors of study boards and others) and external stakeholders. He prepared a report (with observations and recommendations for further quality enhancement) following each visit.

The aims of CBS' quality work

The quality work undertaken by CBS and integrated in the CBS vision, mission and strategic goals, aims at:

- developing CBS as a learning university;
- empowering CBS students to be reflective practitioners;

- educating students who are competitive on both the national and international job markets;
- developing an internal quality culture safeguarding institutional autonomy and public accountability;
- stimulating internal capacity for self-reflection and change;
- promoting the exchange of ideas, experiences and good practice.

The quality system developed at CBS

Attempting to balance quality at both national and European levels and also trying to balance external quality assurance with internal quality assurance and quality improvement presented a challenge to CBS's new Vice-President in 1994. She adopted the above-mentioned Green and Harvey stakeholder-related concept of 'quality' in the following ways.

Quality in the sense of 'exceptional'

According to its mission statement, CBS aims to be an internationally recognised business university at the European top level, which means of an exceptional quality. For CBS as an international university, for academic partners in national, regional and international networks, for corporate partners, both national and international, for the Ministry and Parliament funding CBS and for both national and international students deciding at which university they want to study, it is very important to know how exceptional CBS is. The learning features or quality assurance activities used for that purpose are:

- CRE-Audit (1996), CRE Follow-Up Visit (1998); (CRE now EUA)
- EQUIS[2] Accreditation (1999–2000);
- EQUIS Re-Accreditation 2004–5;
- ESMU[3] Benchmarking Programme (since 2002);
- internally initiated research evaluation at departmental level (ongoing since 1994);
- EVA[4] evaluations (at national level) on subject and programme level – latest 2005;
- the NOQA Comparative Analysis of Systematic Quality Work in Nordic Higher Education Institutions 2004–5;

- AMBA[5] Accreditation 2007;
- AACSB[6] Accreditation (ongoing);
- ranking;
- national programme accreditation from 2008.

The control of these activities is placed with various people within the university depending on relevant qualifications and formerly under the supervision of the Vice-President, now under the supervision of either the Dean for Education or the Dean for Research.

To illustrate the standards at CBS, Table 2.1 outlines the results the CBS has achieved in the ESMU benchmarking. It needs to be stated that

Table 2.1 ESMU benchmarking outcomes for CBS

ESMU benchmarking subject areas	CBS result	Best result
Strategic Management, Policy and Strategy (2001)	5	5
Management of Teaching, Learning and Assessment (2001)	4	4+
Marketing the University (2001)	3	3
Management Information Systems (2002)	3.8	4
Internal Quality Assurance (2002)	5	5
Student Services (2002)	4	4.5
E-Learning (2003)	2	5
External Funding (2003)	4	5
Institutional Research (2003)	3	4
Research Management (2004)	5	5
The University Creating a Regional Knowledge Base (2004)	4	4
Change Management (2004)	4	4
Internationalization (2005)	4	4
Strategic Partnership (2005)	4	4
Governance and Structures (2005)	4	4
Designing New Masters and Doctorates (2005)	4	4
Marketing Higher Education Institutions (2006)	4	4
Innovative Teaching and Learning (2006)	5	5

Source: ESMU Assessors Reports 2001–2006.

all the reports listed in the table arc currently strictly confidential, despite an intense debate among ESMU members concerning making the reports publicly available.

As will be evident from the above, CBS has generally done comparatively well in the benchmarking reviews, often being best or second best in class. However, both in these cases and in cases where CBS has done less well, the benchmarking projects have stimulated reflection and led to decisive action learning from good practice. The report on Marketing the University (2001) was a contributing factor in the decision to establish a strengthened communication platform; the report on E-Learning (2003) has resulted in an ongoing effort to formulate an overall operational CBS strategy for e-learning; and the report on Student Services (2002) has contributed to the establishment of a major initiative on student services. The report on Institutional Research (2003) has, inspired by the University of Amsterdam, resulted in an eight-page newsletter published four times a year by a newly established Business Intelligence Unit.

Quality in the sense of 'perfection'

In a CBS context, the notion of quality as perfection refers to the strategic development as a learning university. It is important to CBS that the staff, academic and administrative, have the competence to manage their job in a 'perfect' way and are enabled and encouraged to keep improving the effectiveness of their professional effort. The stakeholders are academic staff, administrative staff and students. The quality activities are:

- staff recruitment;
- annual appraisal interviews at individual level;
- staff development supported by the CBS Learning Lab;
- benchmarking (internal and external);
- development of a CBS quality culture (places the onus on everyone to maximise the quality of their services and outputs);
- a campus-wide quality development project on student services.

At CBS, the Learning Lab is responsible for staff development in relation to teaching and learning. The internal benchmarking is a transfer of 'good practice' from one environment to another as part of the staff development programmes, while external benchmarking refers to some of the ESMU themes of relevance to the CBS administration.

There is a simultaneous concern for promoting quality activities through propagation of a quality culture, the nurturing of responsibility among the greatest possible number of 'actors', encouragement of initiatives and innovation and the spread of good practice. The overall aim is organisational learning.

CBS sees 'quality culture' in institutions as more important than formal quality assurance procedures. The emphasis is on development of learning rather than institutionalising of bureaucratic procedures. Quality is seen as a concept of multiple significance, distinct for each of the various stakeholders involved. To a large extent, quality development or quality improvement is a question of information and motivation and thus of strengthening the mutual confidence between the levels and environments involved. In the context of CBS, quality initiatives are seen as part of a process of continuous quality improvement, satisfying the various stakeholders that these initiatives lead to change and improvement. Creating a quality culture requires providing a context in which to facilitate quality improvement.

Quality in the sense of 'fitness for purpose'/ relevance/employability

To the stakeholders in the business community, to the employers of CBS graduates and to national and international corporate partners, the notion of quality as 'fitness for purpose' is important. CBS uses the following quality initiatives while striving for increased partnership with business:

- dialogue with the business community;
- dialogue with corporate partners;
- dialogue with graduates (alumni);
- advisory boards;
- networking;
- careers office (graduate placement, individual career plans for students);
- internships/mentorships;
- life-long learning.

Many degree programmes and many departments attach advisory boards to their activities to have a continuous dialogue with the business community about the profile of knowledge and skills of their graduates. The control of these activities is with the departments or the study boards. As part of its strategy, CBS has set up several business research centres and a great deal of the networking with the business community occurs within these centres. An important group of stakeholders is also the CBS alumni, who give feedback to CBS about the quality of their education after having gained some work experience. CBS has a formulated alumni policy under the control of the corporate relation officer together with the Communications Department.

Quality in the sense of 'value for money'/ accountability – payback to stakeholders

Although CBS has a very strong focus on enhancement or improvement, it is also necessary to demonstrate accountability as part of the quality management process. Accountability means the requirement to demonstrate responsible actions to one or more external constituencies. These may be: governments providing funds to CBS; the Ministry of Science, Technology and Innovation; Parliament; taxpayers; CBS students; graduates using their knowledge and skills from CBS in a job situation; or employers offering jobs to CBS graduates. All these examples refer to quality as 'value for money'. The Danish Evaluation Institute's (formerly the Danish Centre for Quality Assurance and Evaluation of Higher Education) self-adopted strategy has been to combine the perspective of improvement with that of accountability. The institute has not had a substantial impact on the continuous internal quality monitoring at the institutional level, although the Danish evaluation model does provide a great deal of information that could form the basis for very useful procedures for internal quality monitoring including students, graduates and employers. As mentioned above, the independent Danish Accreditation Agency took over in 2007 the responsibility for accrediting both new and existing disciplines and programmes on a cyclical basis. At CBS, greater responsiveness to external demands for accountability, transparency and credibility are not seen as antitheses to self-regulation but, rather, as elements of public responsibility and safeguarding autonomy.

The quality assurance activities in this respect include the following:

- external evaluations by the Danish Evaluation Institute now replaced by external accreditation by the Danish Accreditation Agency (ACE Denmark);

- performance indicators;
- performance agreement between the Ministry and each university;
- internal evaluations: feedback to students on the CBS website;
- multiple focus group interviews with employers and alumni regarding drop-out rates, curriculum development, competencies of graduates;
- bi-annual qualitative study of the 'learning environment' at CBS.

It is important to establish a proper balance between internal improvement functions and external accountability functions and several CBS disciplines and programmes have been subject to external evaluation. The study board has been responsible for the self-evaluation reports and organising the peer-review visits, while the recommendations of the final public report have been dealt with by the relevant study board. Performance indicators have been set up within several areas, for example, research publication, student exchange, and numbers of PhD students.

CBS sees the 'Performance Agreement' (2007) with the Ministry for Research and the Ministry of Education, now taken over by the Ministry of Science, Technology and Innovation, as the first step towards the principle of 'management by objectives'. CBS must annually report on the fulfilment of the success criteria set up in the Agreement; however, so far this has not been linked to funding. Aims, means and success criteria within all strategic areas of CBS have been formulated in the Agreement, and with the annual reporting system it is possible for CBS to keep the aims, means and success criteria up to date and to argue for change, if needed. The content of the Agreement is communicated throughout the university via senior and middle management.

Quality in the sense of 'transformation'

As a learning university, the most important aim of the teaching and learning at CBS is to enhance and empower students, which refers to the notion of quality as 'transformation'. CBS needs to ensure that students develop knowledge, skills and abilities, but also that they are empowered as critical lifelong learners. In 2008, the Board of Directors approved the Learning Strategy developed by the CBS Learning Lab. With this new strategy the following views on students and teachers were codified:

- students are *partners*;
- students have an identity and care about their *learning process*;
- teachers are persons who *facilitate* students' learning processes;

- teachers discuss with students their way to *achieve their goals*;
- students learn in relation to their *past* experience and their *thoughts* about their *future life and career*.

The stakeholders are the students, the teachers/researchers and the external examiners safeguarding the learning outcomes of the students. Quality activities in this respect are:

- continuous quality improvement;
- a pedagogical profile according to the CBS Learning Strategy leading to student-centred learning (transformative learning);
- competence profiles and impact on curriculum development;
- ongoing student evaluation of disciplines and programmes;
- benchmarking (internal and external);
- use of an external expert, ongoing since 1994.

A crucial element in the development of transformative learning is staff development. All assistant professors (equivalent of lecturers) take part in a development programme that has a compulsory core and a range of optional elements. The core focuses on four dimensions of the assistant professor's progress, against which they are assessed: pedagogical, personal, didactic and developmental. The first relates to the assistant professors' understanding of pedagogy and their ability to structure learning sessions, communicate and manage dialogue. The personal includes voice projection, body language, facial expression, timing, empathy, and contact with the students. The didactic includes the analytical and practical understanding of basic concepts, such as the ability to formulate teaching and examination goals, to adapt a theme to the level of the students and to be able to take account of resources. The final dimension involves the ability to appraise one's own development and potential as a teacher. Overall, the assistant professor is evaluated on the relationship between academic content, objectives, mode of teaching and level of study and how the assistant professor's activities impact on student learning.

Distributed leadership

CBS has adopted a multi-faceted approach to quality, with a strong emphasis on the learning university, both in the sense of the university as a learning organisation and as an academic environment focused on enabling student learning. The key throughout all this has been the primacy of leadership of quality, not the management of quality. For more than a decade the senior managers at CBS have had a clear desire to take the university forward, to develop a culture of continuous improvement and to transform the institution into a major European business school. This has involved a long-term vision, which has been helped by a period of relative stability in senior positions. Although the vision of the leadership and the enthusiasm and encouragement of the senior team are important, the transformation of CBS could not have been achieved without significant leaders at all levels of the organisation, including department heads, innovative lecturers and committed students.

It is important that the quality system chosen is not a bureaucratic burden but a system able to inspire and motivate stakeholders. For the leaders there must be a drive, imagination and desire to use quality assurance and quality enhancement as necessary tools to prove effectiveness and efficiency within the organisation.

Leaders are effective if their integrity and trust is respected at all levels in the university. They need to be good communicators and engaged in quality initiatives at both national, European and global levels enabling them to get inspiration for further development of their own practices. While this applies to senior managers in the institution, it also applies to leaders at all levels if a quality culture is to develop.

At CBS, as in other Danish universities, divided leadership exists for full-time academic staff members. The Head of Department is responsible for selecting staff with the right competences. The Decree (2007) states 'the head of department shall be an acknowledged researcher and have teaching experience' (MSTI, 2007, paragraph 17). At the same time, the study board (discussed below) is responsible for the quality of the teaching and learning. If student questionnaires or other kind of formative or summative evaluation reveals that a teacher does not perform in an adequate way the study board Director must inform the Head of Department who will arrange for the necessary staff development or other kind of support.

The development of CBS into a high quality learning university has been achieved because it has encouraged leadership and ownership of quality. Rather than impose a set of bureaucratic quality procedures, CBS has adopted an initiative-led approach, encouraging academics, administrators and students at all levels to get involved in a variety of quality-related projects. This process has worked with those innovators and groups who want to develop ideas and approaches and in many circumstances they have acted as leaders in the development of a quality culture.

One area where distributed leadership has been particularly effective is the role of students, especially on study boards. Each programme has a study board, a little like the boards of study programmes in UK universities. However, in Denmark, and particularly at CBS, study boards are far more influential than their British counterparts. The study boards at CBS consist of between 4 and 10 members, depending on the size of the programme. Membership is made up of 50 per cent academics and 50 per cent students and members are elected to the boards by their peers. Boards meet regularly (approximately monthly) and their primary function is to address issues that arise and to plan the development of the programme. The study boards have, within Danish law and institutional mission, considerable power to affect the nature and direction of study programmes. The Decree, as set out in the Ministerial order (MSTI, 2007, paragraph 18), states, *inter alia*:

> ... Each study board shall comprise equal numbers of representatives of the academic staff and students [with] a chairman from the academic staff and a vice-chairman from the students... .
>
> The study board shall recommend a head of studies to the dean ... [who] shall undertake the practical organisation of teaching and tests and other assessment forming part of the exams. ... The study board shall ensure the organisation, realisation and development of the study programme and teaching. Its main objectives are to ... ensure and develop the quality of the study programme and the teaching ... produce proposals for curricula and changes ... approve the organisation of teaching and ... assessment ... process applications concerning credit transfers ... make all statements on all matters of importance to the study programmes... .

Student participation is not just nominal, as in many countries, but a potent force in change (Riddersholm and Kjersner, 2002).

Conclusion

CBS has been on a long quality journey in which leadership rather than management or bureaucracy has been the watchword of quality. A quality culture developed that approached the ideal of being 'invisible', part of the everyday landscape. Strong and stable senior leadership along with a distributed leadership including students, based around an initiative approach that encouraged and supported new ideas and gave those involved delegated responsibility and trust, have been at the root of the transformation of CBS, resulting in the institution winning a number of international awards in quality. However, the university is not resting on its laurels, and its next stage is to create a completely integrated total quality process.

Notes

1. CRE – acronym for standing Conference of Rectors, Presidents and Vice-Chancellors of European Universities; now European University Association (EUA).
2. EQUIS – acronym for the European Quality Improvement System.
3. ESMU – acronym for the European Centre for Strategic Management of Universities.
4. EVA – Danish acronym for the Danish Evaluation Institute.
5. AMBA – Association of MBAs.
6. AACSB – Association to Advance Collegiate Schools of Business.

References

Harvey, H. and Green, D. (1993) 'Defining quality', *Assessment and Evaluation in Higher Education*, 18(1): 9–34.

Ministry of Science, Technology and Innovation (MSTI) (2007) *Ministerial Order concerning the Act on Universities* (the Universities Act). Consolidation Act no. 1368 of 7 December 2007 (English translation). Ministry of Science, Technology and Innovation, Danish University and Agency, case no. 08–046981.

Riddersholm, O. and Kjersner, M. (2002) 'Improving the quality and direction of universities through student involvement', Seventh Quality in Higher Education International Seminar: Transforming Quality, Melbourne, Australia, October 2002.

A leadership model for higher education quality

Fernando F. Padró

Abstract

This chapter presents a possible approach for leaders in higher education quality based on typical demands faced by many universities today. The narrative identifies the course of action a university takes from the point of view of leadership brought by the CEO, senior administrators, faculty governance, key faculty leaders, and the rank-and-file members of the faculty. Traditionally, higher education has recognised the perspectives and approaches from the accountability and assessment movements. Ideas and notions from the field of quality are less accepted and, actually, seen more in terms of a fad. However, the quality framework is here to stay as reflected by what external standards in auditing and/or accreditation procedures reflect and represent. This is a discussion of the benefits for university leaders to adopt a quality framework as a means of not only coping with, but succeeding in maintaining institutional agility and autonomy in an age of uncertainty brought about by constant change.

Key words: accountability; assessment; quality framework; faculty; senior university administration; regulatory frameworks; change management.

One scenario at Stable State University

There are changes in the air for Stable State University (SSU). The external review process is changing its criteria and overall framework of review. In addition, the institution is getting a new chief executive officer intent on making sure the university remains an important member of the state's higher education system and to take the institution to the next step.

Over the past twenty-five years, SSU has had a very good record in terms of enrolment, increase in programmes and physical infrastructure, enhanced reputation of its faculty research, demand for graduates in the workforce, and good standing with accrediting bodies and government agencies. Not as critical in the university's thinking and priorities have been the areas of student support programming or service outreach. More to the point, the senior administrative team has become comfortable and complacent about the state of the university and its ability to represent its interests to the state coordinating board. The team has felt no impetus to change the institutional vision toward its academic and organisational performance, relying primarily on enrolment forecasting projections as a means of bolstering their monitoring of their current input elements.

SSU is a typical public teaching university whose funding is based on a full-time equivalent funding formula. Women and other traditionally under-represented groups make up a proportionate number of the student population at the undergraduate level and most students are dependent on financial aid, mostly in the form of loans, scholarships, or other forms of assistance.

At the same time, as a new chief executive officer (CEO) is coming to the campus, the university has been apprised of changing regulatory and accreditation expectations and procedures which has perplexed and annoyed senior administrators and the key senior faculty leading the faculty governance system. The new CEO is taking the job with the understanding that this institutional sense of complacency cannot last any longer. The CEO's homework prior to deciding to come to SSU identified the changing regulatory environment along with a changing political and economic landscape that suggests higher education is not what it is supposed to be and that SSU is not doing as good a job as its senior administration thinks the institution is doing. The incoming CEO has identified three additional concerns that can have a negative impact on the university. First, there are some elected officials who feel the university is not being held properly accountable because it does not clearly demonstrate how it benefits students, employers, and the community. Second, these politicians do not fully understand the role of faculty at a teaching university, especially when it comes to issues such as grading and selection of books for classes taught. Consequently, there is a lack of trust that faculty are doing what they should be doing. And third, many employers within the university's traditional service area feel that SSU is not doing enough to make sure their needs for fully trained graduates are met.

When it comes to changes in regulatory oversight, there are significant changes in a number of licensing bodies that will impact programme delivery and focus of many of the professional development programmes within SSU. However, the senior administrative team is minimising the potential impact of these changes while the new CEO feels that there are definite challenges to the institution along with opportunities for the university. The state protocols are changing to require more annual reports linked to student learning results based on identified outcomes and the state coordinating board wants to add learning results to a report on institutional stewardship of resources. Furthermore, there are changes in the licensing requirements in a number of professions that impact on curriculum and programme accreditation guidelines. And if this was not enough, institutional reviews by external bodies are also changing the criteria by which higher education institutes (HEIs) are being measured. Once again, the emphasis is switching to a results-based approach to institutional and programme performance based on learner outcomes. Still in debate is a change in the external review environment where the importance of the self-review process in favour of a review based on a set of external standards is being considered, making the review process more of a quality audit.

All this has aggravated both senior administrators, who regarded the changes as nothing more than a general nuisance, and the key faculty leaders who were not aware of changing developments, only finding out from the administration at key faculty governance committees. This created an environment where senior administration did not care about faculty feelings in this regard, and their complacency made faculty feel that (1) the changes were a direct attack on the institution itself, and (2) the new demands were unrealistic and inappropriate because these did not take into account the institution's unique mission. As a result, faculty were unhappy not only because senior administration did not treat faculty as partners in academic concerns, but because they felt that the new demands demonstrated a complete lack of understanding of the nature of teaching, instruction, and the relationship between instructor, student, and learning.

Issues and action points involved in the scenario

This approach is an amalgam of different but actual scenarios that are not that unique in today's higher education. The basis of the approach is the USA-style president as CEO rather than the rector or ceremonial chancellor model. Part of this model is an interaction with a significant central administration, with faculty–administration relationships ranging from what Birnbaum (1988) classified as collegial to anarchic in structure. The issues this situation brings forth represent the importance of a central administration that can make substantive decisions, the difficulty in balancing the recognition and role of faculty through a faculty governance structure, and the importance of and the challenge to institutional autonomy and agility to meet the institutional mission.

Agility and autonomy are the two main issues involved in this scenario. The incoming CEO sees the need to pursue institutional autonomy, while the incumbent senior administration and key faculty leaders perceive the changing external environment more as a threat to institutional autonomy. What is not an issue is that incumbent senior administrators and key faculty leaders want to hold SSU to high standards because what is reflected is an illustration of John Gardner's (1990) concern of not pursuing continual renewal as a means of avoiding complacency.

Within the scenario, the incoming CEO has the following action points to consider.

- Getting buy-in for the new vision from incumbent senior administrators and key faculty leaders/faculty governance structure. As a corollary, define how to work with the senior administration team, the faculty governance structure, and determine the role of faculty in the university's decision-making schema.

- Change the organisational culture to one that is comfortable with a continuous improvement philosophy based on the notion of demonstrating how much learning is happening *by design*.

- Establish a relationship with external stakeholders that enhances confidence and trust in the university's mission, how it is achieved, and its viability in an environment more intent in linking higher education experiences with workforce development concerns. The corollary here is acting as an advocate for maintaining or enhancing institutional autonomy in light of national or state protocols/legislative changes and their supporting regulatory modifications, and changing external review schema that are more and more interested in pursuing evaluation through imposed external standards.

- Review the vitality of the university's mission and vision. Follow up with the review, re-energising, and possible updating of the university's strategic plan and decision-making processes.

- Identify and provide appropriate and sufficient resources to assure changes necessary to maintain a higher degree of agility to meet changing academic practices as well as external expectations and identified opportunities.

For a CEO at an HEI that is directly responsible to a board of trustees or its equivalent, there are two additional layers of action plans reflecting their legal obligations. At one level, action plans have to reflect the role of the board relative to external stakeholder relationships and interaction with the different campus constituencies. At the other level, the CEO has to be focused on issues of board composition, expertise, and their oversight responsibility over the CEO. For example, the National Association of College and University Business Officers (NACUBO) established a set of guidelines in support of legislature passed in the USA pertaining to good business practices in the running of an HEI. Thus, additional action plans the CEO might have to consider based on NACUBO recommendations include the following.

- Ascertaining the economic standing (e.g. bond rating) and viability of the HEI to meet future needs.

- Reviewing the effectiveness and soundness of the university's business practice and reporting procedures that are typically reviewed and signed off by the board of trustees (e.g. financial statements).

- Reviewing and adapting board recruitment and membership criteria and practices to maximise stakeholder interactions and relationships.

- Working out board review criteria for the CEO and other senior administrators.

- Establishing a code of ethical practice binding on all members of the campus community. As a corollary, the CEO also works on tending and managing the relationships between the administration and the board (Balderston, 1995).

Action points for senior administrators at SSU are different in nature. Aronowitz (2006) suggested that administrators have become a professional managerial class. Previously, Blau (1994) suggested that while the role of senior administrators has more in common with those in traditional industries, the role faculty plays within a campus in terms of line functions is different. 'Management is about work planning and work performance' (Millett, 1980, p. 147). Barzun (1968) put it in a slightly different way: in the abstract, senior administrators (such as central administration and deans) have one object, to distribute the university's resources to their best advantage. For Barzun, administrator decisions affect 'budget-making, communication, speed of change, expenditure and waste, student relations, and faculty loyalty – in short, morale and efficiency combined' (p. 104). Consequently, senior administrators should:

- Establish a process for identifying, measuring, and analysing meaningful data from the three campus endeavours: academic affairs, student services, and business affairs.

- Ensure the points in the strategic plan are translated into action and that these have led to desired results.

- Review the soundness of the university's decision-making processes, especially the effectiveness of the input and support from the faculty governance structure.

- Re-evaluate the network of contacts with external stakeholders to ensure that these are providing useful and timely information of upcoming changes in legislation, protocols, and/or regulations so that the university has adequate time to respond to changes. As a corollary, re-evaluate the network of contacts to make sure that the institution is receiving appropriate feedback, especially if it is negative, to allow for corrective action that is deemed credible. Ask unit heads and other mid-level administrators to do the same. In other words, check the effectiveness of how the university receives feedback and how it uses that information.

- Determine if there is an appropriate number of faculty and professional staff participation in the university's faculty governance structure. Re-examine and evaluate the effectiveness of the internal recognition and reward structures for faculty and other professional staff (e.g. student services) to determine whether recognitions and rewards are in alignment regarding the degree of buy-in and participation in formal university-wide decision-making schema or other informal, more personal contributions to campus performance.

Discussing action points for faculty is a more complicated issue because it depends on an HEI's structure as to whether or not the university is dominated by the faculty or controlled to a greater extent by a central administration structure, with or without a formal faculty governance structure that is in place to go along with academic and student service unit participation. As Blau (1994) pointed out, the role faculty plays within a campus in terms of line functions is different than that found in business enterprises. Typically, faculty has a greater say at the academic unit level because they represent the interests of their individual disciplines or professions in the preparation of students in those fields.

Academic units represent faculty's main point of reference and locus of activity (Balderston, 1995). Depending on how the university is structured, there are varying levels of faculty autonomy in decision-making, at least when it comes to academic matters ranging from almost complete to merely being what Rhoades (1998) and Slaughter and Rhoades (2004) referred to as managed faculty.

According to Birnbaum (2003), *governance* in higher education refers to the structures and processes that academic institutions invent to achieve an effective balance between the claims of two different, but equally valid, systems of organisational control and influence: the legal authority vested in oversight boards and professional authority, and the professional authority that justifies the role of the faculty. In their study of faculty governance at universities in the USA, Tierney and Minor (2003) have found that the tradition of shared governance rests on the assumption that faculty should hold a substantive role in decision-making, with the relationship between faculty and the institution subscribing to one of three approaches: *fully-cooperative decision-making, consultative decision-making*, or *distributed decision-making* (i.e. when decisions are made by discrete groups responsible for specific issues, faculty have a right to make decisions in certain areas, the administration and board in others).

Kennedy (1997) pointed out that there is a disparity between the faculty's role as governors of their institution and their role as salaried employees. Faculty, as academic professionals, are defined and evaluated in terms of their individual focus on research and their pursuit of knowledge through the discipline, how their work demonstrates quality through peer review, and the establishment of reputations through international professional associations (cf. Rice, 2006). Therefore, faculty involvement with campus affairs and governance issues in particular varies in accordance to what each faculty member believes he or she gets out of it. These views range from those who prefer a strong administration to those rejecting a strong administrative role in the running of a university (Williams et al., 1987). Of particular concern are those faculty members who can be classified as disengaged because they prefer to focus on scholarship rather than what they see as academic politics to succeed.

In today's higher education environment, '[t]he issues at hand [for faculty] are professional control of pedagogy and curriculum, work load, training and skills, jobs, salaries, and programme evaluation' (Rhoades, 1998, p. 177). The role faculty plays is therefore linked to institutional health and, as such, the action items mentioned below must be considered from the points of view of the faculty as a whole and from that of the individual faculty member. Within these action points are some issues faced by contingent faculty (especially part-time) reflecting the challenges they face in engaging within the academic unit activities as well as the university's shared governance structure.

Challenges for CEOs, senior administrators and faculty leaders

How does all of this come together? The new CEO has a significant challenge based on trying to establish a new organisational climate. On the other hand, senior administrators and key faculty leaders within and outside the shared governance structure already have vested interests based on institutional history and desire to continue what is seen as a successful educational enterprise. The different players come to the table with different and legitimate agendas, perceptions and skill sets. The key is the table, which in this case is composed of the call for educational reform and the need for the university to be seen to meet the challenges of reform.

According to the 2009 World Conference on Higher Education (UNESCO, 2009), goals important for higher education include: access, equity, quality and relevance. This scenario addresses three of the four goals: access, quality, and relevance. All these issues must be worked on simultaneously in order to meet social needs. Access and relevance are tied to quality, and under this approach to higher education, quality is directly linked to quality assurance. Not only is quality assurance (QA) a *vital function* of higher education, it requires the creation of QA systems, patterns of evaluation of performance and results, and the promotion of a quality culture that also includes all stakeholders, internal and external. Education reform, therefore, has become calibrated through the concerns of quality and those issues that challenge quality. The emphasis now is on results based on what the students demonstrably learn and not just on good institutional stewardship over resources and their allocation. It is all about institutional as well as student learning, improvement, and meeting external expectations beyond those based on disciplinary/ professional concerns. The focus now is about the impact universities have outside the campus walls. In other words, as important as student learning are the contributions the university's graduates provide to their employers and by extension to the communities in which they live.

In that context, while the CEO's background, experience, and training do much to shape the university's response, the CEO is only one person in what is an interdependent set of formally identified and informal players that have to come to agreements about how to make effective, positive change happen.

Academia, for the most part, has tagged educational reform to concerns and approaches provided by the accountability and assessment movements. There is a tension between the notions of accountability and improvement that has to be worked out, but working out the distinctions helps to define what assessment is. Ewell (2002) also suggests that for the movement to become part of an institution's culture two things must happen: [1] 'shifting assessment's conceptual paradigm from an evaluative stance that emphasizes checking up on results to an emphasis on assuming active and collective responsibility for fostering student attainment,' and [2] 'evolving a largely top-down, management-oriented use of information in planning and decision making toward a culture that more fully embodies the principles of a learning organization' (p. 24). This last point echoes Kanji's (1998) assertion that higher education systems have to be guided by top management leadership and core concepts in order to achieve excellence.

These two movements within the topic of education reform provide important technical aspects of what is required to generate positive change within the changing external environment; however, in themselves these may not be enough. As Stake (2006) points out, the notion of quality is about two things: the characteristic of the object and goodness (i.e. the degree of excellence). Both movements tend to focus primarily on one over the other, not always both.

It can be argued that accountability focuses on what is happening and does not necessarily focus on improvement. As seen, improvement is an essential component of institutional performance under the new way of looking at universities. Ewell (as quoted in Zemsky et al., 2006) talks about the need to bring the notion of *value added* to the performance equation. Zemsky, Wegner and Massy refer to Trow's belief that there is a conflict between accountability and improvement. Trow argues that 'no review could be both supportive and evaluative' and that 'externally driven evaluative reviews trigger evasive strategies and produce much noise but little improvement' (Trow, 1996, p. 148). The effect of external reviews is that these frame institutional response from the perspective of a *minimaxing regime* – minimising regret while maximising opportunity to maintain one's capacity to protect what is deemed important (Padró and Hurley, 2008).

Changing the assessment model's conceptual paradigm as in higher education, Ewell (2002) referred to, reflects a tension between the role of central administration as management and of shared governance as a key element of interdependent responsible parties in academic decision-making. Senge (2006) made the point that a learning organisation is built through reflectiveness, deep aspirations, the desire to see systematic barriers and enacting systems more in line with what people wanted to create. Yet using the suggested classic top-down approach leads more towards a managed faculty model (cf. Rhoades, 1998) for the sake of institutional efficiency. There is a tension between the need for the institution to provide *vertical integration* of efforts to help create an institutional identity and that of *horizontal representation* when faculty represent their disciplinary interests, based on a healthy conflict of interests requiring faculty and administrative units to come together to provide a balanced view of effective priorities and definition of appropriate – quality – performance (Padró, 2004).

Shulman (2007) asserted that assessments enrich the narrative of the story being told. He tied together assessment with accountability, with the former providing technique while the latter emphasises the storyline of what is being told. Mentowski (1998) believed that assessment information helps to continuously improve programmes. For her, 'effective conversations about assessment move quickly to probing educational commitments, goals, and values' (p. 270). Nevertheless, something seems to be missing from the assessment discussion. Cameron's (1986) view about inherent paradoxes in organisational effectiveness was that it is non-linear, full of contradiction and disconfirmation. The preference is to focus on efficiency and those measures telling that story. In university environments that can be described in terms of Birnbaum's (1988) anarchic organisational environment, strictly focusing on assessment (and accountability for that matter) does not fully reflect the influence institutional dynamics and structural elements of a university have over the language used, goals set, and approach toward setting those goals. 'What becomes tightly or loosely coupled in this symbolic system is related to a mixture of collegial interactions, bureaucratic structures, ongoing coalitions, chance, and cognitive processes by which people make inferences and judgments under conditions of uncertainty' (p. 160).

What is missing is a broader systems perspective, a viewpoint that is found in the quality movement. With similar historical timelines to the assessment movement, it is nonetheless a movement that has not been easily accepted in academic circles because of its roots within business and industry. It provides a systems perspective that merges internal and external environmental concerns with a focus on people as well as techniques and end results. As Ouchi (1981) wrote in his seminal *Theory Z,* the objective is to develop 'the ability of the organization to coordinate *people*, not technology, to achieve productivity' (p. 97).

Benefits from adopting the quality model

O'Brien (1998) warned that universities have to develop a clearer sense of intellectual focus, a clearer sense of their own capabilities and values, and social significance so that they do not become purely market driven or alternative sites for commercial training programmes. Yet, when it comes to quality, there are different perspectives from different stakeholders that are looking for dominance. 'This is not a different perspective on the same thing but different perspectives on different things with the same label' (Harvey and Green, 1993, p. 10). SSU has to demonstrate that it is 'creating an environment where educators, parents, government officials, community representatives, and business leaders work together to provide students with the resources they need to meet current and future academic, business, and societal needs' (Arcaro, 1995 as cited in Goldberg and Cole, 2002, p. 10). Student and other stakeholder satisfaction has to play a significant role in its decision-making processes based on the current perception that universities are feeders of the knowledge industry rather than traditional disseminators and creators of information (Padró and Horn, 2008).

SSU's enemy is time, as many changes sought by leaders take long debate. Shifts in attitude from their subordinates, associates, and organisational culture are slow (Gardner, 1990). The university has to be concerned about what Kegan and Lahey (2001) called *competing commitment*, especially from faculty, even when they may hold a sincere commitment to change and improving the way they teach, do research and perform service. The problem here is that resistance to changes is externally mandated and does not really help improve quality and efficiency (Costa and Lorente, 2007). For some, the disconfirmation of what they stand for is based on the view that Quality sees higher education as a professional service although recognising its difference from other services. This is in part due to the field subscribing to Bertalanffy's (1969) systems theory construct that a good theory applies across the board. Nevertheless, higher education warrants separate treatment because it is at the pure service end of the good-service continuum, characterised by a higher degree of interpersonal contact, complexity, divergence and customisation (Srikatanyoo and Gnoth, 2005).

Owlia and Aspinwall's (1996) six quality dimensions of higher education focus on service satisfaction: tangibles, competence, attitude, content, delivery and reliability. Concerns are for issues such as time, timeliness, completeness, courtesy, consistency, accessibility and convenience, accuracy and responsiveness (Kontoghiorghes, 2003). The emphasis is on reduction and refinement of immediate tasks and indirectly – depending on the climate established by leadership (Amabile et al., 2004) – on creativity and issues on what and how to teach. However, only two of the quality dimensions provide data in a traditional Birnbaum (2000) *Ur-Management* environment (tangibles and competence). The remaining dimensions reflect indicators and measures not typically used as performance measures; yet, elements of two other dimensions (content and delivery) are used in some national systems to demonstrate university performance or as documentation of faculty performance (hiring, tenure and promotion). The remainder are elements deemed appropriate and are becoming embedded within the new guidelines for documenting institutional performance and excellence.

Finally, the chapter investigates the benefits of adapting a quality perspective from the lens of Kotter's (1995) eight steps for transforming an organisation. For the CEO, using a quality framework helps him or her *establish a sense of urgency, create a vision with strategies* and *form a powerful and guiding coalition* of board members (if these are part of the equation), administrators, academic staff (faculty), students and stakeholders to lead the change effort through effective teamwork. '[T]he job of the leader is to accomplish transformation of his organization' (Deming, 1994, p. 116). Transformation is assisted by establishing a philosophy based on a systems perspective that allows the different units to see themselves as integrated and interdependent. The importance of a systems perspective is that it provides connectivity to SSU because it helps develop unifying principles that bring the different elements of the organisation together (cf. Bertalanffy, 1969). It begins by redefining the university's system and its extent and then, as Deming (1994) pointed out, it makes the aims of change clear to all members of the system. Looking at the action points the incoming CEO has to put in play, it becomes apparent that he or she will require nothing short of a comprehensive philosophical structure that also provides specific technical elements to make sure that positive change happens based on the changing notions of success in these times of uncertainty in the support of higher education. More importantly, the need is to get buy-in and willing and supporting participation, especially from the faculty ranks.

Using a quality framework allows senior administrators the ability to *communicate the vision and strategies* necessary for change and *getting rid of obstacles* to change by changing systems or structures seriously undermining the vision. This way, senior administration can *encourage risk-taking and nontraditional ideas, activities, and actions* to meet the newly identified demands, making SSU more agile in meeting the ever-changing external environment. A legitimate strategy in the quality model is continuous improvement, a combination of short- and long-term planning and commitment to mission and established goals and outcomes. Translating to Kotter's (1995) transformation model terminology, quality allows for *planning for and creating short-term wins* in order to demonstrate (*plan for and create*) *visible improvement* as well as pursue the necessary linkage to long range planning based on a plan–do–evaluate–improve cycle. Part of the short- and long-term planning activities should also *recognise and reward those individuals involved in making the improvements.*

An important act for senior administrators that can be derived from the identified action plans at the beginning of the chapter is to *consolidate improvements* and *produce even more change by using gained credibility* to continue changing that which does not fit the vision. Included in this consolidation process is the hiring, promotion, and development of faculty and other staff who can implement the vision. Also important is to reinvigorate the process with new projects, themes, and change agents to embed a culture of continuous evaluation and improvement. Quality as a schema, especially quality assurance, is not the same thing as programme outcome evaluation because there is also a focus on process along with results (Royse et al., 2010). Quality assurance in particular is often based on compliance to a set of standards, be these internal or external.

Faculty governance participants, other key faculty leaders, and individual faculty, unfortunately have to undergo what Weick (1995) referred to as a 'sense-making process' to determine if the vision and strategies communicated are appropriate and legitimate, and that the processes created by senior administration are getting rid of the obstacles to genuine change that benefits SSU as an institution and its student body as a whole. This has to be done while maintaining a balance between valid disciplinary/professional and other pedagogical concerns and public policy steering pressures to provide a workforce in the fields that are the 'flavour of the day'. The action plans of faculty governance and key faculty leaders are the mirror opposite of what senior administration has to provide; nonetheless, the adoption of a quality framework provides faculty with a collaborative structure that extols participation and a legitimate recommending voice from those responsible for facilitating the learning taking place at SSU. What is important here is that individual faculty members see the elimination of obstacles and the focus on recognition and reward as factual rather than suggestive. A careful application of the quality model (cf. Sebastianelli and Tamimi, 2003) provides a greater role for faculty in the processes leading to decisions about institutional quality. Quality is defined by the beholder. Definitions and expectations of quality are different according to one's role within the university (cf. Padró, 1988); therefore, the action plans of faculty have to (1) be based on their perceived ability to provide actual participation and influence on SSU processes and (2) establish that there are tangible benefits to active cooperation and participation with other faculty and administrative structures.

As indicated earlier, this approach is an amalgam of situations different universities have had to face. In many regards, the issues are quite generic, which at one level is rather daunting. The university described in this chapter decided to use a quality framework as a means of navigating through the uncertainty of the changing economic circumstances, of changing demographic patterns of student enrolment, and of changing external review requirements and mandates. The CEO has recognised the very complex set of events that typically occur within a university campus and, to be proactive, brought everyone together – including external stakeholders – to see how the institution could maintain its agility and autonomy. The university has successfully navigated the miasma of uncertainty and has increased its reputation and standing in the process.

Bateson (2002/1979) suggested that learning is a stochastic process. Education thus acts as a governor of a kind, and herein lies the challenge for educators at all levels. Focusing on accountability and assessment can do the job, but it does not bring all elements together because it does not redefine the system to encompass the external environment and the hold it has on organisational behaviour (Pfeffer and Salancik, 1978). Adopting a quality model can assist that. Moreover, it can allow all elements within SSU and other universities to come together and establish a united vision and form of action that will balance the interests of the different parts of the campus as well as stakeholders from the outside. Furthermore, the emphasis on continuous improvement and participation may provide a strategy that would allow any university to maximise its ability to meet changes and to legitimise its demand for autonomy based on responsible stewardship of resources, social responsibility, and academic integrity and excellence.

References

Amabile, T.M., Schatzel, E.A., Moneta, G.B. and Kramer, S.J. (2004) 'Leader behaviors and the work environment for creativity: Perceived leader support', *The Leadership Quarterly*, 15: 5–32.

Aronowitz, S. (2006) 'Should academic unions get involved in governance?', *Liberal Education*, 94(2): 22–7.

Balderston, F.E. (1995) *Managing Today's University: Strategies for Viability, Change, and Excellence* (2nd edn). San Francisco: Jossey-Bass.

Barzun, J. (1968) *The American University: How it Runs, Where it is Going*. New York: Harper & Row.

Bateson, G. (2002/1979) *Mind and Nature: A Necessary Unity*. Cresskill, NJ: Hampton Press, Inc.

Bertalanffy, L. von. (1969) *General System Theory: Foundations, Development, Applications* (revised edn). New York: George Braziller.

Birnbaum, R. (1988) *How Colleges Work: The Cybernetics of Academic Organization and Leadership*. San Francisco: Jossey-Bass.

Birnbaum, R. (2000) *Management Fads in Higher Education: Where They Come From, What They Do, Why They Fail*. San Francisco: Jossey-Bass.

Birnbaum, R. (2003) 'The End of Shared Governance: Looking Ahead or Looking Back'. Paper presented at the Research Forum on Higher Education Governance, 12–14 June 2003 in Santa Fé, New Mexico. Available at: *http://www.usc.edu/dept/chepa/gov/roundtable2003/birnbaum.pdf* (accessed 11 May 2009).

Blau, P.M. (1994) *The Organization of Academic Work* (2nd edn). New Brunswick, NJ: Transaction Publishers.

Cameron. K. (1986) 'Effectiveness as paradox: Consensus and conflict in conceptions of organizational effectiveness', *Management Science*, 32(5), 514–539.

Costa, M.M. and Lorente, A.R.M. (2007) 'ISO 9000:2000: The key to quality? An exploratory study', *Quality Management Journal*, 14(1): 7–18.

Deming, W.E. (1994) *The New Economics for Industry, Government, Education* (2nd edn). Cambridge, MA: MIT Press.

Ewell, P.T. (2002) 'An emerging scholarship: A brief history of assessment', In T.W. Banta (ed.) *Building a Scholarship of Assessment*, pp. 3–25. San Francisco: Jossey-Bass.

Gardner, J.W. (1990) *On Leadership*. New York: Free Press.

Goldberg, J.S. and Cole, B.R. (2002) 'Quality management in education: Building excellence and equity in student performance', *Quality Management Journal*, 9(4): 8–22.

Harvey, L. and Green, D. (1993) 'Defining quality', *Assessment and Evaluation in Higher Education*, 18(1): 9–34.

Kanji, G.K. (1998) 'An innovative approach to make ISO 9000 standards more effective', *Total Quality Management*, 9(1): 67–78.

Kegan, R. and Lahey, L.L. (2001) 'The real reason people won't change', *Harvard Business Review*, 79(10): 85–92.

Kennedy, D. (1997) *Academic Duty*. Cambridge, MA: Harvard University Press.

Kontoghiorghes, C. (2003) 'Examining the association between quality and productivity performance in a service organization', *Quality Management Journal*, 10(1): 32–42.

Kotter, J.P. (1995) 'Leading change: Why transformation efforts fail', *Harvard Business Review*, 73(2): 59–67.

Mentowski, M. (1998) 'Higher education assessment and national goals for education: Issues, assumptions and principles', In N.M. Lambert and B.L. McCombs (eds) *How Students Learn: Reforming Schools Through Learner-centered Education*, pp. 269–310. Washington, DC: American Psychological Association.

Millett, J.D. (1980) *Management Governance, and Leadership: A guide for college administrators*. New York: AMACOM.

O'Brien, G.D. (1998) *All the Essential Half-truths about Higher Education*. Chicago: University of Chicago Press.

Ouchi, W. (1981) *Theory Z: How American Business Can Meet the Japanese Challenge*. Reading, MA: Addison-Wesley.

Owlia, M.S. and Aspinwall, E.M. (1996) 'Quality in higher education – a survey', *Total Quality Management*, 7(2): 161–71.

Padró, F.F. (1988) Quality Circles and Their Existence in Present-Day School Administration. Unpublished dissertation. Tucson; University of Arizona.

Padró, F.F. (2004) 'Vertical Integration v. Horizontal Representation: The clash of cultures in university environments and how these impact institutional standards and their assessment of quality'. *Proceedings for the 7th 'Toulon–Verona' Conference on Quality*, 2–4 September 2004, pp. 135–44. Toulon: University of Toulon-Var.

Padró, F.F. and Horn, J. (2008) 'Leaving academia to become part of the knowledge industry: The unintended consequence of diminishing creativity', *Journal of the World Universities Forum*, 1(4): 113–20.

Padró, F.F. and Hurley, M.M. (2008) 'Assessing Institutional Learner Outcomes', *Journal of the World Universities Forum*, 1(3): 65–72.

Pfeffer, J. and Salancik, G.R. (1978) *The External Control of Organizations*. New York: Harper and Row.

Rhoades, G. (1998) *Managed Professionals: Unionized Faculty and Restructuring Academic Labor*. Albany, NY: State University of New York Press.

Rice, R.E. (2006) 'Faculty work and the new academy', *Liberal Education*, 92(4): 6–13.

Royse, D., Thyer, B.A. and Padgett, D.K. (2010) *Program Evaluation: An Introduction*. Belmont, CA: Wadsworth CENGAGE Learning.

Sebastianelli, R. and Tamimi, N. (2003) 'Understanding the obstacles to TQM success', *Quality Management Journal*, 10(3): 45–56.

Senge, P.M. (2006) *The Fifth Discipline: The Art and Practice of the Learning Organization* (revised edn) New York: Currency Doubleday.

Shulman, L.S. (2007) 'Counting and recounting: Assessment and the quest for accountability', *Change*, 39(1): 20–5.

Slaughter, S. and Rhoades, G. (2004) *Academic Capitalism and the New Economy*. Baltimore, MD: Johns Hopkins University Press.

Srikatanyoo, N. and Gnoth, J. (2005) 'Quality dimensions in international tertiary education: A Thai prospective students' perspective', *Quality Management Journal*, 12(1): 30–40.

Stake, R.E. (2006) *Standards-based and Responsive Evaluation*. Thousand Oaks, CA: Sage Publications.

Tierney, G.T. and Minor, J.T. (2003) *Challenges for governance: A national report.* Los Angeles: Center for Higher Education and Policy Analysis. Available at: *http:// www.usc.edu/dept/chepa/pdf/gov_monograph03.pdf* (accessed 11 April 2009).

Trow, M. (1996) 'Trust, markets and accountability in higher education: A comparative perspective', *Higher Education Policy*, 9(4): 309–24.

UNESCO (2009) *2009 World Conference on Higher Education: The New Dynamics of Higher Education and Research for Societal Change and Development.* Paris, France. Available at: *http://www.unesco.org/fileadmin/ MULTIMEDIA/HQ/ED/ED/pdf/WCHE_2009/FINAL%20 COMMUNIQUE%20WCHE%202009.pdf* (accessed 10 October 2009).

Weick, K.E. (1995) *Sensemaking in Organizations.* Thousand Oaks, CA: Sage Publications.

Williams, D., Gore, W., Broches, C. and Lostoski, C. (1987) 'One faculty's perception of its governance role', *Journal of Higher Education*, 58(6): 629–57.

Zemsky, R., Wegner, G.R. and Massy, W.F. (2006) *Remaking of the American University: Market-smart and Mission-centered.* New Brunswick, NJ: Rutgers University Press.

A framework for engaging leadership in higher education quality systems

Lorraine Bennett

Abstract

This chapter is set against a landscape in higher education dominated by quality-driven funding models and accountability. It describes the development of the Engaging Leadership Framework (ELF) which provides a strategic and practical framework to assist leaders oversee change and improvement. The ELF is presented as a powerful visual model which incorporates complex but interrelated concepts of leadership into a simple, easy to apply leadership tool. It is an outcome of the 'Leadership for Implementing Improvements in the Learning and Teaching Quality Cycle' project funded by the Australian Learning and Teaching Council (ALTC).

Key words: Engaging Leadership Framework (ELF); Australian higher education; quality-driven government funding models; Centre for the Advancement of Teaching and Learning (CALT); excellence; continuous improvement, responding to stakeholder feedback; evidence-based planning and decision making.

Introduction

During the last ten years, more than ever, universities in Australia have operated in a constantly changing environment. These changes have been driven largely by increased public scrutiny and subsequent government reforms demanding greater rationalisation and accountability of the activities and practices of higher education institutions.

The introduction, in the twenty-first century, of overt quality-driven government funding models to support teaching and research were early indicators of a policy shift. New funding models reflected the popular view that universities need to clearly demonstrate their value to society. The Learning and Teaching Performance Fund (LTPF) linked university funding to student performance and satisfaction indicators and the Research Quality Framework (RQF), proposed assessing and funding research on quality and impact outcomes. A change in the Commonwealth Government saw both the LTPF and the RQF superseded by new funding schemes, but the focus on measurement and providing evidence of outcomes still remain the key criteria for determining the allocation of the funds.

The establishment of two national agencies in the early 2000s – the Australian Universities Quality Agency (AUQA) which merges into the Tertiary Education Quality and Standards Agency (TEQSA) in 2011, and the Australian Learning and Teaching Council (formerly the Carrick Institute for Learning and Teaching in Higher Education) – further illustrates the fluid and quality-driven nature of the environment in which universities operate.

The above examples highlight the need for leaders across the university sector to be strategic and nimble in order to respond to and capitalise on the opportunities that arise from constant change. However, equipping leaders with the skills and capacity to successfully lead change is complex and an ongoing challenge. It was a search for a systematic strategy to lead such change and improvement which led to the development of the Engaging Leadership Framework (ELF), described in this chapter.

The ELF was nominated as the main deliverable for a project proposal entitled 'Leadership for Implementing Improvements in the Learning and Teaching Quality Cycle' funded by the ALTC. Specifically, the purpose of the project was to develop a tangible leadership tool, in the form of a framework, which would identify and bring together in a practical way key elements which underpin effective leadership of change and improvement.

Background

The thinking behind the framework was initially informed by work undertaken in the period 2002–6 while developing and implementing new programmes in a single-department faculty in one of Australia's largest universities. The challenges for the faculty leadership were framed by the imperative to quickly adapt to mature-aged cohorts of students, requiring alternate entry pathways, new enrolment and payment systems, and customised courses. However, implementation of the new programmes was hampered by insufficient support infrastructure, inflexible and unwieldy information management systems and restrictive policies and procedures.

In addition some academic staff, who perceived that they were already overworked, were asked to adapt their teaching strategies to accommodate experience-rich, study-poor, mature-aged students, wanting to undertake their studies in multiple modes (face-to-face and online), in concentrated periods of time and often at workplace locations.

The lessons about leading innovation and managing change from the faculty experience were captured in an Emerging Leadership Framework (Appendix A). The 'emerging' framework contained the elements that were thought to be essential to achieving effective change. The selection of these elements was decided by identifying the factors which seemed to facilitate the smooth introduction of the new programmes and by reflecting on what was missing when problems occurred.

The initial emerging leadership framework contained the following drivers and constructs: relationship building; academic excellence; management systems, policy and planning, quality and communication. It also acknowledged that leadership occurs at, and is influenced, by what happens at the operational, institutional and external – community – levels. The entire framework was presented as an integrated teaching, learning and research model.

This framework formed the basis for a leadership project proposal from the university's Centre for the Advancement of Learning and Teaching (CALT) to the then Carrick Institute for Learning and Teaching in Higher Education Ltd, now the Australian Learning and Teaching Council (ALTC). The intent was to take the initial assumptions about leading change and test, develop and refine the Emerging Leadership Framework. The plan was to draw on aspects of action-research methodology to advance the team's knowledge and understanding of 'leading excellence'.

The process

Over the course of the project the leadership framework evolved organically, through at least six visual iterations (Appendix B). These were developed and informed by cycles of targeted literature searches and reviews, consultations, case study observations, reflection, discovery and synthesis.

The literature searches spanned studies and research on organisational leadership, change management and quality improvement. The focus was on reviewing material that addressed team and organisation-wide leadership as distinct from individual leadership. Examples of effective data-driven leadership practice which reported findings in terms of quantitative and qualitative outcomes were sourced and reviewed.

In the consultation cycles, feedback on drafts and elements of the framework was sought from academic and professional staff across the university, from within other universities and from outside the sector. The team consulted with Deans and Associate Deans (Education), with senior university staff (Deputy Vice-Chancellors and Pro Vice-Chancellors), with faculty and divisional/centre managers, with teaching and professional staff, with students and with external consultants who specialise in leadership and change management. Often this feedback was extremely frank. One group of academic staff criticised an early version of the framework, describing it as static, dull and overly managerial. This feedback prompted further work to seek examples of leadership frameworks which were more 'organic' in their approach. Reactions to draft frameworks highlighted issues of ambiguity, lack of clarity and complexity. Other feedback, particularly on the later framework drafts, was confirming of the approach and encouraged pursuit of this line of thinking.

The willingness of so many people to comment on the framework and contribute to its evolution proved to be very helpful in the efforts to reconceptualise and refine the critical elements that needed to be incorporated into the framework.

Other significant inputs into the development of the framework were the observations and reflections on the various unit (subject) improvement intervention strategies (case studies) implemented simultaneously in faculties across the university. A template was developed for these interventions based on a quality cycle of 'plan', 'act', evaluate' and 'improve'. The reports on these activities, as well as the pre- and post-test findings, were instructive and led to the decision to rotate the customary order of the quality cycle so that the ELF starts with the 'evaluation phase' – confirming the framework on data-driven planning and decision-making.

Throughout this project reflective practice and discovery were viewed as complementary activities. Reflective practice sometimes led to an 'ah ha!' moment, but more often was used as a way of making sense of the various sources of information and of conducting a stock-take of what had been discovered thus far. The use of reflective practice techniques was often quite subtle. For example, on occasions, reflective practice framed by hypothetical questions such as: 'what if ...' was used to test out ideas, to open new doors and to look for synergies and connections.

A key to the success of this project lay in the way it could bring together all the findings and present them in an accessible and effective framework. The major challenge was to find a way to synthesise the theoretical underpinnings with the various pieces of observation, feedback and discovery that had been collected along the way. The challenge was not only to identify the key elements and drivers of change but to bring them together in a graphic which could explain the framework and show the inter-relatedness of each component without being too cluttered and complex. The visual iterations, referred to earlier (for further detail, refer to Appendix B), provide a story board illustrating the progressive stages in building the framework.

The product

The final outcome was the Engaging Leadership Framework illustrated in Figure 4.1. This consists of three key components which were identified and tested in the project as being critical factors in leading improvement in higher education.

Figure 4.1   Framework for Engaging Leadership

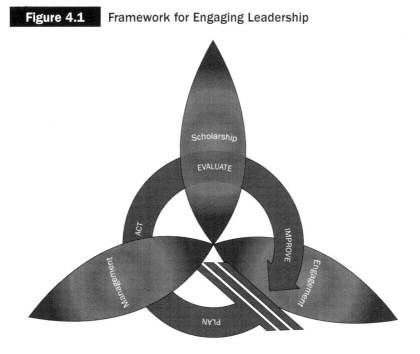

The first component is the 'trilogy of excellence' – excellence in scholarship, excellence in engagement and excellence in management which embody the mission, values and aspirations of the university.

The second component provides the process for change. It builds on continuous quality theory. It utilises a variation of the quality cycle, starting with the evaluation and review phase, emphasising the importance of drawing on institutional data to guide change and improvement.

The third component, which is depicted in the visual framework by the three diagonal stripes, reflects the importance of shared leadership responsibility for effective change. It was reinforced by the literature on distributed and dispersed leadership theory. The three stripes represent inputs from the operational, the institutional and external perspectives.

The strength of the framework is the interrelatedness of the three areas of excellence, their location both within and outside the quality cycle, and the potential for diverse leadership inputs (operational, institutional and external). The framework is primarily driven by evidence-based planning and decision making, as part of a quality improvement process.

The 'trilogy of excellence'

The 'trilogy of excellence' represented in Figure 4.2, was identified as an important driver for effective leadership at Monash University. The first 'blade', *excellence in scholarship*, was selected because it involves the pursuit of academic excellence and encompasses the mission and values of the institution. The decision to privilege scholarship was influenced by the work of many contemporary educators and researchers (Biggs, 2003; Ramsden, 2003; Prosser and Trigwell, 1999).

Findings confirmed and elaborated on the positioning of 'scholarship' as one dimension of the trilogy of excellence. There was broad agreement from educators that 'scholarship' needs to be redefined more broadly from research expertise in a subject area or discipline to include expertise in the scholarship of learning and teaching. Other propositions (Baldwin, 2007) uncovered during the course of this project relevant to the notion of scholarship include:

- that the 'knowledge era' is changing curriculum content and skills;
- that the skills of analysis, evaluation, and synthesis are becoming more important than mastery over a body of knowledge;
- that employability skills and vocational education need to recognise the social context of learning;

Figure 4.2 The key components – trilogy of excellence

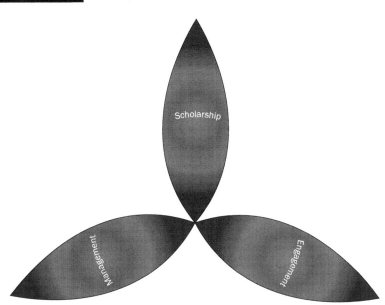

- that leadership at multiple levels of the university needs to support the goal of scholarship of learning and teaching;
- that innovation often emerges from the teacher–student interface; and
- that the practices of academic heads of departments appear to be pivotal to developing an environment that fosters a culture of improvement of learning and teaching excellence.

Excellence in engagement, the second strand of the 'trilogy of excellence', recognises the importance of relationship building and communication for effective leadership. In the early version of the Emerging Leadership Framework, the importance of relationship building and communication were nominated as key elements for effective leadership of learning and teaching. As the Leading Excellence project developed through various consultation and reflection phases, the significance of these two concepts was reinforced. As it was often difficult to distinguish between the actions of relationship building and communication, the term 'engagement' was chosen to encompass the thinking and practice exemplified by both: engagement implying participation and involvement in any activity – learning or organisational development.

The literature suggests that 'engaging' students in the content, management and evaluation of learning and teaching leads to improved learning outcomes (Trigwell and Prosser, 1991; Krause, 2005). There is also strong support for the view that the 'engagement' of staff with issues related to learning and teaching and planned implementation of changes is equally important for sustaining cultures of improvement (Scott, 2007). Similarly, the implementation of change strategies needs to recognise local context and the use of existing expertise to build trust and shared values. While these concepts have been reported in educational literature for some time, evidence of their sustained application in leading change is less apparent. Indeed in the consultations and discussions undertaken in this project, lack of participation and engagement were often cited as the missing or poorly executed elements in endeavours to lead improvement in learning and teaching.

Excellence in management was identified as the third element in the 'trilogy of excellence'. In terms of effective leadership, it means providing the appropriate infrastructure, policies, systems and resources to support learning and teaching excellence.

The suggestion that a focus on 'management' has been divisive in higher education was a recurring theme in the literature and consultations undertaken in the project (Sheehan and Welch, 1994; McInnis et al., 1995; Biggs et al., 2000; Ramsden, 2003; Anderson, 2006). The divide being between academic leaders who subscribe to discourses associated with 'academic freedom' and institutional managers who talk about values, action plans, targets, accountability and best practice. The contention in the ELF is that strong management systems and practices are needed to support, encourage and reward excellence in the scholarship of learning and teaching and to address underperforming areas (Marshall, 2006). Some of the management systems and practices identified as being at the heart of quality leadership included: provision and alignment of IT systems, resource allocation, the structure of learning spaces, attention to student–staff ratios, promotion criteria, recruitment and selection criteria, job descriptions, and workload models that recognise time commitments involved in leadership and intervention processes.

The quality cycle

The *quality cycle* (Figure 4.3) is an important element of the ELF. It was incorporated into the framework as a result of the accumulated learning from this project. It became clear that effective leadership and improvement in learning and teaching in higher education is enhanced if a quality cycle

Figure 4.3   Quality cycle

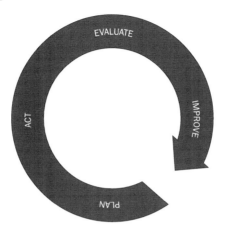

is used to drive the process. The application involved modifying the more common practice (Monash University, 2004) of beginning a quality cycle process with the 'plan' phase to starting with the interrogation of the data, placing the focus on evidence-based planning and decision-making. Thus the suggested sequence becomes: evaluate, improve, plan and act followed by the next rotation of the cycle.

The intention is that data informs discussions and focuses decisions about what needs to be improved or addressed. Starting with the evidence opens the conversation. It allows such questions as: 'what is working well and what is not?' It also enables discussion to draw out contextual and local information which may not be obvious initially. Once the target(s) and priorities for improvement are identified and agreed upon, the planning and implementation of the 'intervention' strategies and actions become much clearer. This approach also reinforces the critical importance of monitoring and reporting back on the outcomes of interventions, as part of a continuous improvement process.

The literature suggests there has been resistance from some academics to valuing feedback from students as an indication of teaching quality and also to the use of measurement (survey) tools on the basis that they cut into class time, do not adequately reflect learning, lower standards and can pander to students (Sheehan and Welch, 1994; Anderson, 2006). Despite ongoing scrutiny, contestation and scholarship focused on the best way to measure quality, the measurement of student learning outcomes remains a key quality indicator in higher education. In this project the team found the student feedback to be a very fruitful way to commence quality improvement conversations and to provide some structure and targets against which to measure intervention strategies.

Diverse leadership perspectives

The final element of the ELF recognises the importance of shared leadership and the role leaders play throughout the organisation in terms of influence, interactions and responsibility for improvement (Ramsden, 1998). In the ELF, this element is described as *diverse leadership perspectives* and acknowledges the importance of thinking about leadership as occurring at multiple levels – at the operational, institutional and external levels (Figure 4.4). The operational level refers to the leadership required in departments, faculties and central student support units where the main interface with students happens. The institutional level refers to the leadership demonstrated by the Council, Vice-Chancellors, Deputy Vice-Chancellors, Pro Vice-Chancellors, Academic Board members, Deans and Faculty Managers as they interact with key stakeholders within the organisation. The external level refers to the leadership required to keep abreast of and engage with government departments and agencies, business and employer groups, professional associations, voters and other external stakeholders. Leadership may be vested in individuals and/or shared by teams (committees).

The concept of leadership 'dispersed throughout an organisation' or 'distributed leadership' is prominent in the literature concerning higher education (Gronn, 2000; Richmon and Allison, 2003; Woods, 2004). The contention is that leadership occurs at many levels where decisions and responsibility lie within the organisational structure. The literature on distributed leadership supports a context-dependent model of leadership where improvement in teaching and learning practices is shown to be situated in a collaborative and collegiate environment.

Figure 4.4   Leadership perspectives

The underlying assumptions of the ELF and its application have been heavily influenced by thinking initially reported by Drucker (1974), and later Garratt (1995) and others. They argue that strategic leadership is about the setting of directions, identifying and choosing activities, and committing resources to create compatibility between internal organisational strengths and the changing external environment within which the university operates. This underlines the need for institutional leaders in particular to keep abreast of and engage with external stakeholders, funding bodies and global socio-economic and political trends.

The ELF in practice: unit improvement

The practical context for the creation of the ELF was leadership of unit improvement. The poster depicted in Appendix C describes the application of the framework using the 'scholarship' aspiration.

The ELF approaches improvement by initially asking the question: *What does the data say?* It interrogates evidence from students and other stakeholders and sources in terms of the quality of the scholarship of learning and teaching – this generally involves looking at feedback on curriculum content, learning materials, assessment and pedagogy and 'benchmarking' it against best practice.

The data identified and interrogated in step one informs and frames conversations and discussions with the relevant stakeholders around the next step which deals with the improvement phase. The key question here is: *What needs to change?* Often this step involves 'drilling down' into the issue and prioritising the areas that need addressing. For example, if the general area of concern was around assessment and there was evidence of high levels of plagiarism. The answer to the question *What needs to change?* would tease out strategies around education of teachers in minimising and detecting plagiarism and education of students on the correct use of source materials and referencing the work of others.

The third step in the process is to do with planning. The question addressed in this phase is: *How will we get there?* Action plans need to be developed which address issues of identifying specific tasks, methodologies, timelines and performance targets. Often it is useful to focus on aspects which can be turned around relatively easily and in a short timeframe. In the ELF project, being able to see and measure improvement as a result of a burst of intensive intervention activities was a great motivator for more extensive reform. Another important part of the planning phase is to draw on the diverse leadership perspectives of the framework.

This involves consideration of leadership inputs, interactions and responsibilities at the operational, institutional and external levels.

The fourth phase in the ELF is the action or implementation phase. It addresses the question: *What will we do?* It is about execution of the plan. During this phase, it is important to document the actions undertaken and to make notes on any changes to the plan that were implemented or any unexpected impediments that impacted on the actions. The ability to accurately monitor and report on these actions is critical to the next rotation of the quality cycle and contributes to the notion of continuous improvement.

After working through the four phases described above in relation to the 'scholarship' element, the next step in applying the framework is to repeat the quality cycle process for 'excellence in engagement' and 'excellence in management', the other aspirations within the trilogy of excellence.

A number of techniques for recording the outcomes of each of the stages were trialled in this project. These included: entering details of the main evidence (data), discussions, decisions and actions into a matrix. Other suggestions included using a task checklist, and project management tools such as a Pert chart, a Gantt chart or customised flowchart. Work on refining guidelines for these possibilities is still in progress but it is highly recommended that some technique for recording each phase is utilised so that the improvement can be tracked and reported.

Conclusion

This chapter describes the development phases and the final product, the Engaging Leadership Framework (ELF), which was nominated as the key deliverable for the 'Leadership for Implementing Improvements in the Learning and Teaching Quality Cycle' project.

The ELF recognises the challenges involved in leading improvement and brings three key aspects of leadership and change together into an integrated model. The 'trilogy of excellence' reinforces the importance of a shared academic vision and purpose across the organisation and the need to embed and support this vision with effective engagement and management systems, policies and practices. The inclusion of the evidence-based quality cycle provides the engine to drive the change, and the diverse perspective 'stripes' of the framework are a reminder that leadership is a shared responsibility and takes place at the operational, institutional and external levels across an organisation.

The ELF concept both informed and was informed by case studies which focused on unit (subject) improvement. However, over the course of the project, it was discovered that the potential applications of the ELF were far wider than unit improvement. The recommendation is that it can be applied as a leadership tool to address a range of change and improvement scenarios. These might include, for example: leading organisation-wide cultural change; addressing faculty and department strategic issues; providing direction for programme and course improvement and shaping individual professional development. This view is supported by one of the institution's academic leaders who declared that 'the ELF has a lot to offer ..., both as a strategic and practical tool in the current higher education climate characterised by rapid change, globalisation and quality assurance'(Shoemaker, 2008).

One of the main advantages of the ELF is that it provides a holistic, strategic and practical approach to leading improvement. Not only does it have the potential and capacity to help reshape the way leadership is conceptualised in learning and teaching, but it can also be applied across the higher education sector and to other organisations. The ELF is designed so that based on their needs, leaders can use the framework as a road map, customise it to suit their workplace and apply it to a range of micro or macro improvement challenges.

The plan for the next phase of the project is to disseminate and consolidate the ELF by assisting four other university sites to grow their leadership capacity by applying the framework to a quality improvement issue that has been identified as a concern in stakeholder satisfaction or performance data. The issue may have surfaced in performance, survey or focus group data or as a result of an internal or external review of some aspect of learning and teaching on the campus.

Future activities will focus on working with each of the organisations to jointly develop customised ELF resources, materials and professional development activities to support the application of the ELF to address the leadership capacity building challenge identified at each of the locations.

Acknowledgements

The project described in this chapter has been funded by the Australian Learning and Teaching Council (ALTC). Further information on the Leadership for Excellence in Learning and Teaching Program is available at: *http://www.calt.monash.edu.au/leadership/index.php*

The ELF project was led by Dr Lorraine Bennett and she would like to thank Christine Tasker, Joy Whitton and Cassandra Eadie for their invaluable support in the project.

Appendix A

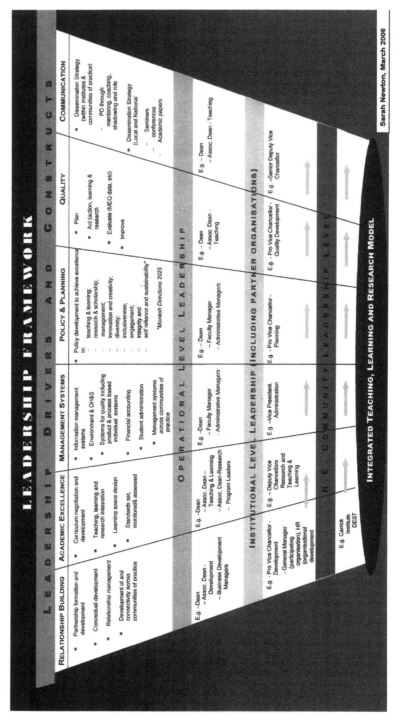

LEADERSHIP FRAMEWORK

LEADERSHIP DRIVERS AND CONSTRUCTS

RELATIONSHIP BUILDING	ACADEMIC EXCELLENCE	MANAGEMENT SYSTEMS	POLICY & PLANNING	QUALITY	COMMUNICATION
• Partnership formation and development • Conceptual development • Relationship management • Development of and connectivity across communities of practice	• Curriculum negotiation and development • Teaching, learning and research integration • Learning space design • Standards set, monitored & assessed	• Information management systems • Environment & OH&S • Systems for quality including product & process based individual systems • Financial accounting • Student administration • Management systems across communities of practice	• Policy development to achieve excellence in: – teaching & learning; – research & scholarship; – management; – innovation and creativity; – diversity; – inclusiveness; – engagement; – integrity and – self reliance and sustainability* *Monash Directions 2025	• Plan • Act (action, learning & research • Evaluate (MEQ data, etc) • Improve	• Dissemination Strategy (within institutes & communities of practice) – PD through mentoring, coaching, shadowing and role • Dissemination Strategy (Local and National) – Seminars – conferences – Academic papers

OPERATIONAL LEVEL LEADERSHIP

E.g. – Dean – Assoc. Dean – Development – Business Development Managers	E.g. – Dean – Assoc. Dean – Teaching & Learning – Assoc. Dean-Research – Program Leaders	E.g. – Dean – Faculty Manager – Administrative Managers	E.g. – Dean – Faculty Manager – Administrative Managers	E.g. – Dean – Assoc. Dean – Teaching	E.g. – Dean – Assoc. Dean - Teaching

INSTITUTIONAL LEVEL LEADERSHIP (INCLUDING PARTNER ORGANISATIONS)

E.g. - Pro Vice Chancellor - Development - General Manager (participating organisation), HR (organisational development	E.g. – Deputy Vice Chancellors Research and Teaching & Learning	E.g. –Vice President, Administration	E.g. - Pro Vice Chancellor - Planning	E.g. - Pro Vice Chancellor - Quality Development	E.g. –Senior Deputy Vice Chancellor

H.E. COMMUNITY LEADERSHIP LEVEL

E.g. Carrick Institute DEST					

INTEGRATED TEACHING, LEARNING AND RESEARCH MODEL

Sarah Newton, March 2006

Appendix B

Evolution of the Engaging Leadership Framework (ELF)

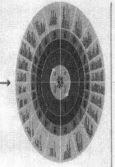

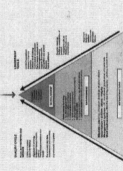

ELF VERSION 1

The initial version of the leadership framework originated in the Faculty of Education in 2006 and was known as the Emerging Leadership Framework (ELF-1). The framework proposed an integrated teaching and research framework and nominated six chairs crucial to effective leadership of improvement of learning and teaching. These were: relationship building, academic excellence, management of systems, policy and planning, quality, and stakeholders. The framework identified key change to be effective: the goals of tension need to be aligned and support each other at these levels — the operational level, the institutional level and the external level.

ELF VERSION 2

The second iteration phase of the Engaging Leadership Framework (ELF) overlayed the phases of the Monash University Quality Cycle — plan, act, evaluate and improve — into the framework. The aim was to underpin the framework structure with a clear and logical process for implementing improvement.

ELF VERSION 3

The next version of the framework moved away from the matrix format and tried to visually depict the drivers (ambition) and tools within a pyramid structured ELF-3. While the structure brought out the importance for effective leadership of the 'image of excellence' — excellence in scholarship, engagement, and management — the power of the quality cycle became lost in the framework.

ELF VERSION 4

ELF-4 was an attempt to recognise the quality cycle. By doing so, the purpose of the cycle was clarified and a decision was taken to start the cycle with the data-gathering process as the evidence. However, the framework then failed to capture the essence of leadership within the higher education sector.

ELF VERSION 5

After further consultation, reflection and review ELF-5 was created. This framework proposed a circular design where the Quality Cycle was shown as the fulcrum around which the dimensions of scholarship (combining the personal drivers of academic excellence and quality and relationship building, balancing stakeholder and communication and influences) of leadership, policy and planning and management systems) turned. This captured the engaged and systematic approach sought, however it was considered too complex to be a useful tool.

ELF VERSION 6

Finally, a professional graphic designer was briefed and after experimenting with a number of images and concepts, the Engaging Leadership Framework (ELF6) was created. ELF6 provides a simple, easy-to-follow visual solution to a number of complex concepts and principles that were raised through the course of the project as being essential to effective leadership of improvement in learning and teaching.

Appendix C

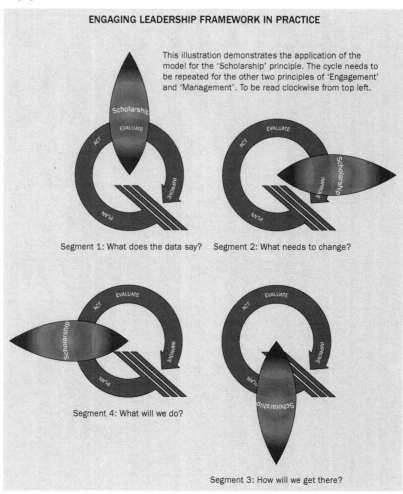

ENGAGING LEADERSHIP FRAMEWORK IN PRACTICE

This illustration demonstrates the application of the model for the 'Scholarship' principle. The cycle needs to be repeated for the other two principles of 'Engagement' and 'Management'. To be read clockwise from top left.

Segment 1: What does the data say?   Segment 2: What needs to change?

Segment 4: What will we do?

Segment 3: How will we get there?

References

Anderson, G. (2006). 'Assuring quality/resisting quality assurance: academics responses to "quality" in some Australian universities', *Quality in Higher Education*, 12(2): 161–73.

Baldwin, G. (2007). *The Teaching Research Nexus*. Melbourne University, CSHE. Available at: *http://www.cshe.unimelb.edu.au/pdfs/TR_Nexus.pdf* (accessed 9 April 2008).

Biggs, J. (2003). *Teaching for Quality Learning at University: What the Student Does*, 2nd edn. Berkshire, UK: The Society for Research into Higher Education and Open University Press.

Biggs, J., Davis, M. and Coady, T. (eds) (2000). *Why Universities Matter*. St Leonards, NSW, Allen and Unwin.

Drucker, P. (1974). *Management: Tasks, Responsibilities and Practices*. London: Heinemann.

Garratt, B. (1995). *Learning to Lead: Developing your Organisation and Yourself*. London: HarperCollins Publishers.

Gronn, P. (2000). 'Distributed properties: a new architecture for leadership', *Educational Management and Administration*, 28(3): 317–38.

Krause, K. (2005). *Understanding and Promoting Student Engagement in University Learning Communities*. Melbourne University, CSHE. Available at: *http://www.cshe.unimelb.edu.au/pdfs/Stud_eng.pdf* (accessed 11 May 2008).

Marshall, S. (2006). *Issues in the Development of Leadership for Learning and Teaching in Higher Education*. Occasional paper, the Carrick Institute for Learning and Teaching in Higher Education. Available at: *http://www.carrick institute.edu.au/carrick/webdav/users/siteadmin/public/grants_leadership_ occasionalpaper_stephenmarshall_nov06.pdf* (accessed 16 April 2008).

McInnis, C., Powles, M. and Anwyl, J. (1995). 'Australian academics' perspectives on quality and accountability', *Tertiary Education and Management*, 1(2): 131–9.

Monash University (2004). *Quality at Monash, Values and Principles*. Available at: *http://www.adm.monash.edu.au/cheq/quality/quality-at-monash-values-principles.html* (accessed 12 April 2008).

Prosser, M. and Trigwell, K. (1999). *Understanding Learning and Teaching: The Experience in Higher Education*. Buckingham, UK: SRHE and Open University Press.

Ramsden, P. (1998). *Learning to Lead in Higher Education*. London: Routledge.

Ramsden, P. (2003). *Learning to Teach in Higher Education*, 2nd edn. London: RoutledgeFalmer.

Richmon, M. and Allison, D. (2003). 'Toward a conceptual framework for leadership inquiry', *Educational Management and Administration*, 31(1): 31–50.

Scott, G. (2007). 'Learning leaders in times of change', *Campus Review*, 9(4): 8–9.

Sheehan, B. and Welch, P. (1994). 'International Survey of the Academic Profession, Australia'. University of Melbourne, paper prepared for the Carnegie Foundation.

Shoemaker, A. (2008). *Leading Excellence: A Report on the 'Leadership for Implementing Improvements in the Learning and Teaching Quality Cycle' Project*, Monash University. Available at: *http://www.calt.monash.edu.au/ leadership/index.php* (accessed March 2009).

Trigwell, K. and Prosser, M. (1991). 'Improving the quality of student learning: the influence of learning context and student approaches to learning on learning outcomes', *Higher Education*, 22(3): 251–66.

Woods, P. (2004). 'Democratic leadership: drawing distinctions with distributed leadership', *International Journal of Leadership in Education*, 7(1): 3–26.

Part 3
Approaches of managers to quality in higher education

Quality management in higher education: a comparative study of the United Kingdom, the Netherlands and Finland

Laurie Lomas, Christine Teelken and Jani Ursin

Abstract

This chapter examines lecturers' perceptions of the balance between quality assurance and quality enhancement in three case study higher education institutions in different European countries. Where quality initiatives emphasised assurance rather than enhancement, this was taken to indicate a significant limitation on a lecturer's autonomy in the quality management process. In-depth interviews using a semi-structured schedule were conducted with 20 randomly selected academic staff in each of the three higher education institutions. The results from the interviews demonstrated a very wide range of views among the interviewees. However, generally, it was found that there was a high level of disappointment with only limited transformation of teaching and learning through quality enhancement. This sense of disappointment was particularly acute in the UK and Dutch institutions where many interviewees expressed concern that quality assurance approaches tended to dominate. In the Finnish higher education institutions, there was a more positive attitude towards quality initiatives with a far higher proportion of interviewees considering that lecturers had significant control over the quality management process and they felt that there was an appropriate balance of quality assurance and quality enhancement.

Key words: quality management; UK higher education; Finnish higher education; Dutch higher education; quality assurance; quality enhancement.

Introduction

This chapter is based on case studies in the United Kingdom (UK), the Netherlands and Finland. In all three cases, the research question was, 'What do you think of first when I say the phrase: quality in higher education?' Every care was taken by the researchers not to influence the respondents in any way and no leading questions were asked. The respondents were academic members of staff in a variety of Higher Education Institutions (HEIs) in each of the countries. They had varying amounts of experience and came from a wide range of academic disciplines. In all three countries the sample included lecturers, senior lecturers, a few heads of departments and in Finland also several students. All three countries are signatories to the 1999 Bologna Declaration which aims to create a highly competitive supra-national European Higher Education Area, in part through the convergence of the various national structures (Bologna Declaration, 1999).

In order to examine the respondents' views on quality management, an analytical framework was used which was based on the two main types of quality: Quality Assurance (QA) and Quality Enhancement (QE). QA has also been described as Type I and QE as Type II. It is acknowledged that there are potential problems in employing this dualism as it does not encapsulate all of the complexities related to quality management. However, the views of the academic staff in the three case studies highlight how opinions can vary along a continuum from QA at one end to QE at the other.

Where there was found to be a greater emphasis on QA, this was taken as an indication of reduced lecturer autonomy because of the pronounced influence of external government agencies on quality management. The general views of academic staff on quality management in the three countries are detailed and the similarities and the differences between the three cases are identified. This leads to an understanding of the degree of autonomy that academic staff have in managing quality in the European countries under review.

The authors will briefly define quality management and assess its impact on higher education before making a link with managerial autonomy, the research method and the results of the case studies in the three countries.

Quality management

'Quality refers to the standards that must be met to achieve specified purposes to the satisfaction of customers' (Ellis, 1993, p. 4). The management of quality can be considered under two broad headings: QA, which has a managerial focus and stresses fitness for purpose and accountability; and QE, which is collegial and concerned with enhancement. QA and QE coexist in HEIs with the particular blend being situational and varying over time and from one HEI to another. Knight and Trowler (2000) argue that QA has a managerial focus because of its maintenance function which is based on the achievement of specified targets and the need for assurance. QE emphasises collegiality, discussion and the sharing of ideas. This should lead to a concentration on creativity and enhancement. A further distinction is that QA is retrospective and stresses compliance and accountability (Hodson and Thomas, 2003) and this contrasts with QE which is prospective and involves continually striving for improvements in teaching and learning (Biggs, 2003). Making use of Harvey and Green's (1993) categories of quality management, QA addresses issues of fitness of purpose and consistency whereas QE aims for transformation.

QA processes include accountability, audit and assessment which are designed to control quality by means of influencing the relevant people in higher education in order to meet externally imposed standards (Elton, 1992) while QE utilises empowerment, enthusiasm, expertise and excellence (Elton, 1992). The extent of quality enhancement will vary greatly in terms of its impact and effectiveness as this is dependent to a large extent on the initiatives of particular HEIs as well as those of government agencies (Hodson and Thomas, 2003). At the individual level of the lecturer, enhancement involves strengthening, augmenting or improving existing practices. Lecturers are more likely to achieve these aims if their HEIs are able to develop and then sustain a quality enhancement culture (Hodgkinson and Kelly, 2007).

In most countries national government agencies have established frameworks and procedures that are designed to establish and maintain high standards in higher education. West European quality management systems tend to be based on a model which includes a national agency, self-evaluation, quantitative data, peer review and a published report (Van Vught and Westerheijden, 1993). The UK Quality Assurance Agency (QAA) is a good example of such a national agency. Established in 1997, its mission statement envisages quality largely in terms of accountability and compliance and these are achieved, for example, through subject benchmarks and codes of practice (Hodson and Thomas, 2003). Examples of QE initiatives in the UK include the support by HEFCE (2006), Centres for Excellence in Teaching and Learning (CETLs) and the Higher Education Academy sponsorship of National Teaching Fellows who are seen as purveyors of excellent practice (Higher Education Academy, 2006).

In the Netherlands HEIs are accountable to the Ministry of Education with the Education and Research Act (1993) and the Adult and Vocational Education Act (1996) being of great significance in terms of quality management. Similarly, in Finland the Ministry of Education and the Finnish Higher Education Evaluation Council (FINHEEC) are the major central agencies of quality monitoring and change management.

Quality and its links with autonomy and the freedom to manage

Shore and Wright (1993) and Hoecht (2006) argue that the QA auditing process is a clear example of Foucaultian panoptic surveillance of lecturers. However, Shore and Wright also claim that academics are not always victims as many know how to 'play the game' and are not in any way damaged by the QA process. They are able to circumvent the control measures. However, Morley (2003) strongly disagrees, stating that QA is generally about surveillance and control and these are key elements of a 'command economy in higher education that threatens to produce self-policing, ventriloquising apparatchiks, as opportunities for self-agency are reduced' (p. 162).

QA has been the dominant form of quality management because of the development of an audit culture in HEIs (Power, 1997) and this has forced them to adopt managerialist systems, structures and processes which more closely resemble business approaches (Delanty, 2001). The increased pressure from external agencies for audit has made many HEIs move towards the rationalisation of structures and decision-making which has led to increased central administrative control of HEIs' organisational management. This in turn has brought about a reduction in lecturer autonomy so that they now have less influence on quality in their departments (Henkel, 2000).

Approach

The research in each of the three countries involved in-depth interviews with twenty randomly selected academic staff. In the UK since 1992 there has been no binary divide between universities and polytechnics. However, in order to canvass the views of staff in a wide range of HEIs, interviewees were drawn from both modern (post-1992) and the older and more traditional universities. In the Netherlands, there is a binary divide between traditional universities and professional universities. Both types of institution were represented. As in the Netherlands, a binary divide exists in Finland. There are 48 HEIs of which 20 are universities and 28 are polytechnics (universities of applied sciences). In Finland the interviewees were only from the university sector.

Semi-structured interviews were chosen as the research method as they allowed similar questions to be asked of all respondents. Also, they provided the opportunity to follow up any interesting points through the use of supplementary questions (Gillham, 2005). All interviews were audio taped, transcribed and then analysed using the Constant Comparative Method (Strauss and Corbin, 1998). This involves assigning meaning to each particular point in an interview and then comparing it with the other points in the interview. When similarities of meaning are found, they are grouped into themes. If no similar meaning is found during a comparison, then a new theme category is created.

Findings from the case studies

The UK

A most significant feature of the views of the sample of lecturers, senior lecturers and heads of departments in traditional and modern UK HEIs was that 44 per cent of the respondents specifically remarked that quality initiatives were largely related to QA. A physics lecturer in a traditional university even went as far as to say that QA could be likened to the quality control systems used in industry from the 1950s to the 1970s. An American studies lecturer in a modern university was concerned that quality initiatives based on assurance were designed to provide standardisation and conformity in universities at a time when diversity was being encouraged. The lecturer mentioned that Scott (1998) had noted that although there were more than a dozen different types of HEI in the UK, the external quality initiatives were largely the same for all HEIs and argued that quality initiatives were not sensitive to the great variety of mission statements.

Many of the respondents made the point that quality initiatives in higher education tended to concentrate on processes rather than on content. A business studies lecturer in a modern university said that he spent a lot of time in his university collecting and passing on to central departments statistics that, it was claimed, showed the students were receiving a good quality education. However, he thought that the collection of these statistics was about building up an audit trail of paper when the time could be used more purposefully to improve his lecture notes and design more effective ways of engaging his students.

A computer science lecturer in a traditional university had the same view of the quality management statistics that were collected, saying that it was not always possible to be confident about the accuracy of some of the data disseminated by quality units. There was often a temptation to 'be creative with' the figures so that they showed higher satisfaction levels. It was sometimes difficult to resist this temptation because of the need to attract greater numbers of students with the associated increase in fee income and funding.

An English lecturer in a traditional university was concerned that the consistency and conformity associated with QA procedures and clear targets stifled essential elements of higher education such as creativity and criticality. She was reflecting the concerns expressed by Barnett (1997) and Rowland (1999), among others, about the changing emphasis in higher education. A psychology lecturer in a modern university supported this view, arguing that quality seemed to be far more related to a managerial (QA) rather than a professional (QE) model and this meant that there was relatively little concern with the curriculum and how students learn. However, she noted that there had been some good work here by the Psychology subject network of the Higher Education Academy but this professional approach to quality was not seen as much as she would have liked.

A general view of many of the academic staff in the sample was that there had been an increase in customer-orientation among higher education senior managers and administrators and this had led to an increase in the use of performance indicators to gauge whether customer needs were being met. There were performance management, league tables and benchmarking which were all examples of 'hard' indicators that purported to show whether students were receiving high quality education. A number of respondents thought that the strong emphasis on QA rather than QE was because the Government is under pressure to respond to a wide range of stakeholders such as the students, their parents, employers and taxpayers who are looking for evidence in the form of indicators to show that universities are effective and efficient and represent good value-for-money.

A politics lecturer in a traditional university warned that older academics often hark back to a 'golden age' of the 1970s when they perceived that higher levels of autonomy existed. This may lead them to have a relatively negative view of current quality initiatives even though lecturers still enjoy far higher levels of autonomy than their colleagues in compulsory and further education and those working in other public sector organisations such as the National Health Service (NHS) and local government. He said academic staff in HEIs were less constrained by benchmarking, standards, service level agreements and protocols than employees in other public sector organisations.

A few respondents had a more positive view of quality initiatives in terms of their impact on the curriculum and students. An accountancy lecturer in a modern university agreed that there was an emphasis on QA but she believed that there were clear advantages as well as some disadvantages. The prescriptive aspects of QA meant there was very little ambiguity for the lecturer because clear indicators, such as subject benchmarks and the National Qualifications Framework, were provided for lecturers, students and universities. The QAA's published results of audits were most helpful for lecturers not only for the evaluation of programmes but also for planning curriculum developments and initiatives. She supported Williams' (2002) point that quality enhancement can result from clear quality processes and changes in programme content, delivery or assessment leading to improvements in the students' experience. She also said that QA processes provided a system for managing academic risk. Higher education was heavily subsidised by the Government and many people who did not use it were paying towards it. This is why it was perfectly reasonable that risks were identified and appropriate action taken. This accountancy lecturer emphasised the accountability function of quality initiatives giving the example of the first Director of the Quality Assurance Agency, being determined to identify those academics who were not up to standard and who were putting the students' education at risk.

An engineering lecturer in a traditional university supported this view of the impact of QA on improvements to the curriculum and teaching. She considered that the major purpose of quality management was to ensure that standards were high and regular quality reviews provided useful information which could then help identify areas for improvement. Programme team members had the information from the QA process that put them in a position to address any shortcomings that had been identified. She also felt that staff time spent reviewing, evaluating, collating data and planning was time well spent.

Overall, many of the respondents spoke of the problems rather than the advantages associated with QA. Although QE was not mentioned directly, a couple of respondents implicitly highlighted the relationship between

QA and QE which often led to the enhancement of teaching, the curriculum and the student experience.

The Netherlands

The Dutch respondents had a wide range of views on the quality of research and teaching but in general they felt that the current developments at HEIs were not related to enhancement. Instead, they indicated that developments in quality management put much more emphasis on quality in terms of assurance and control. The extent of this pressure on performance did vary from one HEI to another and between departments and research groups in particular HEIs.

The respondents accepted that some kind of steering mechanism is required and that a structured approach to quality provides clarity of systems and structures and leads to a thorough review of existing practice. However, the respondents were more inclined to emphasise the undesirable consequences of the control associated with QA. They considered that the control process seems to take precedence over the content of teaching and research. The accreditation model is the main driving force and teaching and research need to fit in to this model. However, this is not always appropriate.

A number of respondents claimed that the importance of image and the desire to attract students seemed to detract from an attention to 'real quality' issues such as teaching students in such a way that they are able to fulfill their potential.

It was also mentioned that lecturers often very easily find ways around quality systems, and they consider it to be of little or no value. One lecturer stated that the accreditation process takes little account of the quality that exists in an institution. It is more a façade than anything substantial. The concern seems to be more about whether the boxes can be ticked to show that procedures are being followed. Another lecturer at a Hogeschool (a University of Applied Sciences) stated that he had mixed feelings about the accreditation system for academic programmes. He argued that the strength of the accreditation process was that it facilitated the implementation of competence-based learning. He highlighted that the system involved transparency about what is required of the students and lecturers. On the other hand, it encouraged a teaching approach which can be too rigid and can result in a mechanistic 'tick-box' approach. Although this may be good for weaker students, it can severely constrain the better ones. He believed that striving for 'real quality' would be more likely to occur if lecturers had greater autonomy because professionals can enhance the quality of their teaching through reflection, professional development and peer review.

Another problem identified was that not everything is evaluated. Lectures are evaluated but dissertation and thesis supervision and workshops are not. As far as the evaluation of lecturers is concerned, if a lecturer is inadequate very little seems to be done to address this.

Teaching is not the only area of their work for which academics are held accountable. In traditional universities in particular, it is research which matters more. With research, there is often more emphasis on the quantity rather than on the quality of publications. Many Dutch respondents felt that it was the expectation of a high output of research papers which leads to promotion and career progression. However, this pressure affects the quality of the work as there is insufficient time to be as critical and challenging as they would like.

In general, the Dutch respondents identified numerous problems with the current quality system. They saw the value of a national quality system but generally they did not believe that it had a significant impact on improving quality. There seemed to be more rhetoric than reality (Teelken and Lomas, 2009).

Finland

Unlike the UK and the Dutch samples, the Finnish respondents highlighted the point that quality has features of both QA and QE. This was particularly evident when the participants elaborated upon their understanding on 'quality'. The QA element of consistency was mentioned twelve times by respondents, and fitness for purpose on eleven occasions. Consistency was understood by the respondents to be achieved through the rules, regulations and agreed instructions which were designed to guide academics, administrators and students in all matters related to the institution's academic programmes. As an example, a lecturer in a natural sciences department noted how the importance of clear, transparent and easily understandable rules reduced the level of misunderstanding and ambiguity related to academic work and activities. The fitness for purpose referred to the congruency of the work carried out by staff and students and how it fitted with their goals and those of the HEI. A student who was interviewed mentioned that students should know exactly what to expect from teaching in order to get the best out of the course. The lecturer's and student's views here support Brennan and Shah's (2000) positive view of QA that it increases transparency in HEIs.

Quality was perceived by sixteen participants to include elements of both QA and QE. They saw QA as a means of monitoring the quality of various activities. A lecturer said that teaching should have follow-up actions so that both the students and the lecturers can evaluate how well the goals for teaching and learning have been met. Those respondents who stressed the importance of QE argued that the purpose of quality initiatives is not just to guarantee minimum quality or monitor teaching and learning as is the case with QA, but rather QE should constantly develop and improve curriculum development and teaching activities. This was the essential contribution of QE.

Only four of the respondents viewed QA specifically as a form of control. A lecturer in the field of engineering said that QA is concerned with watching over the educational and research processes so that the demands of society are met. He believed that by closely controlling an HEI's functions, the basic tasks of the institution can be better performed. He was highlighting the positive rather than negative features of this control.

The Finnish respondents considered that the determinants of quality were more internal than external to the HEI with internal factors being mentioned almost twice as often. Internal determiners included the scientific community, academic staff and students. The scientific community was important especially in defining the quality of research whereas the students were acknowledged for their significant role in helping to develop teaching and learning. There were external factors which are related to society, financiers and legislation. A lecturer in a natural sciences department highlighted the importance of feedback from society at large because, if this was not acted upon, he feared that inadequate higher education would be provided leading to a workforce unable to cope effectively with the challenges of the twenty-first century.

Raising financial issues, a lecturer in the field of biology highlighted the point that the Finnish Government is the primary funder of higher education and therefore it has the right to demand that the resources it allocates are used purposefully. This respondent considered that while the responsibility for academic activities of good quality rests with members of the HEI's academic community, upon the formal structures and its decision-making bodies, HEIs are responsible to society and so it is perfectly reasonable that the accountability element of QA is not neglected.

The case studies: similarities and differences

There are a number of similarities and differences between the quality management approaches in the three countries which are helpful in explaining the range of responses of the academic staff in the sample.

Compared to the Dutch and Finnish systems, there is far greater compliance in the UK (Hodson and Thomas, 2003). In the UK generally the respondents talked about the external influences on quality. Newton (2002) refers to the burgeoning of the 'quality industry' throughout Europe but with UK HEIs being subject to a larger number of audit criteria than elsewhere in the world (Billing, 2004). Hodson and Thomas (2003) argue that in the UK the balance between institutional autonomy and public accountability has shifted towards the latter with a consumerist approach leading to a concern to meet the needs of higher education stakeholders such as students, their parents, prospective students, employers and government agencies. The QAA has brought about a culture of conformance with academic departments providing paper audit trails to make it abundantly clear that they observed the Agencies' requirements (Evans, 2002) and evidence has to be gathered to show that there are sound systems and structures designed to assure the quality of academic programmes and the students' learning (Gordon, 2002). McNay's (2006) research revealed rather alarmingly that 77 per cent of academic staff thought that QA procedures had encouraged conformity in teaching and discouraged innovation.

Dutch and Finnish HEIs have traditionally enjoyed higher levels of autonomy. However, the relationship between the state and HEIs has changed in all three countries with a movement away from a situation of relatively light control by government to one of greater central control (Brennan and Shah, 2000). Nevertheless, there has been more significant and more radical change in the UK than elsewhere in Europe (Theisens, 2004). This is possibly because quality management systems were introduced earlier to UK HEIs than in the Netherlands and Finland. The UK Council for National Academic Awards was formed in 1965 to scrutinise the provision of higher education in polytechnics (which became modern universities in 1992), but in the Netherlands quality management was not introduced until the 1980s (Hoecht, 2006). In Finland it was not until the early 1980s that decision-makers started to pay attention to 'quality' issues (Saarinen, 2005).

Academic departments in Dutch HEIs enjoyed a relatively large amount of autonomy (De Boer and Goedegebuure, 2001) but, with the introduction of the 1997 Modernisering Universitaire Bestuursorganisatie (MUB) Act (the law for modernising universities' administrative structures) HEIs became accountable to a supervisory body called the Raad van Toezicht (Board of Governors). This consisted of five non-academics who were accountable to the Minister of Education. Representative councils remained at institutional and faculty levels but, overall, academic staff lost much of their power. Although power shifted towards the centre because of the Act, the extent of the centralisation was not as great as was expected. De Boer and Goedegebuure (2001) believe that this was because central command structures did not work particularly well in Dutch HEIs and thus when managerialist approaches, systems and structures were introduced, it was difficult to sustain them.

Although the Finnish quality management culture is historically based on a collegial enhancement approach, in recent years the conception of quality as QA has become far more significant (Simola and Rinne, 2006). Through FINHEEC, there is a QA 'fitness for purpose' approach in Finland as well. The balance of QA and QE in the Finnish Higher Education sector is seen clearly in how evaluative information that is gathered is used. Not only is it used to indicate the existence of particular high quality activities (QA), it is also used as part of self-evaluation to identify and inform development activities (QE) (Lomas and Ursin, 2009).

To summarise, there are a number of similarities between the three higher education systems but, comparatively, during the last thirty years the changes in UK HEIs have been more radical. Consequently, it would appear that academics in UK HEIs now have less autonomy in managing quality than their Dutch and Finnish counterparts. Observers of European higher education systems such as Harvey and Newton (2007), Rosa et al. (2006) and Stensaker et al. (2007) suggest in their analysis that academics have relatively little power and, in terms of quality, there has been disappointing progress in the improvement of students' teaching and learning experiences. Using Harvey and Green's (1993) definitions of quality, transformation of teaching and learning has rarely occurred.

Conclusions

The empirical research, particularly with academic staff, in the UK reflects the disappointment that only limited transformation through QE has been achieved. Many UK academics have not seen the desired emphasis on the conception of quality management based on a collegial, enhancement-led approach as the respondents have generally perceived quality management to be externally determined by government agencies and with the process involving a degree of supervision and control. With the few exceptions of the academics who appreciated the clarity and high standards of control, nearly all respondents disliked the consequences of an increased emphasis on quality assurance which have been forecasted by, for example, Barnett (1997) and Rowland (1999).

In the Netherlands it is the general opinion that quality management in its current shape and character does not suit the individual academic, neither their teaching nor their research. While the respondents are not so much against the general idea of quality management they dislike the manner in which it is being carried out. Dutch academics complained about 'window dressing', increased workload and lack of attention to the implicit, 'real' quality in teaching and research. The academic staff in the sample generally felt that the outcome of quality management initiatives has been little or no enhancement of the quality of teaching and research. There are similarities here with the views of the UK respondents and this fits with the analysis of Harvey and Newton (2007), Rosa et al. (2006) and Stensaker et al. (2007).

The situation is rather different in Finland as only a few academic staff perceived QA as a form of control and most of them reported a reasonable balance between QA and QE conceptions. According to Finnish participants both managerial (QA) and collegial (QE) features co-existed. Hence, academics in Finland seem to retain control with the quality matters largely remaining in their own hands even if they recognise and accept the managerial conceptions and the aims associated with QA.

From the perspective of European higher education, the question is how will quality management develop in the future as a result of the Bologna Declaration and Process? Will there be a continued drift towards a QA approach? Or will there be greater emphasis on a more balanced approach similar to that of the Finnish system which would allow lecturers greater control over the management of quality? Further research involving a longitudinal study using the same methodology in, say, five years' time would help answer this question.

References

Barnett, R. (1997) *Higher Education: A Critical Business*. Buckingham, SRHE/ Open University Press.

Biggs, J. (2003) *Teaching for Quality Learning at University*. Buckingham: SRHE/Open University Press.

Billing, D. (2004) 'International comparisons and trends in external quality assurance of higher education: Commonality or diversity?', *Higher Education*, 47, 113–37.

Bologna Declaration (1999) *European Higher Education in a Global Setting: A Strategy for the External Dimension of the Bologna Process*. Available at *http://www.dcsf.gov.uk/londonbologna/uploads/documents/ExternalDimension-finalforconference.doc*.

Brennan, J. and Shah, T. (2000) *Managing Quality in Higher Education*. Buckingham: SRHE/Open University Press.

De Boer, H. and Goedegebuure, L. (2001) 'On limitations and consequences of change: Dutch university governance in transition', *Tertiary Education and Management*, 7(2), 163–80.

Delanty, G. (2001) *Challenging Knowledge*. Buckingham: Open University Press.

Ellis, R. (1993) 'Quality Assurance for University Teaching: Issues and Approaches', in R. Ellis (ed.) *Quality Assurance for University Teaching*, pp. 3–15, Buckingham: Open University Press.

Elton, L. (1992) 'Quality enhancement and academic professionalism', *The New Academic*, 1(2), 3–5.

Evans, G. (2002) *Academics and the Real World*. Buckingham: SRHE/Open University Press.

Gillham, B. (2005) *Research Interviewing – A Range of Techniques*. Maidenhead: Open University Press/ McGraw-Hill Education.

Gordon, G. (2002) 'The roles of leadership and ownership in building an effective quality culture', *Quality in Higher Education*, 8(1): 97–106.

Harvey, L. and Green, D. (1993) 'Defining quality', *Assessment and Evaluation in Higher Education*, 18(1): 9–34.

Harvey, L. and Newton, J. (2007) 'Transforming Quality Evaluation: Moving On', in D. Westerheijden, B. Stensaker, and M. Rosa (eds) *Quality Assurance in Higher Education*, pp. 225–45, Dordrecht, the Netherlands: Springer.

Henkel, M. (2000) *Academic Identities and Policy Change in Higher Education*. London: Jessica Kingsley Press.

Higher Education Academy (2006) *National Teaching Fellowship Scheme – Individual Awards*. Available at *http://www.heacademy.ac.uk/NTFSindividual.htm* (accessed November 2009).

Higher Education Funding Council for England (HEFCC) (2006) *Funded Centres for Teaching and Learning*. Available at: *http://www.hefce.ac.uk/learning/tnits/cetl/final/* (accessed November 2009).

Hodgkinson, M. and Kelly, M. (2007) 'Quality management and enhancement processes in UK business schools: a review', *Quality Assurance in Education*, 15(1): 77–91.

Hodson, P. and Thomas, H. (2003) 'Quality Assurance in Higher Education: Fit for the new millennium or simply year 2000 compliant?', *Higher Education*, 45, 375–87.

Hoecht, A. (2006) 'Quality assurance in UK higher education: Issues of trust, control, professional autonomy and accountability', *Higher Education*, 51(4), 541–63.

Knight, P. and Trowler, P. (2000) 'Editorial', *Quality in Higher Education*, 6(2): 109–14.

Lomas, L. and Ursin, J. (2009) 'Collegial or managerial? Academics' conceptions of quality in English and Finnish universities', *European Educational Research Journal* 8(3), 447–60.

McNay, I. (2006) *Beyond Mass Higher Education.* Maidenhead: SRHE/Open University Press.

Morley, L. (2003) *Quality and Power in Higher Education.* Maidenhead, SRHE/Open University Press.

Newton, J. (2002) 'Views from below: academics coping with quality', *Quality in Higher Education,* 8(1): 39–61.

Power, M. (1997) *The Audit Society: Rituals of Verification.* Oxford: Oxford University Press.

Rosa, M., Tavares, D. and Amaral, A. (2006) 'Institutional consequences of quality assessment', *Quality in Higher Education,* 12(2): 145–59.

Rowland, S. (1999) 'The role of theory in a pedagogical model for lecturers in higher education', *Studies in Higher Education,* 24(3): 303–14.

Saarinen, T. (2005) 'From sickness to cure and further. Construction of "quality" in Finnish Higher Education policy from the 1960's to the era of the Bologna process', *Quality in Higher Education,* 11(1): 3–15.

Scott, P. (1998) 'Massification, internationalisation and globalisation', in P. Scott (ed.) *The Globalisation of Higher Education,* pp. 108–29, Buckingham: SRHE/Open University Press.

Shore, C. and Wright, S. (1999) 'Audit Culture and anthropology: neo-liberalism in British Higher Education', *The Journal of the Royal Anthropological Institute,* 5(4): 557–75.

Simola, H. and Rinne, R. (2006) 'Koulutuksen laadunarvioinnin yhteiskunnallisten vaikutusten tutkimisesta' [On researching the impacts of quality assessment of education], *Hallinnon tutkimus,* 25(2): 66–80.

Stensaker, B., Rosa, M. and Westerheijden, D. (2007) 'Conclusions and Further Challenges', in D. Westerheijden, B. Stensaker and M. Rosa (eds) *Quality Assurance in Higher Education,* Dordrecht: the Netherlands, Springer, pp. 247–60.

Strauss, A. and Corbin, J. (1998) *Basics of Qualitative Research: Techniques and Procedures for Developing Grounded Theory.* Newbury Park: Sage.

Teelken, C. and Lomas, L. (2009) 'How to strike the right balance between quality assurance and quality control in the perceptions of individual lecturers: A Comparison of U.K. and Dutch Higher Education Institutions', *Tertiary Education and Management* 15(3), 259–75.

Theisens, H. (2004) *The State of Change: Analysing Policy Change in Dutch and English Higher Education.* Enschede, the Netherlands: University of Twente Publications.

Van Vught, F. and Westerheijden, D. (1993) *Quality Management and Quality Assurance in European Higher Education: Methods and Mechanisms.* Luxembourg: Commission of the European Communities.

Williams, P. (2002) 'Anyone for enhancement?', *QAA Higher Quality,* 11(1): 1.

Towards a culture of quality in South African higher education

Nicolene Murdoch and Anci Du Toit

Abstract

Institutions all over the world are faced with change forces, impacting on their reputation and even threatening provision of quality services to students in all regards. Quality is still defined in various ways, and there are also perceptions that existing quality mechanisms which are in place are sufficient. There is a range of concerns and barriers that are evidently impacting on the establishment of a culture of quality in higher education. Among the most crucial links in the chain of successful implementation of a quality culture at a university are the support of management, sound governance structures, but ultimately the individual employee, since implementation of policy is in his or her hands. Even in unstable environments, institutions should embark on this process of establishing an embedded quality culture. The challenge is to apply research findings, observations, lessons learnt and information obtained from the literature to design a strategy aimed at establishing a culture of quality. Most importantly, however are those utilised for embedding quality into institutional cultures in an ever-changing and unstable environment in order to ultimately display evidence of true improvement?

Key words: embedding quality culture; issues and barriers; ever-changing higher education environment; improvement; South African higher education.

Introduction

The South African higher education landscape has undergone major restructuring over the last ten years. This is, however, not unique to this country; globally, universities are grappling with 'change forces' (Fullan and Scott, 2009) which have huge implications for institutions and their functioning within their respective environments. Most of the major changes in the South African context relate to 'profound and moving policy platforms' (Jansen, 2004). This led to the establishment of the current national quality assurance system.

The White Paper (titled *A programme for the transformation of Higher Education*), released in 1997, identified quality as a 'critical principle' in South African higher education. It stated that 'the pursuit of the principle of quality means maintaining and applying academic and educational standards, both in the sense of specific expectations and requirements that should be complied with, and in the sense of ideals of excellence, that should be aimed at' (Department of Education, 1997).

Around the same time, the Council on Higher Education (CHE) was constituted to *inter alia* advise the national Minister of Education on higher education matters and undertake quality assurance activities through the Higher Education Quality Committee (HEQC). The HEQC was constituted in terms of the South African Higher Education Act 1997 as a permanent sub-committee of the CHE with the mandate to:

- promote quality assurance in higher education;
- audit the quality assurance mechanisms of higher education institutions; and
- accredit higher education programmes.

The HEQC was formally established in 2000, and a founding document was released in 2001, outlining its goals, functions and terms of reference. The HEQC released documents delineating the programme accreditation and institutional audit criteria and frameworks in 2004 (CHE, 2004). Fully fledged institutional audits commenced in 2005, followed by various national programme reviews.

South African higher education institutions soon realised that their continued success and reputations are dependent on the integration and accommodation of these external requirements into the internal institutional environments. This not only requires changes to institutional policies, processes and systems, but also implies adjustments to the institution's 'frame of reference' and traditions. This chapter will investigate the development and implementation of a strategy aimed at facilitating what Fullan and Scott (2009) refer to as a 'change-capable culture'.

A culture of quality

Adoption of new initiatives to answer to external demands necessitates changes to institutional cultures. It is clearly an institution's own responsibility to implement certain key elements to realise such a 'change-capable culture' (Fullan and Scott, 2009). Srikanthan and Dalrymple (2005) illustrated the difficulty of effecting change or altering aversion by relating the anecdote used by a president of a university in the United States who said: 'Trying to change an educational system is like trying to move a cemetery; there is not a lot of internal support for it.'

Predominantly external accountability-based approaches to quality monitoring only have 'an initial impact on quality improvement', warned Harvey (1998). Alternative internally driven approaches are needed to ensure a continuous improvement cycle. He advised that the tensions between the external accountability requirements and the internal commitment to the enhancement could be countered by empowering staff to take initiative and find their own ways to improve. This would result in a culture fostering innovation and encourage staff to act as professional enhancers of learning (Hencliffe, in Harvey, 1998).

Gordon (2002) stated that an effective quality culture, by definition, 'involves the articulation of shared perspectives, values, procedures and approaches to practice'. According to Lueddeke (in Srikanthan and Dalrymple, 2005), a change in culture can only be accomplished when implicit and silent assumptions are brought to the surface and confronted. Only then is it possible for a change-capable institution to emerge, which is not defensive, responsive, strategic and outcomes focused (Fullan and Scott, 2009).

The above requires commitment and acknowledgement that all staff should be involved and agree to a common understanding of and 'an underpinning philosophy, beliefs, values and basic assumptions' pertaining to quality. This is, according to Lomas (2004), an important pre-requisite for embedding a quality culture in a university.

Hodgkinson and Brown (2003) agreed with various other authors that the following procedures are the most useful in establishing a learning organisation aimed at a change in culture:

- Raise awareness of the issues and possible solutions through formalised and structured interactions and interventions.
- Dissolve the barriers between academic, administrative and support staff through discussion, sharing of information and joint ownership of problems and solutions.
- Listen to staff from all levels of the organisation, and consider the quality of all proposals, irrespective of the source.
- Keep everyone informed of new developments and challenges.
- Report, recognise and celebrate achievements and successes.
- Managers should demonstrate their commitment to the quality process by regular attendance and involvement in interventions and activities.
- Lastly, look for ways of removing any possible barriers to quality enhancement.

More recently, Fullan and Scott (2009) added to the above-mentioned list of attributes of change-capable universities.

- Calm and evidence-based responses should be provided to crisis situations and collective problem solving.
- Vigorous, transparent decision-making and determination of priorities.
- Clear lines of accountability and recognition of the various stakeholders who function effectively as a collective.
- Simplified approval processes which are outcomes-focused.
- Strategic networking and benchmarking.

The need to make resources (which include physical, psychological, human, infrastructural, etc.) available to support the change process is stressed by Senge et al. (in Srikanthan and Dalrymple, 2005). Further support to creating a quality culture through organisational and operational initiatives includes structural changes, refined designs for work processes, reward systems, information networks and empowered task teams.

When the dialogue within an institution gains momentum, it will result in the development of the ability to reflect on patterns of behaviour and enable stakeholders to see and discuss the bigger picture (Srikanthan and Dalrymple, 2005). These acquired skills and capabilities would in turn result in the development of positive 'attitudes and beliefs' and confidence when staff realise the opportunity to participate and play a role in shaping the future of the institution.

In her analysis of several case studies, Wilkinson (in Strydom et al., 2004) confirmed some of the above findings, and highlighted the following as specifically true for 'change-capable' institutions in the South African context:

- culture change necessitates well planned staff development activities;
- ownership of quality assurance processes is crucial and can be developed by well-designed self-evaluation procedures; and
- changing attitudes is a gradual process.

Referring to several UK and South African studies, Strydom et al. (2004) also warned that implementation of a quality system is doomed to failure unless it has the full support of the university's leadership. Barnett, in Lomas (2004), supported this view by making an important distinction between the management *of* quality and management *for* quality. The latter employs an approach of 'inform and involve', rather than an approach of 'command and control'. Ramsden (Lomas, 2004) postulates that transformational leaders who 'are able to provide a guiding vision and gain commitment, engage the hearts and minds of staff and are thus indispensible in any attempt to effect a change in culture'.

It is clear from the above that change is a cyclical and not a linear process which should be driven by reflective and active leaders. The implication is 'earning by doing' which is crucially important during the establishment of a quality assurance system, together with the firm commitment and involvement from management. Such leaders will ensure that quality policies and structures are continuously evaluated and improved by means of critical self-evaluation procedures. Strydom et al. (2004) further concluded that up-skilling, education and training of staff should thus be recognised as a complex developmental learning process and not an event or a singular compliance exercise.

Research

Purpose and methodology

It is evident from the literature that informal quality assurance systems are often implemented by staff. Different views of quality are also held by staff. The purpose of the first phase of the research project was to conduct a situation analysis among both academic and support staff at a South African institution to:

- ascertain the prevalent notions of quality;
- establish the level of ownership of quality displayed;

- establish the level of importance awarded to quality in the institutional context;
- identify existing quality improvement mechanisms and procedures; and
- identify areas of concern regarding quality.

The research was conducted by means of a structured questionnaire distributed to a non-probability sample of employees on all campuses of a large public institution in South Africa.

The purpose of the second phase of the research project was to identify the constituents or critical success factors of existent creative and productive quality systems present in higher education institutions. This was done by means of Appreciative Inquiry workshops. This research method is aimed towards identifying existing strengths and competencies within a particular context and seeks to create meaning by drawing from concrete success stories and thus emphasises the positive (Reed, 2007).

Research findings

The following is a summary of the main findings of both the above phases of the research project relating to the notions of quality, mechanisms currently utilised to enhance quality and prevalent concerns regarding quality.

Notions of quality

The respondents were asked to define 'quality' within their own work context and the results are shown in Table 6.1. It is clear from the table that staff on different levels, in some instances at the same or different institutions, hold diverse views of what quality entails. The findings clearly indicate that there is a range of views. On the one hand it is described in philosophical, intangible terms, and on the other hand more direct and measurable aspects are emphasised. The above notions cover a wide range of perceptions, and this should be taken into account in the development and refinement of the quality culture within an institution. It clearly demonstrates that the institution needs to determine and recognise the various views in order to derive a common understanding of what quality would entail in their particular context.

Table 6.1   Notions of quality

Notions of quality	Description
Fitness for purpose	Relevant attributes and values, as embodied in the institution's mission and related statements
Fitness of purpose	Compliance of the mission with expectations of relevant policy and stakeholders
Value for money	Responsiveness, cost effectiveness and efficiency
Transformation	Social development, employability and economic growth
Benchmarking	Comparability to other acclaimed institutions
Addressing stakeholder needs	Awareness of the changing needs of clients and application of innovative approaches
A 360 degree philosophy	An all-encompassing quality system with overall involvement of all staff in all activities at all levels
Student development and support	Assisting students to reach their highest potential to interact with the immediate environment and beyond
Integrated and applied research	Relevant, applicable, cutting edge, peer reviewed research that culminates in publication and recognition of the institution
Professionalism	Excellent levels of service quality to all stakeholders
Effective and progressive management	Planning based on informed decision-making and timely communication and consultation
Reliable management information systems	Data quality and institutional research capacity to inform planning and decision-making
Human resource management	Support and investment in staff as key resource
Financial management	Sound financial management to ensure viability and sustainability
Work environment	A safe, secure and comfortable work environment
Partnerships	Mutually beneficial relationships with stakeholders and community engagement
Subject-specific and teaching expertise	Sound pedagogical principles displayed by discipline experts

Mechanisms utilised to enhance quality

The mechanisms shown in Table 6.2 were identified as already employed in the work context to enhance quality. They would all, or at least in part, be familiar and recognised by higher education practitioners all over the world. These are typical and traditional minimum quality assurance requirements, and in some cases evidence can be provided to demonstrate that these formal mechanisms are in place at a particular institution. The proper and effective implementation of the above within a particular context is however a different question. It is often found that it is randomly applied, but does not reach its full potential in terms of the utilisation of the information that is gathered during these processes.

Concerns regarding quality

Table 6.3 shows concerns raised regarding quality. Some of these may be specific to the South African higher education context, but evidence may be found in other countries as well. It is clear from the table that there

Table 6.2 Existing mechanisms to enhance quality

Mechanism	Description
Benchmarking, networking, and sharing best practice	National and international benchmarking, networking and market research to obtain up-to-date information on current trends and developments, according to performance indicators and standards
Human resource management and staff development initiatives	Honest and constructive feedback on performance and subsequent remedial action, as well as encouragement of increased personal and professional competencies
Surveys and evaluations	Instruments to obtain feedback regarding expectations and satisfaction levels of internal and external stakeholders to improve quality of service
Peer review and consultation	Feedback and expert advice from internal and external specialists
Reflective practice	Reflection and subsequent reviews which result in innovative adjustments to improve
Participative management	Management, characterised by delegated responsibility, regular consultation and open discussions

Table 6.3   Concerns about quality

Concern	Description
The under preparedness / readiness of students	Indications that the quality and preparedness of students are deteriorating, specifically related to reading and academic writing skills necessary for tertiary studies
Academic staff workload	Increased workloads and research or administrative related expectations render staff incapable of delivering high quality teaching
Lack of knowledge of the higher education context	Failure to keep track of and react to changes in the higher education landscape, not having a broad perspective and see the bigger picture, both nationally and internationally
Lack of effective communication	Lack of both formal and informal communication channels within institutions
Failure to 'close the quality loop'	Lack or perceived lack of responsiveness to concerns raised and information gathered through self-evaluation and review activities
Lack of support from management	Ineffective or incompetent leadership displaying a lack of commitment and support
Incapable quality practitioners	Lack of credibility, personal attributes, attitudes and skills of those who aim to effect change and lead quality related initiatives

are still very real concerns regarding quality related activities. Some of the respondents still perceived quality management to be a political prescription that endangers intellectual autonomy. Quality initiatives (such as programme reviews) were seen by some as merely a 'paper burden'. A number of respondents labelled the governmental bodies as bureaucratic and felt that while academics are expected to 'bow down' to the requirements of these bodies, it does not ultimately have a real effect on the quality of education.

Establishing a culture of quality

In light of the above, it is clear that the establishment of a culture of quality is no easy task. It might have been expected that the higher education sector generally has matured in this regard over the last few years, but from the above it seems that concerns must be continuously addressed and managed in this process. Creating a quality culture is often viewed as a journey to the 'promised land', which will never be reached, completed or achieved. Managers in higher education are often not even bothered to embark on this journey, or alternatively, they view it as something that can be accomplished in a short period of time with limited input and effort. The challenge is to apply all the above research findings, observations, lessons learnt and information obtained from the literature to design a strategy aimed at establishing a culture of quality in a higher education institution functioning within an ever-changing environment. It is important that a structured approach is determined and systematically implemented.

When considering the strategic intent of an institution, it is preferable that specific mention should be made of 'quality improvement' in the vision, mission and strategic goals of an institution. Alternatively, reference should be made to similar concepts such as 'efficiency' and 'effectiveness'. If this is the case, it indicates that quality is a strategic priority and that quality initiatives are supported by management, which is crucial for establishing a quality culture.

This, however, needs to be translated into practice and it is advisable that a member of the executive management should be assigned responsibility for quality assurance and promotion at the institution. It is also necessary to display this commitment by other executive members attending meetings, events and discussions regarding quality, thereby visibly showing their support and the importance of quality in their portfolios. Executive management should be knowledgeable on both national and international quality imperatives, role players as well as trends in the quality domain related to their particular field, e.g. research. Quality improvement should be high on their operational agenda and regularly be discussed with those reporting to them, which relates to the importance of effective governance structures which allows for such constructive discussions.

It is recommended that institutions follow an all encompassing, systematic approach when striving to embed a quality culture. This is contrary to the suggestion by Lomas (2004) that an institution should initially concentrate on only one of the core activities. There is support in the literature for both the above approaches. An all-embracing approach strengthens the concept of quality being 'everybody's business'. An institution is by definition a multi-faceted entity and the proposed all-inclusive approach will counter the perception that certain functions are regarded as more important than others, e.g. research is more important than teaching. A lapse in the quality of any service rendered by an institution has a detrimental effect on its entire functioning and, ultimately, its reputation.

Even though universities are subjected to various external forces and functioning in modernised societies, they are for the most part still very traditional and hierarchical in nature. On the one hand they consist of organisational units that are structured in terms of administrative responsibilities, and on the other hand they comprise academic communities working towards transferring high level skills and producing educated minds. Governance structures in higher education institutions are increasingly mirroring those of corporate entities necessitated by the environments they are functioning in. As previously mentioned, the governance structures should create opportunities for constructive discussions and informed decision-making.

Typically, the institutional council is ultimately accountable. It is crucial that even at that level, the council should be informed regarding key national legislative imperatives, as well as the quality initiatives and practices within the institution. In most institutions across the world, the senate (or its equivalent) is the ultimate internal custodian of academic quality. It is responsible for final approval quality-related policy and must ensure that it is implemented satisfactorily.

On the next level there is often a structure, such as a quality committee, that steers quality management on behalf of the senate. This structure's functions usually do (or should) include quality management not only of the academic provision, but also of the support services. Governance structures and committees are usually present in institutions, at least on paper. Elaborate documents are found which describes levels of accountability, terms of reference, frequency of meetings, etc. The meetings are however often not constructive, time consuming and non-productive. Fullan and Scott (2009) emphasise this by saying that 'universities often spend too much time discussing what should change and too little time figuring out how to make desired changes happen'.

In order to establish a culture of quality, effective governance structures should be designed by means of an extensive process of consultation to ensure ownership and participation. Furthermore, meetings should be chaired effectively to ensure inclusion of the relevant items on agendas, as well as the identification of action points and assigned responsibility to a particular unit or individual with clear timeframes for feedback. It is important that the culture of quality is displayed not only in an effectively designed governance structure, but also during actual meetings.

Typically, there is a unit or division at the university which is responsible for the institutional execution of quality-related responsibilities. Careful consideration should be given to the team appointed in this unit, especially to those who interact directly with staff, since the personal characteristics of the individual who strives to effect change are viewed as the key to success. If at all possible, different staff members should be appointed to take the primary responsibility for the different portfolios, e.g. academic programmes and/or departments and support services. This will reiterate the equal levels of importance afforded to the different functions of the university.

Lomas (2007) warned that the staff employed in such a unit might be seen as pariahs, or purely as administrative staff, due to their association with the unit rather than with academic or specific support departments. To counter the resultant negative attitudes towards quality initiatives, the staff responsible for the quality management of the academic departments and programmes should have some experience in this regard. Similarly, those responsible for the quality of research activities should be well respected in research cadres. This would reduce the psychological distance between the quality management unit and the academic or research staff.

Even where credible and competent quality practitioners are appointed, ownership and ultimate responsibility for quality management reside with the deans and executive directors, their line managers and finally with each individual staff member, thus those closest to the services rendered. The quality unit's role should be mainly coordinating and facilitating both quality improvement and accountability initiatives and is there to support the staff in any way possible.

It is critical to create a universal frame of reference for the institution to ensure that there is a common understanding of the goals, aims and objectives with regard to quality on the different levels. This should be custom made for a specific institution and be formalised in terms of official and approved documentation. The documentation should typically include a quality policy and procedures, a quality plan that is aligned with the strategic intent and plan of the institution and guideline documents or manuals for the various quality processes. These documents should be developed in consultation with the various stakeholders in the institution to ensure buy-in from all concerned. It should also follow the approval processes as applied within the governance structure of the particular institution. It is recommended that an advisory committee or consultative forum be established to aid discussion and ensure eventual informed consensus.

The development of the relevant documentation and policy documents is, however, only the first step. The even bigger task lies in spreading the message and convincing every individual staff member to implement what is contained in the policy documents and manuals in his or her everyday conduct. Staff from all spheres and levels in the university should be invited to join discussion forums or to serve on advisory committees, which may vary in size and specific purpose. To initially establish and then further stimulate dialogue and debate, it might be advisable to put the identified concerns and issues on the table. Discussions should, however, then be constructively led in a positive direction by focusing on possible solutions and tapping the creative minds of staff.

At the heart of a successful strategy is the effective dissemination of accurate information at all levels. It is imperative that staff should be made aware and informed of the bigger picture of quality management and its role, not only on an institutional level, but also within the higher education context. This could be achieved by the above-mentioned suggestion of active participation, or by inviting guest speakers and experts, international and national, internal and external, to address staff on quality-related trends and experiences in the similar domains. All staff should be invited and encouraged to attend and participate in these seminars and discussions. The increased exposure to the bigger picture, as well as to external expertise will provide a greater understanding of the necessity of related activities on an institutional level. Seminars, training and information sessions should be scheduled for different times of the day, month and year, taking into account the academic calendar, and to accommodate the largest possible target audience. These sessions should also afford staff members the continuous opportunity to ask questions, raise matters of concern or make suggestions for improvement.

Old communication favourites and proven strategies such as staff newsletters, campus newspapers and regular institutional publications should also be utilised, but it is necessary to complement these and also find new and innovative ways to communicate. This can include alerting staff by mobile phone messages to important circulars or deadlines, making use of 'pop-up' screens on the web page, electronic rotating screens displayed in common areas and creating awareness by means of competitions and incentives. The communication campaign should employ printed and electronic media and should be a balanced mix of upward and downward communication.

The most valuable communication is however on a personal level, which reverts back to the characteristics and attitude of a person most likely to succeed in effecting change in institutional culture. Favourable attributes are: having a positive attitude, no self-interest, being self-motivated, pro-active, passionate, persevering, solution-oriented and willing to help. This person should have excellent inter-personal relations, be well-liked and most importantly, treat people with respect. It is essential for a person in this position to be knowledgeable, credible, flexible and trustworthy.

It is recommended that the staff member tasked with the coordination of the quality promotion activities in a specific domain starts by discussing quality related matters with the relevant highest authority, i.e. the dean or executive management member. Presentations could then be made to smaller groups such as the management committee, units or departments and eventually to subsections. It is important that all staff members should be informed on the reasoning behind the quality enhancement drive and that individual roles be clarified. The scheduling of activities, e.g. self-evaluation and peer review processes, should be drawn up in consultation with both the management and staff within the unit.

There is a definite need for systematic direct support during the implementation of quality management processes. This could require redesigning current processes as well as support in developing project management plans. Guidance and input is required in the development of relevant documentation, and advice and assistance regarding logistical arrangements may be useful. The support should however not be forced onto the unit or department but should rather be available on request. Support should also be provided to prepare the necessary parties for, for instance, interviews during a site visit. Assistance can be provided in terms of the distribution of information and documentation, e.g. the self-evaluation report should be provided to the executive management member who is responsible for the faculty or division. This kind of support might seem insignificant, but will certainly aid in efficient and less frustrating experiences, and taking ownership of the quality processes at all levels.

The quality management unit should compile an annual institutional report on the trends in all quality related activities, e.g. the self-evaluation and peer review reports, and by doing so bring matters that need to be addressed at institutional level to the attention of the executive management. Examples of good practice during the year should be showcased and shared with colleagues who may face similar challenges. It might be a consideration to introduce a quality award, similar to that of research and teaching awards for significant progress made in this regard.

Conclusion

The South African higher education sector is challenged by various national and political issues. This created instability in the sector and a general lack of a culture of quality. The national government and authorities are often used as an excuse for not even embarking on this process of change or a complete resistance to quality related initiatives. It does seem that institutions in South Africa have fallen into a trap of waiting for a better or more stable time to tackle some of the above-mentioned challenges and quality concerns. The culture is very much categorised by postponement and deferral, which often leads to not doing anything at all.

Some institutions in South Africa view the process of cultural change as such an enormous task and often don't even know where to begin. Institutions are often faced with so many 'real', everyday issues (e.g. unsafe campus environment, lack of financial aid, violent student protests, etc.) that quality is not a priority, and institutions are tied up in a culture of survival at the most. It was recommended previously that a holistic approach should be followed; however, in some instances it might be worthwhile to make some effort to at least be able to demonstrate some change and improvement, even if it is on a smaller scale.

Another evident characteristic in the South African context is that institutions of higher education often play the 'blame game'. Deteriorating quality and unsatisfied students are always the fault of external forces, and institutions seldom take responsibility for unacceptable service quality, ill judgement or reactive crisis management. For example, the school system is blamed for the under preparedness of students. It may take some time for institutions to consider what they can do to holistically support students and not merely sit back and complain about the lack of quality students entering into the higher education encounter in the first instance.

There is, and will probably always be some new framework, policy, legislation, structure, committee, ministry, funding framework, revised institution typologies, debates about consistent nomenclature, and the list goes on and on. And should any or all of the above fail as an excuse, there is always the academic freedom debate which can be revived. The most important aspect of creating a culture of quality within an institution is to take responsibility and be committed to make a difference. In an era of constant change and in a context of transformation, higher education institutions should lead and not lag behind in displaying excellent quality in all respects.

References

Council on Higher Education (CHE) (2004) *Institutional Audit Framework*. Pretoria, South Africa: CHE.

Department of Education (1997) Education White Paper 3. A Programme for Higher Education Transformation. South African Government Gazette.

Fullan, M. and Scott, G. (2009) *Turnaround Leadership for Higher Education*. USA: Jossey-Bass: San Francisco.

Gordon, G. (2002) 'The roles of leadership and ownership in building an effective quality culture', *Quality in Higher Education*, 8(1), 97–106.

Harvey, L. (1998) 'An assessment of past and current approaches to quality in higher education', *Australian Journal of Education*, 42(3): 237–49.

Hodgkinson, M. and Brown, G. (2003) 'Enhancing the quality of education: a case study and some emerging principles', *Higher Education*, 45, 337–52.

Jansen, J. D. (2004) Accounting for Autonomy: How Higher Education Lost its Innocence. *41ˢᵗ TB Davie Memorial Lecture, University of Cape Town*, 1–11.

Lomas, L. (2004) 'Embedding quality: the challenges for higher education', *Quality Assurance in Education*, 12(4): 157–65.

Lomas, L. (2007) 'Zen, motorcycle maintenance and quality in higher education', *Quality Assurance in Education*, 15(4): 402–12.

Reed, J. (2007) *Appreciative Inquiry: Research for Change*. Thousand Oaks, USA: Sage Publications: CA.

Srikanthan, G. and Dalrymple, J. (2005) 'Implementation of a holistic model for quality in higher education', *Quality in Higher Education*, 11(1): 69–81.

Strydom, J.F., Zulu, N. and Murray, L. (2004) 'Quality, culture and change', *Quality in Higher Education*, 10(3): 207–17.

Part 4
Auditing quality in higher education

Auditors' perspectives on quality in higher education

Robyn Harris and Graham Webb

Abstract

This chapter provides an introduction to External Quality Assurance (EQA), including a brief history of the development of EQA models used in higher education around the world. The concepts of 'fitness for purpose' versus 'fitness of purpose' are discussed, as is the notion of 'standards' as the current hot topic in quality worldwide. Standards as they are defined and interpreted in the academic quality discourse are considered and some practical examples of how standards are being implemented by national EQA agencies are discussed. The second part of the chapter considers approaches taken in EQA and the merits and limitations of such approaches are addressed. Recurring short comings and lessons learned from audits are considered based on experience in Australia and elsewhere from the perspective of auditors. The concluding part proposes the need for EQA to evolve to better reflect the contemporary quality improvement practices of higher education institutions.

Key words: quality; quality audit; accreditation; external quality assurance; academic standards; peer review.

Introduction to External Quality Assurance

The emergence of the 'quality control' movement of the 1950s and its progression into the continuous quality improvement movement has been well documented (Juran, 1995; Mouradian, 2002). The meaning of the concept of quality in higher education has been the subject of considerable debate and discussion, with a number of definitions being widely discussed including quality as distinctiveness, quality as excellence and quality as minimum standards (Harvey and Green, 1993; Green, 1994; Goodlad, 1995). Other common notions include quality as 'fitness for purpose' which indicates that an institution of higher education is judged to be of quality when it demonstrates that it is achieving its defined purposes or objectives. This chapter is primarily based on experience with 'fitness for purpose' audit processes in Australia and New Zealand.

Expectations with regard to quality in higher education arise from the legitimate interests and concerns of governments, citizens/taxpayers, employers, students and parents. Most developed and many developing countries now have national external quality assurance agencies overseeing the operation of their higher education institutions. The purpose and methods of these agencies vary considerably. Accreditation systems are based on the assessment of at least minimum standards and have been a feature of the North American and European higher education environment for many years. Concerns about undermining institutional diversity led to the development of national quality audit systems that apply a 'fitness for purpose' model rather than an explicit standards-based approach. In Australia, the Australian Universities Quality Agency (AUQA) has been charged with undertaking 'fitness for purpose' quality audits since its formation in 2000 and is described in AUQA's Audit Manual as follows:

> AUQA uses as its primary starting point for audit each organisation's own objectives and does not impose an externally prescribed set of standards upon auditees. AUQA considers the extent to which institutions are meeting these objectives, and how institutions monitor and improve their performance. AUQA also takes into account the requirements of relevant external reference points established to guide institutions in setting their objectives. This approach recognises the auditee's autonomy in setting its objectives and in implementing processes to achieve them within some overarching parameters, such as criteria set by agreed national or sectoral guidelines. (AUQA, 2009a, p. 4)

Even in this definition, it is clear that an AUQA 'fitness for purpose' audit is imbued with considerations of 'fitness of purpose' in terms of establishing performance against external reference points, parameters and criteria. In recent years increasing emphasis is apparent in Australian higher education policy toward setting and measuring objective standards, evidenced by, for example, the introduction of criteria-based audits for institutions under provisions of the Higher Education Support Act; the Learning and Teaching Performance Fund which has rewarded institutions financially on the basis of results on government defined measures; Excellence in Research for Australia which assesses research quality within Australia's higher education institutions using a combination of indicators and expert review by committees (with some similarities to the Research Assessment Exercise which has been operational in the UK for the past 15 years); and the development and recent strengthening of the National Protocols for Higher Education Approvals Processes and the Australian Qualifications Framework. The recently announced Tertiary Education Quality and Standards Agency (TEQSA) is Australia's first systematic attempt to establish a combined agency to accredit providers and conduct standards based quality audits across the tertiary education sector. It is proposed that this agency, to commence operations from 2010, will develop objective and comparative benchmarks and focus on measuring and reporting institutional performance in areas such as retention, selection, exit standards and graduate outcomes.

There is an inherent tension between the operation of many EQA agencies whose role includes making summative judgements of institutional performance (which might be considered the 'hard' aspect of quality audit) while also having a role in quality development – the 'soft' side of quality audit. Examples of developmental activities undertaken by AUQA include the creation and maintenance of a Good Practice Database which is used to share information across the sector on good practices identified through audits; the initiation and continued sponsorship of an annual national forum for quality practitioners to discuss quality-related matters; and a range of developmental consultancy work within the Asia-Pacific region. In fact use of the term 'audit' is rather misleading in the context of the actuality of activities in Australia over the past decade as audits have not been standards based and there has been a spectrum of developmental activities associated with the audit process. This begs the question of what a truly standards based audit would look like.

Standards

Academic standards have been the 'hot topic' in higher education quality in recent years. In a report written for the UNESCO World Conference on Higher Education, Altbach et al. (2009, p. xi) noted that:

globalization, regional integration, and the ever-increasing mobility of students and scholars have made the need for internationally recognized standards among and between nations more urgent. The explosive growth of both traditional institutions and new providers raises new questions in regard to standards of quality. Quite naturally, 'consumers' of education ... are demanding some kind of certification of institutions and the qualifications they award. Mechanisms for establishing international comparability are still new and largely untested.

Both within Australia and internationally, the definition, measurement, monitoring and reporting of higher education standards is receiving increasing attention. In the USA, the Secretary of Education's Commission on the Future of Higher Education (Spellings Commission: US Department of Education, 2006) recommended that accrediting agencies pay more explicit attention to standards of student performance including completion rates and student learning. In the UK, the Quality Assurance Agency for Higher Education (QAA) recently published results of a series of enquiries in response to public concerns about slipping standards of higher education raised in the media. This focused on five topics including student workload and contact hours; English language requirements for international students; recruitment practices for international students; the use of external examiners and assessment practices (QAA, 2009).

In Australia, the Ministerial Council for Education, Early Childhood Development and Youth Affairs (the nine Ministers of Education from the State, Territory and Commonwealth Governments of Australia) who are the owners of AUQA, have required the Agency to use its second cycle of quality audits to assess and report on the standards an institution is achieving noting that 'AUQA should be able to recommend ... improvement (including at the subject or discipline level) to ensure that acceptable academic standards (based on ... minimum standards or other reasonable measures of graduate outcomes or success) are being met' (AUQA, 2009b). AUQA Cycle 2 audits which commenced in 2008 maintain a fitness for purpose approach but the Agency claims that these audits will 'reach conclusions on the *outcome standards achieved by the institution, in both absolute and comparative terms, in relation to each theme*' (AUQA, 2009a, p. 27; emphasis added). An examination of the eleven university Cycle 2 audit reports released to date would suggest that AUQA has been only partially successful in meeting this aim.

AUQA notes that the definition of 'standards' in higher education is a complex matter:

The word 'standard' is used for many different concepts, including a desirable structure or behaviour, a criterion to measure such behaviour, or an actual measure. For the purpose of Cycle 2 audits, the intended meaning is closest to the third of these concepts: standards are indicators or descriptors of what certain entities should be able to demonstrate. Specifically, AUQA has adopted the following definition:

> A **standard** is an agreed specification or other criterion used as a rule, guideline, or definition of a level of performance or achievement.

The specification and use of standards helps to increase the reliability and the effectiveness of an application or service, and also assists in its evaluation or measurement. In a few places in the Framework there is mention of 'clear processes' or 'transparent procedures for …'. In general, however, adjectives such as 'clear' or 'transparent' are omitted but are to be understood. The Framework should be assumed to commend clarity, transparency and comprehensiveness throughout. (AUQA, 2009a, p. 105)

In a recent paper AUQA (2009b, p. 8) defines an academic achievement standard as:

- an agreed specification or other criterion,
- used as a rule, guideline or definition,
- of a level of performance or achievement.

This definition has two key features. First, a standard refers to a level that is preset and fixed. After that, it remains stable under use unless there are good reasons for resetting it. In higher education this would mean that the standards are not reset for each cohort of students, or for each assessment task. An academic standard is therefore a big-picture concept that stands somewhat apart from particular assessment tasks and student responses. Second, agreement on the specification must be by authority, custom, or consensus, as standards are not private matters dependent on individuals but collegial understandings shared among academics and other stakeholders.

The paper goes on to propose an elaborate process for the development of statements of generic skills and discipline-specific academic attainment requiring extensive review, analysis, modelling, consultation, documentation, new techniques and practices for the measurement of student learning.

Rather than going down this path, an alternative model could be proposed in which 'standards' are equated to good practices to be expected, with performance assessment based on a review of the approach adopted and outcomes demonstrated within a range of accepted performance. This approach would allow for a stronger developmental focus and greater recognition of the diversity and context within which higher education providers operate. In each area, one could make explicit the *value* underpinning the activity; the *approach* to be adopted; the *standard* which should be attained; and the *standard measurement*. To illustrate this, the authors will take the example of the evaluation of teaching. In defining good practice in this area, an EQA would be able to articulate certain values that underpin the activity such as, for example, that those experiencing an activity are uniquely placed to give comment/feedback on aspects of the activity. In undertaking an institutional evaluation, the EQA could assess the degree to which such values are embedded within an institution's approach (e.g. in a policy which might state that there should be a variety of inputs to the evaluation of teaching, including from students). The standard could then relate to the instruments used to gather student evaluation of teaching, ensuring they reflect appropriate levels of validity and reliability; that results are monitored through documented processes and required improvements identified; and that actual improvements are monitored and reported. In determining the standard measurement and range of performance, it could be stated that on an item assessing 'overall quality' of a unit using a five point Likert scale, units with a mean satisfaction rating below 3 for two consecutive deliveries should be designated for improvement action and improvements monitored over the following two delivery periods. Using this approach, an EQA's assessments of institutional performance would be based on explicit shared values about key indicators of the institutional quality management system and its outcomes within an agreed range of accepted performance.

Approaches to External Quality Assurance – costs, benefits and recurring lessons

The 'Guidelines of Good Practice in Quality Assurance' (INQAAHE, 2006) presuppose a method for EQA that has become the dominant methodology for such agencies. This starts with institutional self-review and the preparation of a performance portfolio document, followed by one or more institutional site visits by a panel of external 'peers' appointed by the EQA agency to undertake the investigation on its behalf. The audit panel calls for the submission of additional documentation following its reading of the institutional performance portfolio and then conducts interviews with typically many hundreds of staff, students and external community members. Audit findings are based on this documentary and testimonial evidence. The audit panel attempts to validate the self-review and 'triangulate' its conclusions with the opinions it gathers through interview of staff and others. The panel's findings are communicated to the institution (and usually also the public) by way of a written report.

There is a strong reliance in most EQA models on peer review, which is a common method used in higher education for the assessment of journal submissions, book and monograph proposals, research grant applications and in individual staff confirmation and promotion processes. As Marsh et al. (2008) have observed, there is surprisingly little empirical research on the effectiveness of peer review. In relation to peer review of journal submissions and book chapters, some suggestions of response bias based on institutional affiliation, personal beliefs, and gender have been noted (Peters and Ceci, 1982; Webb, 1994). While there has been some critique of peer review as the basis for quality audit (see Harvey, 1998 and Barrow, 1999), there is a need for work to be undertaken to better understand the dynamics at play in peer review panels for institutional quality audit. EQAs take a number of steps to try to mitigate the possible effects of professional, personal and ideological conflicts of interest on the part of their auditors (including auditor selection processes and comprehensive auditor training programmes) but there is as yet no reliable measure of the extent to which these actions are successful in mitigating a potentially significant limitation in the use of peer review audit panels. In the authors' experience, there have been numerous instances where auditors expect to see activities within the institution being audited, as they exist within their own institution. An example is an auditor from a research-intensive university expecting certain types of research activity and performance and reluctant to acknowledge less traditional forms of investigation as 'proper research', or an auditor from a technology-focused university expecting a utilitarian approach too, for example, like graduate attributes and employability.

As noted above, AUQA adopts a 'fitness for purpose' approach to audit, which allows flexibility for the audit panel to concentrate on those issues that are of particular importance to the auditee. A significant shortfall, as the process is currently applied, is inconsistency in the issues identified for investigation, which can lead to situations where one university may receive a recommendation that it should introduce a system of mandatory teaching evaluation to fill a perceived gap in its suite of otherwise comprehensive evaluation instruments, whereas another university may receive a commendation for taking the first steps in introducing any form of teaching evaluation. In another university that has been undertaking and utilising extensive student evaluation systems for years, this may warrant no mention at all. Blackmur (2008) notes that the external review of AUQA in 2006 found there was a perception within the sector of variability of AUQA's audits in terms of the level of rigour of judgements, and the detail and length of audit reports. AUQA attempts to control for this possibility and ensure consistency of audit findings, through auditor selection and training processes; pairing of agency staff on audit assignments to act as 'peer referees'; and a system for the review and approval of audit reports by staff not directly engaged in the particular audit prior to public release of reports. Nonetheless, there are numerous instances in AUQA audit reports where a practice explicitly commended in one university is not even referred to in the report of another even though it is operating equally as effectively, simply due to the sampling of issues undertaken by the audit panel. The authors are not talking here of peripheral or mission specific activities but activities that are core to all universities. On the matter of sampling the AUQA Audit Manual notes that:

> An audit panel's work depends on well-chosen purposive sampling. … The selection of samples occurs at two levels. The first arises from the panel's analysis of the Performance Portfolio, during which particular areas may be identified as, for example, significant or problematic, and therefore selected for further investigation. Depending on the focus and scope of the audit, panels may choose to sample organisational units, activities, programs, the application of policies, award courses or other activities. Panels may also choose to track some key issues across or through the auditee's organisation. At the second level, the panel agrees on the documentary or oral evidence it needs to sample within these areas, taking account of the need to triangulate evidence … Consistent with the scope of the audit, panels may seek samples that are expected to be typical or samples that are expected to show wide variety (AUQA, 2009a, p. 81).

Audit investigations of large, complex institutions necessarily must employ some form of sampling but the methods by which samples are selected are neither sufficiently transparent nor robust to provide confidence that they produce results truly representative of the entire population (i.e. the university). This is a significant limitation of the current model of operation for EQAs. Agencies need to consider the development of standards and protocols for the application of sampling, including sampling design and size. A study of practices in financial auditing, where such standards already exist, could be of use (such as Auditing Standard ASA530 issued by the Auditing and Assurance Standards Board, 2006). Again, the authors are suggesting that based on values, there are pervasive indicators and measurable performance on these indicators which are in place or could be developed across the sector.

Another limitation of audits is that auditors find it all too easy to become absorbed in the detail and minutiae contained in the volumes of documentation typically provided and fail to concentrate on the 'big issues' that, in the end, will be of most importance to the institution. This can lead to the criticism that audits are simply bureaucratic exercises that deliver little if any 'value add' to the auditee. Just as in auditor training it is common to point out to potential auditors that they should not interpret other institutions through the lens of their own institution, it is also common for auditors to be warned against taking up their individual and personal interests. However, in both cases this amounts to a warning which, months or years later, is quickly forgotten when the auditor comes into the auditing situation. It is an essentially human trait to go back to the familiar in order to interpret and understand a new situation and this is seen repeatedly, despite the warnings, in academic audits. In addition, the testimony of staff interviewed during the audit is often very compelling and for the unwary audit panel, can unduly sway its opinion on an issue, overriding the general picture provided by a study of institutional data. The practice by some EQAs of developing the draft report prior to the institutional site visit and updating it at the conclusion of the visit helps to counter this risk.

Concluding comments

Woodhouse (1998) has noted that 'an external quality monitoring agency should be maximally flexible, maximally cost-effective and minimally intrusive'. Most quality agencies would aspire, if not actually claim, that audit is minimally intrusive and costly to institutions. Experience in Australia to date is that the audit process has been costly in direct staff time and resources and is usually regarded as an 'event' that is divorced from the ongoing and 'real' quality monitoring and improvement initiatives underway within the university. Nonetheless, the establishment of an external quality assurance agency has led institutions to prioritise a consideration of quality issues, which has been of benefit to institutions individually and to the sector as a whole. AUQA's formation in 2000 led many Australian universities to initiate significant reviews of parts of their operations – a notable example being reviews of transnational teaching partnerships – and to act quickly to implement improvements. In the case of transnational operations this led to radical reform in many institutions of the systems and processes used to manage such arrangements and, in some instances, to the closure of some transnational operations. Carr et al. (2005) conclude in the New Zealand context that 'it is exceedingly difficult to quantify the independent influence of EQA ... [but that] EQA does have a powerful initial role as a catalyst, as well as a validation for university-led reform'. Having undertaken one comprehensive audit round and now in the midst of theme-based audits, it can be argued that the benefits to Australian higher education institutions of the current external audit approach are rapidly diminishing. As will be shown in the final chapter of this book, there is a need for the model of EQA to become more attuned to the level of sophistication in quality monitoring and evaluation that is now in evidence within higher education institutions.

References

Altbach, P.G., Reisberg, L. and Rumbley, L.E. (2009) *Trends in Global Higher Education: Tracking an Academic Revolution. A Report Prepared for the UNESCO World Conference on Higher Education.* Paris: UNESCO.

Auditing and Assurance Standards Board (AUASB) (2006) *Auditing Standard ASA 530 Audit Sampling and Other Means of Testing.* Canberra: AUASB.

Australian Universities Quality Agency (AUQA) (2009a) *Audit Manual, Version 6.0.* Melbourne: AUQA.

Australian Universities Quality Agency (AUQA) (2009b) *Setting and Monitoring Academic Standards for Australian Higher Education: A Discussion Paper.* Melbourne: AUQA.

Barrow, M. (1999) 'Quality management systems and dramaturgical compliance', *Quality in Higher Education*, 5(1): 27–36.

Blackmur, D. (2008) '*Quis Custodiet Ipsos Custodes?* The review of the Australian Universities Quality Agency', *Quality in Higher Education*, 14(3): 249–64.

Carr, S., Hamilton, E. and Meade, P. (2005) 'Is it possible? Investigating the influence of external quality audit on university performance', *Quality in Higher Education*, 11(3): 195–211.

Goodlad, S. (1995) *The Quest for Quality. Sixteen Forms of Heresy in Higher Education*. Buckingham, UK: Society for Research into Higher Education and Open University Press.

Green, D. (1994) 'What is quality in higher education? Concepts, Policy and Practice', in D. Green (ed.) *What is Quality in Higher Education?*, Buckingham, UK: Society for Research into Higher Education and Open University Press.

Harvey, L. and Green, D. (1993) 'Defining quality', *Assessment and Evaluation in Higher Education*, 18(1): 9–34.

Harvey, L. (1998) 'An assessment of past and current approaches to quality in higher education', *Australian Journal of Education*, 42(3): 237–55.

International Network for Quality Assurance Agencies in Higher Education (INQAAHE) (2006). *Guidelines of Good Practice in Quality Assurance.* Available at: *http://www.inqaahe.org/main/capacity-building-39/guidelines-of-good-practice-51* (accessed 8 June 2009).

Juran, J.M. (ed.) (1995) *A History of Managing for Quality. The Evolution, Trends, and Future Directions of Managing for Quality*. Milwaukee, Wisconsin, USA: American Society for Quality Control Quality Press.

Marsh, H.W., Jayasinghe, U.W. and Bond, N.W. (2008) 'Improving the peer-review process for grant applications: reliability, validity, bias and generalizability', *American Psychologist*, 63(6), 160–8.

Mouradian, G. (2002) *The Quality Revolution. A History of the Quality Movement*. Lanham, Maryland, USA: University Press of America.

Peters, D.P. and Ceci, S.J. (1982) 'Peer-review practices of psychological journals: The fate of published articles, submitted again', *Behavioural and Brain Sciences*, 5: 187–95.

Quality Assurance Agency for Higher Education (QAA) (2009) *Thematic Enquiries into Concerns about Academic Quality and Standards in Higher Education in England*. London, UK: QAA.

US Department of Education (2006) *A Test of Leadership: Charting the Future of US Higher Education: A Report of the Commission Appointed by Secretary of Education Margaret Spellings*. Washington, USA.

Webb, G. (1994) *Making the Most of Appraisal: Career and professional development Planning for Academics*. London, UK: Kogan Page.

Woodhouse, D. (1998) 'Quality assurance in higher education: the next 25 years', *Quality in Higher Education*, 4(3): 257–73.

Part 5
Academic development and quality in higher education

Academic development as change leadership in higher education[1]

Ranald Macdonald

Abstract

This chapter explores the changing role of academic developers as they engage more broadly in quality agendas in higher education. Understanding the nature of change and the complexity of institutions has led to the development of models and frameworks as the basis for engaging more holistically with the day-to-day realities of universities. A further aspect of the context is the growing emphasis on the *enhancement* of the quality, such as the student learning experience, as well as *assurance* of quality processes and outcomes. These changes have put academic developers very much at the centre of strategy and policy development with regard to learning and teaching and the student experience more broadly.

Key words: academic development; change and complexity in higher education; holistic approaches; quality enhancement; quality assurance.

Introduction

Academic developers have traditionally been involved in promoting quality in learning and teaching through engagement in programme development and delivery, the initial training of new academics through, for example, post-graduate certificates in learning and teaching or academic practice, and evaluating practice with follow-up remedial or developmental support (Macdonald, 2009a).

Increasingly, however, academic developers have to take a far more strategic position and are engaged in developing policy as the basis for changing educational practice. Much of this is in the context of a quality agenda which has moved from purely quality assurance to a greater emphasis on quality *enhancement*. This chapter will explore the nature of change which is required to bring about improvements in the assessment of student learning and provision of feedback across a large metropolitan higher education institution in the UK – Sheffield Hallam University. To set the context, some current understandings of 'quality' in the UK will also be explored as the word is perhaps being used by different people to have different meanings.

Part of the quality context is the National Student Survey (NSS) which all final year students in UK universities are invited to complete. While the overall level of satisfaction has been relatively high, many institutions have received poor evaluations from students on the questions related to assessment and feedback, and the impact of the quality initiative to be described will be measured directly by improvements in future student evaluations.

The Assessment for Learning Initiative (TALI) is led by academic developers, and employs a holistic model of change developed by Macdonald and Joughin (2009) together with a growing understanding of complexity theory and the conditions necessary for emergent change. TALI is engaging with academic staff, administrators, managers and students in changing policy, practice, regulations and systems as they relate to assessment and feedback with the intention of improving both NSS scores and the quality of learning

This chapter is written from the perspective of a UK academic developer and thus, for some, may reflect an unfamiliar use of words which will hopefully be made clear by the context in which they are used.

Academic development – an emerging profession

A consideration of 'academic development' inevitably begins with how to define it as different terms are used in different countries and educational sectors to refer to the same or similar activities (Macdonald, 2009a). Whether it is academic development in Australia and New Zealand, staff or educational development in the UK, faculty, instructional or organisational development in the US, 'academic development' has become ubiquitous in many higher, tertiary or post-compulsory education systems, at least in more developed countries. 'Professional' and 'academic staff' development are also used in various contexts (Macdonald, 2002). For convenience, the term 'academic development' is used as all-encompassing for what will be seen to be a great variety of roles and activities.

There is some debate as to whether academic development is what people 'know' or what they 'do' and whether it is a profession or an activity (Macdonald, 2003). The following quotes, while not necessarily fully inclusive of those engaged in the field or the activities in which they engage, may prove a useful starting point:

> … an academic developer is any person who has a role in which they are explicitly expected to work with academics to assist them to reflect upon their academic role in relation to teaching, research, scholarship, leadership, funding applications and supervision of students. An academic developer may also work at a departmental/ institutional level in a developmental role. (Fraser, 2001, p. 55)

> Academic/educational/faculty development refers to the numerous activities which have to do with the professional learning of academics in post-compulsory, tertiary or higher education. Since academics perform a variety of roles, and are engaged on a variety of contracts, the scope for academic development is wide. (Brew, 2004, p. 5)

Immediately a number of potential tensions are revealed: what do people engaged in the area call themselves, to what extent are they 'real' academics and what is their primary focus – the individual or the institution? Choosing to use the term 'staff development', Webb (1996, p. 1) delineates the area as including 'the institutional policies, programmes and procedures which facilitate and support staff so that they may fully serve their own and the institution's needs'. The tension between fully serving 'their own and the institution's needs' continues to reverberate in the literature. Following from Webb's definition, academic development is taken by many to be activities that are concerned with 'sustaining and enhancing the quality of learning and teaching within the institution' (Hounsell, 1994). What also begins to become clear are the origins of the area in the quality agendas since the 1970s, particularly in relation to improving the quality of teaching and learning through staff development (Hicks, 2007) and a focus on individuals and their development. This engagement with the quality agenda has, at least in the UK, continued until the present day and, if anything, is growing.

An issue of ongoing concern for academic developers is that there are those in their institutions who view them as either an unnecessary overhead intruding into their professional practice as teachers or as a diversion of funding away from the true business of a university – research. This raises challenges when academic development departments are asked to be accountable or to evaluate the impact of their activities, in particular when they are required to show how their activities have contributed to strategically defined outcomes and not just whether they are in line with strategic objectives (Brew, 2007).

As observed by Macdonald (2009a), there have been few studies of the impact of academic development, though notable exceptions include those by Gibbs and Coffey (2004) on the impact of training of university teachers on their teaching skills, their approach to teaching and the approach to learning of their students; Rust (1998) on the impact of educational development workshops on teachers' practices; Rust (2000) on the impact of initial training courses on university teaching; Piccinin and colleagues on the impact of individual consultations on student ratings of teaching (Piccinin et al., 1999) and on the teaching of younger versus older faculty (Piccinin and Moore, 2002); Brew and Lublin (1997, reported in Prebble et al., 2004) on the longer-term effects of informal programmes of teaching development; and Stes et al. (2007) on the long-term and institutional effectiveness of a faculty training programme.

A short case study will perhaps illustrate an approach to evaluating the impact of academic development. The New Zealand Ministry of Education commissioned a team from Massey University to undertake a systematic review on the impact of academic staff development on student outcomes which was reported in Prebble et al. (2004). The report came up with two propositions concerning the relationship between academic development and student learning outcomes: good teaching has positive impacts on student learning; and teachers can be assisted to improve the quality of their teaching through a variety of academic interventions (p. 12). With respect to the second proposition, the study reviewed and summarised the impact of five types of academic development interventions: short training courses; in situ training; consulting, peer assessment and mentoring; student assessment of teaching; and intensive staff development (p. 26). The findings were thought to support further investment in the development of the professional practice of teaching, though with varying evidence to support the various approaches.

The report recommended further research in New Zealand and a successful bid was subsequently made to the Ministry of Education's Teaching and Learning Research Initiative for a project entitled: Unlocking Student Learning: 'The impact of teaching and learning enhancement initiatives (TLEIs) on first year university students'. The three-year project began in 2006 involving partnerships between academic developers with teachers on large first year courses in all eight New Zealand Universities to improve student learning through enhancement initiatives. The author was involved as an international critical friend to the project.

The ongoing final evaluation of the project includes an analysis of the data derived from addressing three questions to see the extent to which academic developers' interventions did have an impact.

1. How can academic developers and teachers work together to enhance student learning experiences and performance?

2. What impact do teaching and learning enhancement initiatives (TLEIs) developed by academic developers and teachers have on students' learning experiences and achievement in large first year classes?

3. How can the impact of academic development on student learning be determined?

While the first question is largely unproblematic, the other two do not provide such clear cut answers. This is not least because the activities of academic developers in relation to student learning are largely of a second order, as mediated by the attitudes, personalities and activities of individual teachers. However, in an increasingly performative higher education culture, the issue of identifying and measuring impact is likely to remain to the fore.

'Quality' in the UK – an academic developer's perspective

As with 'academic development', 'quality' may also be a problematic term, not least as it may be understood and used differently by different people in the same institution. The problem is exacerbated once terms such as 'assurance' and 'enhancement' are appended to it. Elton (2005) contrasted the two as 'doing things better' (quality assurance) and 'doing better things' (quality enhancement). In UK higher education, primary responsibility for ensuring academic standards and quality, and high quality student experiences, rests with independent and self-governing universities and colleges. So, while each institution has its own internal quality assurance procedures, the Quality Assurance Agency for Higher Education (QAA) periodically checks how well they meet their responsibilities, identifying good practice and making recommendations for improvement (QAA, 2009).

The four home nations which comprise the UK have slightly different arrangements. For England and Northern Ireland, each institution is reviewed as part of a six-year cycle of institutional audit, when a judgement is made about the confidence as to the 'present and future management of the quality of its programmes and the academic standards of its awards'. In Scotland, so-called enhancement-led institutional review makes similar confidence judgements but also 'focuses on the effectiveness of each institution's approach to enhancing the learning experience and achievements of its students'. Finally, the institutional review system in Wales examines the ways in which institutions grant awards and aims to ensure that they are 'providing higher education of an acceptable quality and appropriate academic standard'. In all cases review teams comprise senior staff from other institutions and the professions, as part of the so-called evidence-based peer review process. Students are also increasingly being included as members of review teams.

While the QAA is still largely perceived as being engaged in quality assurance, it is trying to focus more on quality enhancement, though some might, perhaps uncharitably, argue that it is just trying to enhance the quality assurance processes. It defines enhancement as 'the process of taking deliberate steps at institutional level to improve the quality of learning opportunities' (QAA, 2006), though some see this as a somewhat limiting definition, not least because of its focus on the institutional level. However, in Scotland the Quality Enhancement Framework has also included a series of Enhancement Themes on which the sector and individual institutions focus for a period of time.

More direct quality enhancement initiatives have been promoted by the Higher Education Funding Council for England (HEFCE) through its Teaching Quality Enhancement Fund (TQEF) which is, at the time of writing, being replaced by a fund for Teaching Enhancement and Student Success (TESS). Reflecting its definition of enhancement above, HEFCE states that:

> The main strategic purpose of this funding is to embed and sustain learning and teaching strategies and activities that have been steadily developing over the last six years to encourage future institutional investment in continuous improvements. (HEFCE, 2006)

The TQEF supported development at institutional, individual and subject levels through a number of initiatives including the development and implementation of institutional learning and teaching strategies, individual National Teaching Fellowships, largely subject-focused projects under the Fund for Development of Teaching and Learning, the Higher Education Academy and its Subject Network of 24 subject centres, and the particularly well-resourced 74 Centres for Excellence in Teaching and Learning (CETLs).

While the final outcomes of all these initiatives is still being evaluated, they have all provided rich opportunities for academic developers to engage in the development of policy, strategy and practice. Not only have academic developers taken significant leading roles but it has provided opportunities for many to move into the field, though they might not necessarily see themselves as 'academic' or 'educational' developers (Macdonald, 2002).

Academic developers have also had a major part to play in the attempt to professionalise and accredit teaching in higher education through the provision of initial training and ongoing professional development for those engaged in teaching and learner support. The UK's Staff and Educational Development Association (SEDA) has been at the forefront of these developments (Beaty, 2006) and they were given greater prominence as a result of the so-called Dearing Report of the National Committee of Inquiry into Higher Education in 1997. A key recommendation of the Dearing Committee was the establishment of a professional Institute for Learning and Teaching in Higher Education (ILTHE). One of the functions of the Institute would be to accredit programmes of training for higher education teachers. Subsequently replaced by the Higher Education Academy, this aim has been continued through the development of professional standards for teaching in higher education. Many of the courses/programmes associated with these developments have been led by academic developers and the emphasis has increasingly moved from mere hints and tips as to how to perform better in the classroom, important though this may be to the new teacher, to a focus on a more holistic notion of academic practice, involving teaching, research, service and academic leadership and management. These courses are seen by many as an integral part of the quality enhancement agenda as they seek to improve the quality of learning and teaching.

The nature of change in higher education

'Change' has become ubiquitous within higher education. So much so, perhaps, that there might even be a failure to ask 'what would happen if we didn't change?' (Macdonald, 2009b). However, many tasked with bringing about change often see it in a linear way, rather than recognising the complexity of universities, not least because of the individuality and autonomy of many working within these universities.

> Complexity thinking shares with these frames the conviction that transformations of learning systems cannot be understood in terms of linear or mechanical terms and that any attempt at such transformations is necessarily a deeply ethical matter that must be undertaken with caution, humility and care. (Davis and Sumara, 2006, p. 130)

In seeking to understand how change could be brought about in the assessment of student learning, myself and a colleague, who was then working in Hong Kong but is now in Australia (Macdonald and Joughin, 2009), drew on the literatures around systems thinking, complex adaptive systems and educational change. Of particular interest was the work of Ralph Stacey (2007) who has written extensively on complexity and organisations. His increasingly familiar Agreement and Certainty Matrix has proved useful to many in understanding why change does, or does not, work in their organisation. The matrix comprises two dimensions – the degree of certainty and the level of agreement. Where the outcomes of management decisions are close to certainty and there is a high level of agreement, so-called technical rational approaches predominate. Here data from the past is used to predict the future and specific paths of action can be planned. At the other extreme, where there is no certainty or agreement, anarchy and chaos will be the norm. However, reality is normally somewhere between the two extremes.

The closer one is to certainty and agreement the better traditional management approaches will work; the further away the more likely individuals are to ignore or avoid the situation. However, between the two extremes is a large area which Stacey calls the 'zone of complexity' and others 'the edge of chaos' (Tosey, 2002). This area perhaps best reflects the reality of many organisations, not least Higher Education Institutions (HEIs), where the complexity of the situation can be daunting if managers and their colleagues do not realise that this is what the world is really like and, while it should be treated with respect, is not necessarily to be feared. Complexity may be contrasted with, or situated between, simple and chaotic and, as such, is more normal than one can perhaps believe. It provides the opportunity for creativity, innovation, risk-taking and even play.

As complex organisations, HEIs comprise large numbers of units, individuals or agents each of which behaves according to some set of rules but adapts according to those with whom it is interacting. This interaction and adaptation leads to the notion of self-organisation which, whilst not chaotic, is neither predictable nor easily controlled. Within complex systems the result of agents interacting and self-organising leads to the notion of 'emergence' and this is unpredictable, reflecting 'the edge of chaos'.

One aspect of change particularly explored by Macdonald and Joughin (2009), through the development of a model, was the necessity to recognise that institutions had to be viewed more holistically and that change involved a number of levels and players. Simplifying it somewhat, the foundational level of the model is the unit of study where learning and assessment happens – variously termed the module, subject, unit or course. The second level of the model represents the collection of those units that constitute the student's overall learning experience – typically the degree programme or a major within a degree. At the third level, academic staff are normally organised into what are variously termed departments, schools or faculties (where the latter term refers to a structural unit within the organisation). The fourth level represents institutional-level entities that support learning, teaching and assessment. Finally, the model acknowledges the important influence of the wider, external context in which universities operate. Use of the model in a number of learning and teaching contexts has shown that it is perhaps necessary to consider the individual student/learner as being the foundational level. However, it is important to recognise that the levels represent a growing distance from where learning, teaching and assessment happens.

The dynamics in the model come from examining the relations between and within each level, together with the influence of any additional factors, such as quality systems, within the institution. No one level is necessarily more or less important or influential than another but they all need to be considered when trying to bring about educational change.

The Assessment for Learning Initiative (TALI): a case study in institutional change

The first National Student Survey, which covers all final year undergraduate students in England, Wales and Northern Ireland, took place in 2005 with the aim of providing information for potential students as to where to study. The survey consists of six 'areas' covering: teaching; assessment and feedback; academic support; organisation and management; learning resources; and personal development. There is also a question asking about 'overall satisfaction' with the quality of the courses the student took. While the overall figures were very satisfactory at Sheffield Hallam University, there was concern about the relatively poor results for assessment and feedback, as was the case in many institutions surveyed.

Over the years, Sheffield Hallam University, no doubt like many others, has made changes to assessment regulations and frameworks, processes and systems, and academic practices without necessarily ensuring that the various aspects are well integrated or that the whole is viewed holistically. There was also concern about how to improve student progression by reducing the amount of reassessment needed. As a result of a number of coffee bar discussions, the author and a senior academic from one of the university's four faculties drafted a paper on Profile Assessment which addressed many of the issues of concern and started a wider discussion across the university about assessment. This led eventually to the setting up of The Assessment for Learning Initiative (TALI), modelled on one of the university's already successful Centres for Excellence in Teaching and Learning (CETLs – see earlier).

TALI became part of a broader university-wide Assessment Project which was established to focus on deliberate actions needed to bring about change in:

■ *assessment practices* – that are learner focused and promote student engagement and attainment;
■ *assessment regulations* – that are clear, consistent and student centred;
■ *assessment processes* – that are efficient and effective.

TALI is reported more fully as a change initiative elsewhere (Macdonald and Joughin, 2009) but, as one would expect in a large institution (more than 28,000 students) with a diverse student and academic population, change has not always gone smoothly. However, to take the example of providing better feedback to students, the Macdonald and Joughin model (2009) has shown that, for there to be a joined up and comprehensive approach to change, ownership and responsibility needs to be taken at various levels, by staff, students and other stakeholders. The approach acknowledged the complex nature of the issue and the context in which it arose and the need to address issues at all levels – student, module/unit, course/programme/subject group, faculty/department, institution and externally.

Locating the initiative within the quality enhancement agenda, one internal paper reported on 'the significant progress achieved to date as the university continues to take deliberate, incremental steps in the quality enhancement of assessment and feedback'. Further, 'our approach, distinct from others in the sector, has been to recognise the complex nature of assessment and to respond with a model for an integrated approach to assessment identifying deliberate action at each organisational level of the university'. Part of the initiative was to appoint secondees on a senior grade to lead in their own faculties to identify the sometimes idiosyncratic nature of different disciplinary and professional areas. These secondees, together with others from the institution's central academic development unit, the Learning and Teaching Institute, formed a dedicated cadre of academic developers who recognised the need to develop their own thinking and skills before they could engage effectively with their colleagues and the faculty and institutional systems. They also worked externally to share the experiences and gather feedback in a variety of different forums.

TALI is ongoing and reflects many of the characteristics of successful change initiatives by focusing on interactions between individuals and groups at different levels. A series of networks and events has provided opportunities for more conversations (Shaw, 2002) which are necessary for change to emerge in a complex situation. While there has been a formal management structure and planning approach, it is recognised that the parallel change approach is key to the success of TALI. One measure of success will obviously be future NSS scores for assessment and feedback, while recognising that many other factors may come into play at local levels.

And finally …

This chapter draws on earlier work by the author on academic development, educational change and complexity. By setting it within the context of the quality enhancement agenda it is possible to see that academic developers have a key role to play in drawing on ideas and concepts from other domains in order to address key aspects of institutional development. Universities are complex organisations with differing agendas and characteristics. No 'one size fits all' approach will work and 'academic development' itself may come to mean many things. However, 'change leadership' means understanding the nature of change and the institutional context in which the change is to take place. As Lewis Elton, quoted earlier, would say, successful change is doing better things and not just doing things better. Effective academic developers understand this and are able to contribute within, and sometimes against, institutional cultures and systems.

Note

1. This chapter draws on materials and ideas published in Macdonald (2009a) on academic development and Macdonald and Joughin (2009) on the nature of change in higher education.

References

Beaty, L. (2006) 'Towards professional teaching in higher education: the role of accreditation', in P. Ashwin (ed.) *Changing Higher Education: The Development of Learning and Teaching*. Abingdon, UK: Routledge.

Brew, A. (2004) 'Editorial: The scope of academic development', *International Journal for Academic Development*, 9(1): 5–7.

Brew, A. (2007) 'Editorial: Evaluating academic development in a time of perplexity', *International Journal for Academic Development*, 12(2): 69–72.

Davis, B. and Sumara, D. (2006) *Complexity and Education: Inquiries into Learning, Teaching and Research*. New York: Routledge.

Elton, L. (2005) 'Scholarship and the research and teaching nexus'. In Barnett, R. (ed) *Reshaping the University: New Relationships Between Research, Scholarship and Teaching*. Maidenhead, UK: SRHE/Open University Press.

Fraser, K. (2001) 'Australian academic developers' conceptions of the profession', *International Journal for Academic Development*, 6(1): 54–64.

Gibbs, G. and Coffey, M. (2004) 'The impact of training of university teachers on their teaching skills, their approach to teaching and the approach to learning of their students', *Active Learning in Higher Education*, 5(1): 87–100.

Hicks, M. (2007) *Positioning the professional practice of academic development: An institutional case study*. Unpublished EdD thesis, University of South Australia.

Higher Education Funding Council for England (HEFCE) (2006). *HEFCE Teaching Quality Enhancement Fund Funding arrangements 2006–07 to 2008–09*. Available at: *http://www.hefce.ac.uk/pubs/hefce/2006/06_11/* (accessed 9 June 2009).

Hounsell, D. (1994) 'Educational development', in J. Bocock and D. Watson (eds) *Managing the University Curriculum: Making Common Cause*, pp. 89–102. Buckingham, UK: SRHE and Open University Press.

Macdonald, R. (2002) 'Educational development: research, evaluation and changing practice in higher education', in R. Macdonald and J. Wisdom (eds) *Academic and Educational Development: Research, Evaluation and Changing Practice in Higher Education*. London: Kogan Page.

Macdonald, R. (2003) 'Developing a scholarship of academic development: Setting the context', in H. Eggins and R. Macdonald (eds) *The Scholarship of Academic Development*. Buckingham: SRHE/Open University Press.

Macdonald, R. (2009a) 'Academic development', in M. Tight, K.H. Mok, J. Huisman and C.C. Morphew (eds) *The Routledge International Handbook of Higher Education*. New York: Routledge.

Macdonald, R. (2009b) 'Is there too much management of change?', in M. Todd and D. Marsh (eds) *Why Social Science Matters: Managing Change in Learning and Teaching*, C-SAP: Higher Education Academy Subject Network for Sociology, Anthropology and Politics. Available at: *http://www.c-sap.bham.ac.uk/resources/publications/wssm.htm* (accessed 9 June 2009).

Macdonald, R. and Joughin, G. (2009) 'What does it take to improve assessment in support of learning?', in G. Joughin (ed.) *Assessment, Learning and Judgement in Higher Education*. Netherlands: Springer.

National Committee of Inquiry into Higher Education (1997) *Higher Education in the Learning Society*. Norwich, UK: HMSO.

Piccinin, S., Cristi, C. and McCoy, M. (1999) 'The impact of individual consultation on student ratings of teaching', *International Journal for Academic Development*, 4(2): 75–88.

Piccinin, S. and Moore, J.-P. (2002) 'The impact of individual consultation on the teaching of younger versus older faculty', *International Journal for Academic Development*, 7(2): 123–34.

Prebble, T., Hargraves, H., Leach, L., Naidoo, K., Suddaby, G. and Zepke, N. (2004) *Impact of Student Support Services and Academic Development Programmes on Student Outcomes in Undergraduate Tertiary Study: A Synthesis of Research*. New Zealand: Ministry of Education.

Quality Assurance Agency (QAA) (2006) *Handbook for Institutional Audit: England and Northern Ireland*. Available at: *www.qaa.ac.uk/reviews/institutionalaudit/handbook2006/* (accessed 9 June 2009).

Quality Assurance Agency (QAA) (2009) *An Introduction to the QAA*. Available at: *http://www.qaa.ac.uk/aboutus/IntroQAAMay09.pdf* (accessed 9 June 2009).

Rust, R. (1998) 'The impact of educational development workshops on teachers' practice', *International Journal for Academic Development*, 3(1): 72–80.

Rust, C. (2000) 'Do initial training courses have an impact on university teaching? The evidence from two evaluative studies of one course', *Innovations in Education and Training International*, 37(3): 254–62.

Shaw, P. (2002) *Changing Conversations in Organizations: A Complexity Approach to Change*. Abingdon, UK: Routledge.

Stacey, R.D. (2007) *Strategic Management and Organizational Dynamics* (5th edn). Harlow: Pearson Educational Limited.

Stes, A., Clement, M. and Petegem, P.V. (2007) 'The effectiveness of a faculty training programme: long-term and institutional impact', *International Journal for Academic Development*, 12(2): 99–110.

Tosey, P. (2002) *Teaching at the Edge of Chaos*. Available at: *http://www.palatine.ac.uk/files/1045.pdf* (accessed 9 June 2009).

Webb, G. (1996) *Understanding Staff Development*. Buckingham: SRHE and Open University Press.

Quality in the transitional process of establishing political science as a new discipline in Czech higher education (post 1989)

Jan Holzer[1]

Abstract

This chapter concerns quality in the Czech political science community and the way in which it has developed since the re-establishment of the academic freedoms in Czech higher education 20 years ago. The main questions that the case study poses are:

In what way is the phenomenon of quality judged within the national political science community (and whether it is assessed at all)?

What are the mechanisms employed?

What are the factors (internal or external) that impact on this?

The chapter also aims to give the reader an insight into the development of the discipline of political science since 1989. It attempts to identify the ways and degrees in which the institutional, organisational, paradigmatic, theoretical and methodological 'self-definition' of a new academic community impacted on the changes in the perception of quality in higher education, particularly in the area of teaching and learning, but also in research.

Key words: transformation of higher education; Czech higher education; Political Science; establishing mechanisms of quality monitoring and enhancement; quality in teaching, learning and research.

Introduction

This chapter focuses on the discipline of Political Science in the Czech Republic, and in particular the transitional process of its development within the 'community' of Czech political scientists. The chapter reflects the experiences of the author as a single representative of this 'community'. The main questions that this chapter poses are:

> In what way and whether at all does the 'community' of Czech political scientists examine the phenomenon of quality?

> If so, then what are the instruments and factors (systemic or non-systemic) that the 'community' utilise in assuring quality.

Prior to discussing the issue of quality in Czech Political Science, it is important to provide the reader with a short outline of the development of the discipline in Czechoslovakia since 1989 (and subsequently the Czech Republic since 1993), in other words, after the fall of the Czechoslovak communist regime of over 40 years. The author believes that the subject of quality and its development has been/is interlinked with the actual process of establishing Political Science in the Czech Republic. The chapter argues that Political Science is a relatively new discipline in the Czech higher education context and thus it is not 'constrained' by the tradition (academic and non-academic) or the 'standards' of scholarship prior to 1989.

In that respect, this chapter attempts to examine the way in which the process of establishing this new discipline, in terms of its theoretical, methodological and paradigmatic self-definition, the gradual formation of the 'sub-disciplines' and of the actual 'community' of political scientists, has impacted on the perception of quality particularly in teaching and learning but also in academic publishing. This will be considered not only from the perspective of the actual practice of individual academics, but also from the more generic perspective of the established parameters of the standards of scholarly work. In that sense the chapter attempts to present an objective evaluation through the author's personal experiences in teaching, research and administration.

Context

Political Science in the Czech context does not have a long tradition as an established academic discipline. In the period of the so-called First

Czechoslovak Republic (1918–38), the topics typically researched and taught in Political Science were incorporated in general Social Science or Studies of the State. During the communist period (1948–89), research in Social Sciences was virtually non-existent. Any political research was based on the Marxist-Leninist ideology, the so-called Scientific Communism, which barred any viable research in Social Sciences. There was a short period of the so-called Prague Spring in the second half of the 1960s, when this total restriction of research in Social Sciences was briefly lifted. In the 1970s and 1980s, Czech Social Sciences were again totally isolated from the West. This was not the case, for example, in Poland or Hungary (Holzer and Pseja, 2002).

This short historic overview is important, as the issues that Czech Social Sciences had to deal with in the early 1990s were related to laying the foundations of social science disciplines, such as Political Science. When forming individual schools of Political Science, the key questions were: What would be the academic make-up of these schools? Who would be the leading figures in establishing Czech Political Science? There were three potential groups: (1) Personalities involved in political dissent during the communist period – these individuals got involved only in exceptional circumstances; (2) Lecturers in Marxism-Leninism – this group eventually did not get involved in the process either; (3) Young or middle-aged generations of lecturers in Modern History or Area Studies who most frequently became involved in the formation of schools of Political Science. The first schools of Political Science were established in 1990 at Charles University and the Czech University of Economy in Prague and at Masaryk University in Brno.

This does not mean that the formation of the 'community' of Czech political scientists was a clear and straightforward process. Nevertheless, the key part in formation of the discipline was played by academics without 'ideological' links to the previous communist regime. In this aspect the community distinguished itself from other related academic communities, such as historiography or law.

In terms of the student population, the first students enrolled in the subject in the academic year 1991/2. Initially, the student numbers were relatively small (around ten people), and these were students already enrolled in other subjects at the university (this was initially even the author's case). The numbers have subsequently grown relatively quickly and have reached hundreds at the turn of the century, and so Political Science entered the era of mass higher education provision.

Where has quality come to play its role in these processes? Frankly, this issue was not considered at the beginning of the 1990s by either side of those involved – students or lecturers – as at the beginning of the formation of this new discipline, the communication between these two groups was relatively 'symbiotic'. This has stemmed from the unique position of the discipline at that time – of a newly formed discipline – where most students and lecturers were learning, discovering and getting access to material and knowledge which was very new. At that time (an era prior to widespread Internet access), every new translation of a book and every lecture by an international expert in the field were exceptionally valued.

This post-1989 emergence of a new discipline created a very specific kind of quality, reminiscent of the Platonic method of lecturing – unconventional, in no specific way formalised, nevertheless (to a degree) naively accepted or taken for granted. However, this form of quality has, inevitably, faded away following the growth in student numbers and related changes in the structuring of the teaching and learning of the discipline.

The questions of *how* to teach and research in this new discipline were not considered at the beginnings of the development of Czech Political Science, let alone in any way institutionalised. This is not to say that the academics who have initiated the development of this discipline have not considered these questions. However, the standard of Czech Political Science in its initial stages has not been 'confronted' by any external regulations or professional bodies but was driven more by the values and efforts put in by individual academics and students.

It is also important to point out that in the 1990s, the academic status of Political Science was questioned. On the one hand, the independent status of Political Science within the Social Sciences was disputed. Some members of the historiographic and legal communities felt that there was no need for establishing a new discipline which could have been no more than a supporting discipline utilising the knowledge of Modern History and Constitutional Theory. On the other hand, there was an even harsher accusation that Political Science faced, of being a new form of Marxism-Leninism. It is therefore not surprising that throughout the entire 1990s a significant effort was devoted to 'existential' questions. 'Defending' the value of the discipline, fitting it into the existing faculty and university structures, gaining respect among other existing disciplines, attaining financial independence, and establishing links with overseas schools and experts – these were the main concerns during the 1990s. Quality permeated all these processes, however, only implicitly through the actions of individual academics who shaped Czech Political Science.

Scholarly output of Czech Political Science and the phenomenon of quality

The first significant event which started changing the character and potentially also the standards in Czech Political Science was the establishing of Czech academic journals in Political Science. And thus, in the mid-1990s, the community was given a platform where they could publish the results of their research. From 1989 until the mid-1990s academic papers were published in political journals aimed at the general public. It is important to remind the reader of the fact that the circumstances were quite exceptional and the Political Science community has realised that this was only a provisional stage.

However, establishing academic journals has not brought up the concern with quality directly. Editorial work at the beginning was typically undertaken by a single person and there was a lack of academic papers in Political Science in the 1990s. The larger schools of Political Science typically also published their own academic journal or journals, most of whose contributors were academics from the school.

A more general standardisation of quality in Czech academic journals was instigated by the Czech Government Research Council in 2008, when it approached all the editorial boards to verify the refereed status of their journal/s. The editorial boards were required to prove that each submitted paper was reviewed by at least two referees and they also had to demonstrate that there was at least a 30 per cent 'drop-out' rate (i.e. a minimum of one third of all submitted papers are rejected by the journal). The list of Czech refereed academic journals that resulted from this exercise will be updated annually, and research papers published in journals without this refereed status are not acknowledged in evaluations of research output of individual schools, which then has a direct impact on institutional funding. In other words, generally the Czech academic community including the Czech Political Science field had reached the stage of formally appraising (first in quantitative terms) their own research output.

This trend has appeared in the last few years, which means that any formal evaluation of academic research output has not been a concern for the Czech Government. The intention of this chapter, however, is not to analyse in detail the changes in the model of funding and evaluating research output in Czech higher education. Nevertheless, there is currently a perceived direct link between funding and quality, and thus the system of state funding in higher education has a fundamental impact not only on the strategies of individual academics but also on the schools which subsequently influence the nature and standard of their research output.

Prior to introducing this model of funding, the main funding bodies for Czech Social Sciences were the Czech Science Foundation (GACR) and Czech Academy of Science (AVCR). Gaining research funding through these organisations represented a measure of success and also a level of regard in the academic community. Being on the board of the GACR represented the highest level of regard in the academic community. Therefore, the changes in the system of funding in higher education were quite closely linked to the changes of perception of quality. In the Czech context, this is associated with the recommendations of the Czech Research Council in their *White Paper on Tertiary Education* which was published in 2008. The Council proposed changes in funding and related requirements for gaining research funding. The changes, for example, include involving international referees and thus more objective decision-making, and a greater accountability for funding linked to outcomes.

To sum up, if Czech Political Science has after 20 years of its existence put 'quality' on the agenda of the debates, then it is in the area of research output. Therefore, the trend of evaluating the quality of research output in higher education has finally reached the Czech Republic. At present, the process is more in the stages of collecting and quantifying data predominantly through the number of citations and publications with some current attempts at standardising the process. However, the link between this evaluation process and the quality of research outcomes is not apparent. This leads to a question: 'Does the increase in quantity necessarily mean increase in the quality?'

Teaching and learning outcomes in Czech Political Science and the phenomenon of quality

Academic life does not only involve research, the area of learning and teaching is regarded as equally important. Identifying quality in this aspect appears more complex for Czech Political Science. Therefore, the author suggests re-formulating the question of *How* was quality introduced and reflected in Czech Political Science? to *Who* was the instigator of the search for quality in Czech Political Science? It is important to point out that evaluating quality not only means *what is being evaluated* and *by what tools*, but equally *who* evaluates. According to Political Science models of power, there are three approaches to this: statist, corporative and liberal. The first approach suggests that higher education ought to be accountable to its key funding provider – the state – and thus the state should be the evaluator. The second approach suggests that the community of political scientists ought to carry out evaluations. The third approach proposes that evaluation should not be institutionalised and that the 'customers' (students) as well as the 'providers' (lecturers) ought to communicate evaluations among themselves.

When examining what was happening in Czech higher education in the 1990s (a transitional period) taking the perspective of the statist model, the role of the state in higher education was minimal. This was clearly a reaction to the previous Communist era, where higher education belonged to the most restricted and regulated arenas. Tertiary and other educational institutions enabled enforcement of ideology. For example, all tertiary students had to enrol into mandatory courses, such as *History of the International Labour Movement and the Czechoslovak Communist Party*, *Marxist-Leninist Philosophy*, *Political Economy* and *Scientific Communism and Atheism*.

Since 1989, the state started respecting academic freedom. However, the state held some control over higher education through not only remaining as the main funding provider, but also establishing the Czech Accreditation Agency. The agency grants accreditations for all tertiary study programmes. Granting an accreditation was conditional on providing quantitative and qualitative evidence by the respective applicants (school, faculty or university). In terms of qualitative aspects, the applicants had to demonstrate, for example, a certain number of associate professors teaching their courses. However, in practice, the agency dealt to a greater degree with the aspect of quantity (demand) than quality. This may be documented by some publicly available data: for example, the total number of applications for accreditation between 2000 and 2006 has grown from 250 to 1,635.

Investigating this growth from the level of personnel, it would be naive to assume that there has been such a significant growth in the numbers of lecturers in individual schools. The phenomenon of the so-called *flying professors*, a term invented by the English writer David Lodge, comes to mind in this context where some associate professors and professors have nominally become guarantors of accreditations in a number of universities. In relation to an extensive growth in demand for tertiary education in the Czech Republic, the number of accreditations has increased significantly, resulting in the Accreditation Agency perhaps being more lenient than might be considered appropriate. Currently, there is a debate in Czech higher education about changing the existing accreditation system so that accreditation would be granted to individual universities rather than schools and disciplines. Accreditation then would be granted to universities which would be capable of demonstrating a viable internal accreditation mechanism, significantly based on the assurance of quality. In these initial attempts at institutionalising quality, the *university* would thus become the guarantor and mediator of quality. Thus, the university would become the mediator of the pressures created by the state, particularly in relation to permanent pressures related to financing the tertiary sector, which would in turn provide disciplines with some space for their initiatives in return for guaranteeing a certain standard.

The author's own institution, Masaryk University in Brno, has started a process of internal evaluations, irrespective of whether the new process of accreditation will be introduced or not. Currently, organisational structures for the purposes of evaluation are being developed throughout the university, i.e. one representative of the faculty leadership team – typically this is the Associate Dean Academic – and one academic are given the responsibility for the evaluation process. The university's aim is to build an effective evaluation system, in case the change in the accreditation system is introduced, and also to be able to have some input into the process of forming a new model of evaluation. The university has commenced this process through pilot evaluations of three selected disciplines, and it is planned that in the academic year 2009/10 one discipline per faculty will be evaluated in this way. This is an indication of the university's ambitions and expectations in relation to the state of becoming a 'partner' in developing a new accreditation system. Masaryk University is at the forefront of the development of the evaluation process in the Czech Republic.

In terms of the cooperative model of evaluating and reflecting on quality, there is not much to be said about the activities of the community of Czech political scientists. There is, for example the Czech Political Science Association (CPSA). However, its activities are restricted to holding a national conference (every three years) and publishing one of the two key Czech Political Science journals (*The Political Science Review*). Nevertheless, not all well-regarded Czech political scientists are members of this association (the membership is optional) and a majority of political science schools do not regard it as essential to their activities.

Therefore, Czech Political Science is not 'corporative' in nature, and the CPSA does not represent Czech Political Science as a whole; instead the community consists of individual schools and their members. Quality in teaching and learning has thus always meant activities of individual academics – their lecturing, preparation of the course material and research activities (and their outcomes presented at conferences). It can be argued that quality in this context is highly subjective.

The only established aspects of academic quality are the key milestones in academic career development: i.e. being awarded a PhD, Associate Professorship and Professorship. Only some schools of Political Science in the Czech Republic have the right to award these titles, and these are awarded largely on the basis of research output, rather than teaching and learning. There are, for example, only three schools in the Czech Republic which have the right to award Professorships: these are the Faculty of Social Sciences (Charles University, Prague), University of Economics (Prague) and Faculty of Social Studies (Masaryk University, Brno). The ultimate guarantor of this title is the state.

Conclusion

The author has attempted to outline the perceptions of the phenomenon of quality in Czech Political Science. The story has not described any major turning points, mainly gradual development through small steps. This might generally relate to the nature of quality as a phenomenon which is not always easily measurable, and so to improve quality may be a matter of small gradual steps.

The only critical moment that Czech Political Science has experienced was the fall of the Communist regime which enabled establishment of the discipline as such. Therefore, quality is being introduced into Czech Political Science and Czech higher education, in general, quite gradually, through particular initiatives of individuals. This presents a permanent challenge to the author and his colleagues, and the absence of 'written' rules of quality does not mean that there is no quality or that the academics would not regard this topic as important.

Given the present state of quality in Czech Political Science, this chapter does not offer any practical 'suggestions'. Therefore, it is fair to say that introducing quality into Czech Political Science has been a gradual process resulting from efforts of individuals, schools, faculties, universities, editorial teams, research councils and various government departments. The fact is that the understanding of quality in Czech Political Science is currently broad and varied. The author believes this to be a positive aspect, indicating the openness of the Czech higher education system to developing a systematic quality approach in the near future.

Acknowledgements

This chapter was written as part of the research project 'The Political Science in Central Europe', sponsored by the Czech Science Foundation (project number GAČR 407/07/0562). The author is affiliated with the Faculty of Social Sciences, Masaryk University, Department of Political Science. Email: *holzer@fss.muni.cz*.

Note

1. This chapter was translated by Dr Patricie Mertova.

Reference

Holzer, J. and Pseja, P. (2002) 'Political Science – Czech Republic', in M. Kaase and V. Sparschuh (eds) *Three Social Science Disciplines in Central and Eastern Europe: Handbook on Economics, Political Science and Sociology (1989–2001)*, pp. 226–45, Bonn/Berlin/Budapest: Social Science Information Centre.

Academic development and quality in Oman: mapping the terrain

Thuwayba Al Barwani and
Mohamed Eltahir Osman

Abstract

Academic development and quality in higher education as a field of practice and scholarship, is increasingly becoming a prominent feature of Higher Education Institutions (HEIs). As a result, HEIs are pressured to improve their academic programmes and ensure compatibility with international standards. Obviously, they respond to their intensifying accountability requirements in various ways. The Sultanate of Oman, for example, proposed a comprehensive and integrated quality management framework for all higher education institutions, and established an Accreditation Council that undertakes a comprehensive review of the requirements for academic quality assurance. Some HEIs have also opted for affiliation with external academic institutions. Being the major higher education institution in Oman, Sultan Qaboos University (SQU) has adopted effective quality assurance policies, and created its own quality control mechanisms. However, as pointed out by Tayler (2009), in all fields that are grounded in practice, diversity in experiences can only enrich our practice and scholarship if it is shared and welcomed as part of the discourse among academic communities. Thus, the purpose of this chapter is to present and share two case studies that highlight the academic development and quality of teaching and learning at Sultan Qaboos University in Oman based on perspectives drawn from different disciplines and units involved in supporting and assuring academic quality. More specifically, this chapter focuses on how academics in two colleges (Engineering and Education) incorporate quality improvement in the design, development, implementation, and evaluation of their courses. The chapter also highlights the continuous quality improvement process for SQU curricula, as well as the teaching quality improvement process, and the role of other supporting units involved in academic development and quality in SQU.

Key words: academic development; quality assurance; quality improvement; mapping the terrain; Sultan Qaboos University; higher education; Oman.

Introduction

Academic development and quality in higher education as a field of practice and scholarship is increasingly becoming a prominent feature of Higher Education Institutions (HEIs). As a result, HEIs are pressured to improve their academic programmes and ensure compatibility with international standards. According to Gosling (2009), academic development is a field in which profound and persisting contradiction is not resolvable as a problem of professional practice, but is the lived condition within which the work is carried out on a daily basis. Brew (2007) argues that this field exists in a time of perplexity. It faces critical issues of identity, purpose and values. However, this is not surprising, because universities are social systems with various functions that take place simultaneously within the same structure, although with different emphases (Castells, 2001). Ellis et al. (2007) point out that although university-wide strategic planning, policy-making and global resource allocation are usually at the centre, the ultimate responsibility for the quality of learning and teaching rests with the faculty and those most closely associated with it, the teachers and students. Nevertheless, when different partners in an institution are responsible for different parts of the academic development and quality, a number of additional management strategies are required to mitigate against disintegration of its cohesion. Working with explicit academic standards for student learning outcomes, for instance, requires a heightened praxis by teachers. It involves designing curriculum and employing teaching methods that will assist the student in achieving certain learning outcomes and developing and implementing corresponding assessment schemes (Carrol et al., 2009). However, to understand how a university may assure the quality of a process in order to improve it and better understand related quality standards, it is important to view quality as both accountability and improvement. Quality as accountability does little for learning in higher education as it cannot help to develop an understanding about processes, which is necessary to understand how to improve them (Biggs, 2001). Laughton (2003) points out that if the academic quality assurance process is seen as an improvement-led initiative as opposed to accountability-led, then it might be well received by the academics as one of the aspects of professionalism and self-improvement. Research evidence suggests that the authority associated with the academics' professional culture remains a strong influence in mediating how policies are implemented (Brunetto, 2001). It appears that any approach to academic quality improvement perceived by academic staff to be managerial in nature is likely to be greeted with scepticism and resistance (Davies et al., 2007). It is important, therefore, to pursue academic development and quality assurance in an environment of cooperation and support.

Higher education institutions respond to their intensifying accountability and quality requirements in various ways. In the Sultanate of Oman, for example, the Government proposed a comprehensive and integrated quality management framework for all HEIs, and established an Accreditation Council that undertakes a comprehensive review of the requirements for academic quality assurance. Additionally, some private HEIs have also opted for affiliation with external academic institutions. Being the major higher education institution in Oman, Sultan Qaboos University has adopted some quality assurance policies, and created its own quality control mechanisms. However, as pointed out by Tayler (2009), in all fields that are grounded in practice, diversity in experiences can only enrich our practice and scholarship if it is shared and welcomed as part of the discourse among academic communities.

The purpose of this chapter is to present two diverse case studies that highlight the span of academic development and quality of teaching and learning at Sultan Qaboos University (SQU) in Oman. More specifically, this chapter will focus on how academics in two colleges (Engineering and Education) incorporate quality improvement in the design, development, implementation, and evaluation of their programmes. The chapter will also highlight existing quality improvement processes for curricula and teaching quality and will also show the role of other supporting units in enhancing academic quality and development.

From an oil economy to a knowledge economy

Since the early eighties, the Sultanate of Oman has invested in what is arguably one of the fastest growing higher education systems in the world. By 2006 the country had 52 colleges and universities, enrolling 42,741 students (Ministry of Higher Education, 2007; Sultan Qaboos University,

2007). This dramatic growth was financed mainly by national oil revenues which in 2007 accounted for 67 per cent of the national budget (Ministry of Finance, 2007). However, 2004 projections were that these oil reserves will be largely depleted within the next ten to fifteen years (Sultanate of Oman, 2004). New extraction technologies and recent discovery of some new oil reserves have extended this horizon, but the country's oil reserves are finite and production is already on the decline (Chapman et al., 2009).

Faced with the loss of oil revenues, Oman is seeking new strategies for sustaining its economy. To that end, Oman is investing heavily in higher education in the belief that its new competitive advantage in the international marketplace could be providing highly educated workers to replace the foreign manpower and perhaps have competitive advantage for employment in other neighbouring countries. Thus Omani leaders are banking on the belief that the drive of neighbouring countries for international economic competitiveness will create a demand for Omani workers in those countries.

The Omani Government's goal is to have at least 50 per cent of the 18–24-year-old age group continue to post-secondary education by the year 2020, up from 19 per cent in 2004 (Council of Higher Education, 2004). This is an ambitious goal, as 38 per cent of the population is below the age of 15 (Ministry of National Economy, 2007).

While the growth of private higher education in Oman has been a major national achievement, there is concern about the quality of the education provided by these institutions and the availability of career opportunities for the country's graduates (Council of Higher Education, 2004). Omani HEIs already produce more college graduates annually than there are new and replacement jobs available in the country, an oversupply projected to get worse as college participation rates increase (Al Barwani et al., 2008). The questions now facing government and higher education leaders are: Where will these graduates find jobs? Are graduates of HEIs well positioned to compete for the jobs that are available on the local and regional labour markets? How does the quality of the HEIs compare with the manpower requirements for a sustainable knowledge economy?

Higher education in Oman: seeking solutions

Believing that the transition to a knowledge economy will require a highly educated workforce, the Government of Oman (GoO) invested heavily in the creation of a public higher education system and strongly encouraged Omanis to pursue post-secondary education. Initially this encouragement came through a combination of policies that provided free higher education to Omani citizens who met admissions standards, assurances of public sector employment for graduates, and strong job protection for Omani citizens once they were hired (Chapman et al., 2009). These policies were effective and the public system quickly expanded. Enrolment growth outstripped the capacity of the public sector to afford such an expansion. Moreover, faced with the prospect of declining oil production, GoO also needed to slow the intake of graduates into public sector employment, preferably without antagonising the citizenry who had come to regard free higher education as a 'right' (Chapman et al., 2009).

To address these issues, GoO, in 1995, legalised private higher education and promoted its expansion through a generous set of incentives to those willing to invest in and/or operate private colleges and universities. The Government provided the land on which to build and exempted those institutions from taxes for five years, provided they allocated scholarships for students from low-income families. Further, in 2006, the Government awarded each of the private universities a capital grant of up to RO 20 million ($52 million). Even though the Government heavily subsidised the start-up and on-going operation of private colleges and universities, the creation of the private higher education system offered relief to government both in terms of the cost of financing higher education and the level of accountability.

Since the establishment of the first private college in Oman in 1995, private higher education has grown rapidly. There are now four private universities and 19 colleges. Enrolment in private higher education went from none in 1995 to 20,353 students in 2007 (Ministry of Higher Education, 2007, p. 200). With rapidly expanding higher education (both public and private) and the increasing number of graduates who have difficulty finding employment, the government began to pay serious attention to issues of quality assurance and quality enhancement. Policy makers came to recognise that traditional academic controls were no longer adequate to today's challenges and that more explicit assurances about quality were required. To this end, a Royal Decree was issued in 2001 to establish the Oman Accreditation Council.

Oman's mechanism for quality: exploring the terrain

As indicated earlier, Oman has a young and fast growing higher education sector. Higher education is offered by a number of providers including the Ministry of Higher Education, other governmental entities and private owners (for profit). The programmes are a mix of locally developed and imported, which had not been assessed and the quality of which had not been determined. It was timely, therefore, that the government established the Oman Accreditation Council (OAC) in 2001 to be the body responsible for the external quality assurance and quality enhancement of higher education institutions and programmes. Among its main responsibilities was to 'Lay down the procedures for the assessment and review of higher education institutions' (Oman Accreditation Council, 2008). In response to this mandate, the OAC took the initial step of developing a document which laid down key elements of the national quality management system. These key elements made up what were considered to be the 'Requirements for Oman's System for Quality Assurance' (ROSQA).

ROSQA, in effect, is the combination of a number of elements of an overall quality system. It includes a system for classifying institutions of higher education; a qualifications and credit framework; institutional standards; and processes for institutional and programme licensing and accreditation. Some of these elements needed to be updated, and missing elements needed to be created. This system was gradually reviewed and updated, based on the goal that the educational system infrastructure will comprise integrated frameworks for fields of study, qualifications and credit, and supporting policies, which will ensure that Oman's education system can interface with the education systems of benchmark countries. The purpose of this goal is to provide the policy infrastructure necessary to transform Omani higher education from a system dependent upon other countries to a mature system capable of providing its own degree programmes at international standards (Ministry of Higher Education and the Accreditation Council, 2006).

Recognising that most HEIs in Oman are currently unlikely to pass provider accreditation, it was decided that the focus for the next few years would be on implementing quality audits after which institutions may progress towards accreditation. Thus, the next several years were considered to be a grace period where institutions were allowed to ready themselves for provider accreditation. It is anticipated that by 2015, no non-accredited institutions will be permitted to offer higher education programmes in Oman (Ministry of Higher Education and the Accreditation Council, 2006).

Starting from 2008, each higher education institution was expected to undergo a quality audit process. This first stage emphasises the evaluation of the effectiveness of the institution's quality assurance and quality enhancement processes against its declared goals and objectives. Quality audit involves a self-study of the institution's activities resulting in a Quality Audit Portfolio followed by verification of the portfolio by an external Audit Panel assembled by OAC. After the verification process, the panel produces a Quality Audit Report containing Commendations, Affirmations and Recommendations.

The second stage involves each HEI undergoing a Standards Assessment which basically measures whether or not the institution has met the Quality Standards published by OAC. The Standards Assessment involves a self-assessment against standards and whether or not the HEI has satisfactorily attended to the Affirmations and Recommendations of the Quality Audit Report. The OAC will then convene an External Assessment Panel to verify the HEI's assessment application. The panel produces an Assessment Report indicating the standards that have not been met and a confidential report for the OAC Board, advising whether or not the HEI has met the standards and has satisfactorily addressed the Affirmations and Recommendations. If the report is satisfactory, the OAC Board will award the HEI a Provider Accreditation Certificate. The cycle is then repeated every four years (Oman Accreditation Council, 2008). As it turns out, Sultan Qaboos University is the first institution that has undergone the quality audit review. It completed its Quality Portfolio early in 2009 and received the Review Panel in May 2009, thus testing the mechanisms involved in the first stage of the national quality assurance framework.

Sultan Qaboos University quality control mechanisms: mapping the terrain

Sultan Qaboos University was established in 1986 as an institution that focuses on student learning, promotes scientific and social research, enhances faculty and staff development in its various forms and exhibits organisational learning as it deals with the challenges facing it. Student learning takes place at the undergraduate and postgraduate levels in an educational environment that integrates Omani culture, rigorous inquiry and scholarship, creative imagination and reflective engagement with society. Specifically, SQU strives to expand the boundaries of knowledge and insight through teaching, research and community service. It also strives to be the leader among higher educational institutions in Oman and the region and to be an institution recognised both nationally and internationally for excellence in research and instruction. In this regard, the university is committed to preserving and disseminating core values including: moral and professional ideals, excellence, institutional growth, innovation, academic freedom, and quality.

SQU consists of nine colleges and other university units located over 9.7 km² in the suburbs of Muscat. At present the university offers 66 undergraduate and 58 postgraduate academic programmes for a population of about 13,410, and 855 undergraduate and graduate students, respectively. In contrast, the number of SQU employees as of January 2008 was 4,294. Out of this number 1,074 are academic staff of whom 654 are PhD holders.

The quality of inputs

Although academic quality is defined differently by different providers, all agree that the quality of any programme output is largely dependent on the quality of its input and processes. Accordingly SQU, as a premier institution, preferentially receives the top general education graduates in the Sultanate. All colleges annually review and send their Student Entry Standards to the Deanship of Admission and Registration. For example, students wishing to apply for any undergraduate programme should possess a General Certificate of Education, a minimum average of (C) grade in all subjects studied, and fulfil the minimum subject requirements for each programme.

Another significant source of input is the quality of faculty who are employed by the university. Two groups of faculty comprise the teaching force: Omani faculty who have mostly received their doctorates from reputable universities in the US, Canada, Europe, Australia and New Zealand; and non-Omani faculty who are hand-picked from international markets to bring in new experiences, ideas and expertise.

SQU offers to its faculty a supportive environment for research, professional development and opportunity to contribute to community service, together with a lucrative salary and other fringe benefits such as sabbatical leave, research leave, conference attendance, etc.

In order to assure and maintain the quality of its programmes, the university also provides a comprehensive system of academic support services that is designed to assist both students and staff in their learning and instructional processes. These services include, but are not limited to: a unique Local Area Network (SQUNet) and Oracle web applications that provide electronic interactivity for all academic transactions such as online registration, campus-wide timetabling, grades, degree audit, probation, postponement, and other status information. The SQUNet has more than 14,000 connections, where all employees and students can access specific dynamically updated information targeted for their needs through SQU Portal, and an e-mail service for more than 20,000 users. In addition, SQU provides a library system that includes about 300,000 volumes, 1,500 printed journals, 14,500 audio visual and digitised items, and about 13,000 electronic full-text journals and e-books, and over 30 bibliographic databases. Moreover, the university promotes the development of flexible instructional and learning approaches through a blended e-learning environment. The Centre for Educational Technology, for example, administers more than 300 courses on WebCT and Moodle Learning Management Systems. SQU also provides additional services through the Student Counselling Centre, the Centre for Career Guidance, and various research centres. Apart from the academic activities, the Deanship of Student Affairs sets up, plans and programmes in areas of culture, sporting and social services as a complementary part of the educational process.

The quality of processes

The missions, objectives, and outcomes of all colleges are in line with those of the university as a whole. Consequently, there are general guidelines for course development at both the undergraduate and graduate levels. Thus, the procedure followed for developing curricula is based on a systematic and systemic quality monitoring and improvement process. Figure 10.1 illustrates that input and feedback may be sought from various constituents such as students, staff, employers, alumni, external advisory boards, and external examiners. For example, all programme proposals are first scrutinised by the relevant curriculum committees, and then discussed in departmental and college boards for recommendation to the academic council in accordance with SQU's Academic Regulations.

Quality procedures are also ensured through University Academic Regulations that address issues of students' progression standards, graduation requirements, etc. Sultan Qaboos University requires an overall grade-point average (GPA) of 2.0 (on a 4 point scale) for graduation. Grades are usually recorded and archived by the Deanship of Admission and Registration. According to the University Academic Regulations,

Figure 10.1 Continuous quality improvement process for SQU curricula

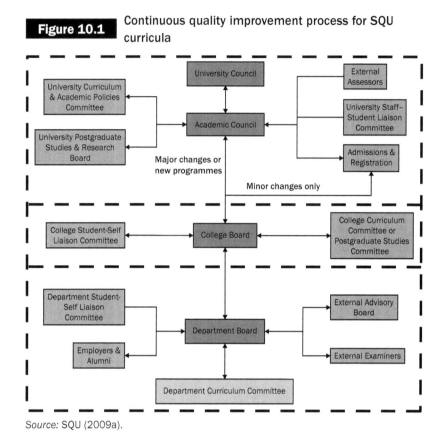

Source: SQU (2009a).

a student who achieves a minimum GPA of 2.0 on both semester and CGPA (cumulative GPA) may continue without interruption in his/her degree programme. However, under certain conditions a student will be placed on probation. For example, when the student's CGPA falls below 2.0 or the CGPA is above 2.0 but the semester GPA is less than 1.0 or the CGPA is above 2.0 but the semester GPA has been below 2.0 for two consecutive semesters, a student is required to take remedial action, which includes limiting the number of credits to 12 in the following semester. Students under probation usually get help and professional guidance from their academic advisers and counsellors. Failing to get out of probation in four consecutive semesters results in withdrawal from the university. Students work very closely with an assigned adviser to ensure that they take courses according to their degree plans. During the student final semester, the Deanship of Admission and Registration provides a degree audit for all graduating students against the requirements for the year they were admitted and coordinates with colleges on issues relating to student status.

As the university requires a GPA of 2.0 for graduation, it maintains a rigorous monitoring system for students at all levels through the advisory system. Advisers keep records of appropriate personal details of students, courses taken and grades awarded. These records are also available to advisers online. In addition, instructors' records of attendance and course work are submitted at the end of each semester to be kept in the department course files. Student e-mail addresses are available to alert students of any progress or attendance concerns that arise at an early stage. The university enforces a strict policy for student attendance. Course instructors are required to warn students who have missed 10 per cent of classes. Students who fail to attend the required minimum 20 per cent of classes are barred from the course.

Furthermore, the university conducts induction sessions for all new students during the orientation week. Considerable additional support is provided to ensure their smooth progression within the programmes. Moreover, comprehensive advising and registration guidelines are also available online (*http://sisinfo.squ.om/* or *http://sis.squ.om.*) This document serves to provide guidance to staff, faculty and students. Normally, a series of seminars and presentations are arranged for the faculty on student advising. The university has also developed an electronic advising system for the faculty, where a student's progress, credits earned, and the number of courses remaining can easily be produced.

In addition, almost all departments rely on advisory boards and external examiners for feedback on improving their programmes and ensuring compatibility with international standards. The quality of teaching is ensured through continuous assessment of teaching performance (by both students and peers) and by the provision of support through professional development programmes offered by different departments and centres.

Promoting a culture of academic quality

Although quality assurance and improvement are embedded in various academic and administrative structures and practices, SQU is keen to make academic quality a routine business and an integrated part of its organisational culture. For example, all faculties are routinely involved in some form of assessment and evaluation process including formative and summative evaluation of courses and programmes. In addition, the university at large underwent several institutional evaluations by teams of international experts covering all aspects of its duties and tasks, including governance, finance and management, learning and instructional environment, research, and community services. Further, several seminars on the subject were held at university and college levels to raise the awareness of quality assurance and improvement within all involved units and departments.

The quality of outputs

Since its inception, the university has awarded degrees to over 24,000 students at the Bachelor's Diploma and Master's levels (Sultan Qaboos University, 2008). A large percentage of these graduates have found employment in the civil service, the private sector, military and security areas and international organisations, while others with entrepreneurial skills have ventured on their own. The university has a record of a number of its graduates who have become leaders in different sectors of society and a significant number who have been appointed to very high level positions in the Government.

While it is clear that the above-mentioned quality assurance processes are mostly at the institutional level, a look at individual colleges reveals that there are significant variations between them. Though much seems to have been done, one would have difficulty in identifying a framework, a pattern or infrastructure for quality that encompasses the whole university. One notes that though elements of the quality assurance process are in place, they are generally haphazard, uncoordinated and without focus. This can be equated to pieces of a puzzle that do not form an identifiable picture or a terrain that has not been mapped. To this end, this paper will explore the diversity of the quality assurance processes at SQU by focusing on two diverse colleges: the College of Education and the College of Engineering. These two colleges can be said to represent individual models from which some form of a university wide model might emerge.

College of Engineering: towards a mature system

The college started its academic programmes in 1986 when Sultan Qaboos University accepted its first batch of students with a mission to provide students with a high quality engineering education, to carry out basic and applied research, and to provide a service to society by taking excellence as its benchmark. In 1991, its first batch of sixty engineers graduated. Since then, the college has steadily increased its new student admission to about 478 students in 2008, and has a total of 126 academic staff. The college currently offers 11 undergraduate degree programmes, and 8 graduate programmes (Sultan Qaboos University, 2009b).

Since its inception in 1986, the College has employed effective quality management and assurance policies for its programmes. Four of the college undergraduate programmes have been evaluated and recognised by the Accreditation Board for Engineering and Technology (ABET). It is the primary organisation responsible for monitoring, evaluating, and certifying the quality of applied science, engineering, and engineering technology education in the United States. Another four programmes have gone through rigorous self-evaluation, and are awaiting an ABET decision.

Quality audit: implanting the culture of self-assessment

The primary processes through which the college programmes meet the ABET engineering criteria include students in good academic standing, a strong curriculum, well qualified faculty members, and excellent facilities. Figure 10.2, illustrates the Continuous Quality Improvement Process (CQIP) for Undergraduate Education, which shows a flow chart of the CQIP at different levels. It identifies basic components of the undergraduate programme, ranging from a specific course offering to the complete programme curriculum. These components include all of the ABET criteria. The CQIP requires periodic review from all involved parties, and recommendations for improvement for each item in the cycle. Assessment activities, for example, include surveys of students, faculty, industry and alumni, student course evaluations, course file assessment, and student grades.

In addition, the college has another assessment and evaluation system which is based on external examiners who visit various departments at the end of each semester. During their visits, which last about a week, the external examiners meet with all departmental staff and many students from each cohort, review the final examination sheets of graduating students, and attend most of the students' final year presentations. After the visit, the external examiners send a comprehensive report evaluating the entire programme and related activities to SQU Administration. Most of the external examiners' recommendations are usually considered

Figure 10.2 Continuous Quality Improvement Process (CQIP)

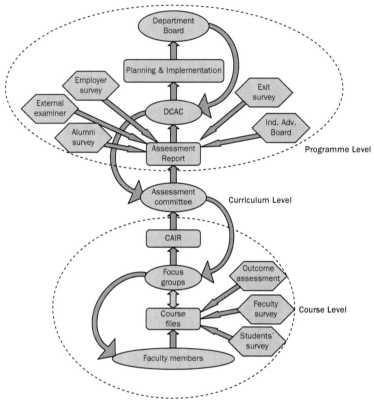

DCAC- Department Curriculum and Accreditation Committee
CAIR- Course Assessment and Improvement Report

Source: College of Engineering, ABET Self-Study Report

for implementation, and fed into the Continuous Quality Improvement Process (CQIP).

CQIP requires that the programme outcomes should be evaluated at least once every year. Table 10.1 shows how each programme outcome is evaluated by all constituents against the stated programme educational objectives. Accordingly, the course coordinators review and improve their course syllabi, including outcome coverage, at least once every year. Furthermore, the Accreditation Committee reviews and improves the complete undergraduate curriculum including outcome coverage,

Table 10.1 Correspondence of outcomes and objectives

Programme outcomes	Programme educational objectives			
	1	2	3	4
a. Knowledge	✓			
b. Experiments	✓			
c. Design	✓			
d. Teams		✓		
e. Problem solving	✓			
f. Ethics			✓	
g. Communication		✓		
h. Breadth			✓	
i. Life-long learning				✓
j. Contemporary issues				✓
k. Modern tools	✓			✓

at least once every three years. It is also required that all departmental committees review and update their strategies at least once every three years.

College of Education: towards the establishment of a system

The College of Education was established in 1986 to prepare and train teachers and professionals needed for the expansion and development of the Omani education system. Today the college has a multi-faceted mission that emphasises preparation of teachers and school administrators, research and consultancy, international collaboration and modelling of excellence in developmentally appropriate educational settings and practices. Currently, the college has a student population of about 2,233 undergraduates, 129 higher diploma and 96 MA students. In addition, it has a total of 140 academic and administrative staff, and offers 11 undergraduate teacher education programmes, 5 higher diploma programmes and 8 MA programmes.

Unlike many other colleges of education in the world, the College of Education at SQU is a high demand college that can afford to admit only the very best candidates into the teaching profession. The college is therefore highly competitive and maintains high admission standards for both the new intake and transfer students.

Unlike the College of Engineering, which has a more established quality assurance infrastructure, the College of Education can be said to be in the early stages of establishing an organised, systematic mechanism for quality assurance and accreditation. While basic quality indicators can be identified and some basic quality components have already been established, the quality assurance map is yet to be defined. The quality culture and quality structures and mechanisms are therefore among the important issues that the college is currently examining.

Academic standards

The College of Education offers a broad range of courses aimed at developing and enriching students' knowledge and instructional competency. Complementing the student degree plan, the courses offered comprise 40 credit hours in the areas of curriculum and teaching methods, psychology, educational technology, and foundations of education. To ensure compatibility of its programmes with international standards, the college went through an external review process conducted by the United Nations Development Programme (UNDP) in November 2005. All eight departments were reviewed by international programme evaluators. Further, the college maintains its own internal quality assurance mechanisms through the College Quality Audit Committee Department, College Curriculum Committees, and Boards.

Assessment: quality indicators

The college is keen to use a variety of assessment methods in all offered courses such as tests, research projects and classroom presentations. Students are required to produce a variety of class work for their courses, including essays, responsive journals, reports, presentations, group assignments and quizzes, for which they receive quantitative and qualitative feedback. The purpose of using various assessment methods throughout the programme is to provide a balanced view of student learning and competence which at the same time ensures fairness and reliability in the assessment. Student evaluations indicate these assessment methods help them clarify their strengths and weaknesses. Teaching Practice Assessment is based on an observation sheet which contains certain criteria checked by a faculty supervisor from the college, the Principal, and a cooperative teacher from the school where the student-teacher practises teaching. The final grade is divided into 80 per cent (60 per cent for actual teaching and 20 per cent for related activities such as designing lesson plans) awarded by the faculty supervisor, with the remaining 20 per cent divided between the school Principal and the cooperative teacher.

Assessment methods have been matched to course outcomes, and they reflect the general learning outcomes of the programme and individual course objectives. Students are provided with feedback on their performance and are able to discuss their evaluation with faculty in all assignments and tests. Departments use the marking criteria and assessment scale published by the university in the various college handbooks. Where faculty employ additional criteria, these are communicated to the students via student handbooks and course syllabi. To ensure that the assessment process is rigorous, objective and fair, a variety of methods, consultations and discussion at various levels are used. Final grades are reviewed by the Examination Committee, and submitted to the head of department for scrutiny, and then to the College Board for discussion and approval. Students have the right to appeal if they feel that they have been assessed unfairly. In such cases, a departmental committee investigates the complaint and reviews the students' assignments and exams.

Quality of learning opportunities

To demonstrate that the college practises what it preaches, a variety of teaching methods are usually used in all offered courses to achieve the intended learning outcomes. Small class sizes (20–30) permit interactive seminar/workshop-style teaching, with some forms of group or pair work commonly used. This allows a high level of interaction and close monitoring of students' development.

Emerging instructional technologies are commonly used in the teaching/learning process. Many courses use computer labs for practical instruction or Internet/electronic database access or training work. Online instruction and/or discussion through WebCT or Moodle are also used in some courses to supplement classroom teaching. Student participation and independent learning are strongly encouraged through student presentations, self-learning, group work and research-based project work. In addition, around 5–10 per cent of the final grade in a number of courses is allocated for student participation. Other opportunities for increased student participation and independent learning come through student groups and societies supported by the college, and the Deanship of Students Affairs.

Quality of learning materials provided

To assure the quality of course contents, the assigned textbooks are reviewed regularly for their relevancy and comprehensiveness by course instructors and a departmental committee and approved by departmental and college boards. Most courses use additional sources of materials to supplement textbooks, such as printed or electronic handouts. Students are also required in some courses to research relevant supplementary materials. In addition, most courses provide opportunities for autonomous learning through assignments, mini-projects and presentations.

Conclusion

It is clear from the above that the two colleges represent precisely two different models or mechanisms for quality assurance. This may well reflect the diversity of processes within the university as a whole. While there is no question that diversity should be nurtured and encouraged, both between colleges and between programmes within individual colleges, the need for a unifying, cohesive, university wide quality infrastructure cannot be underestimated.

What is common between the two colleges is that both have not as yet tackled the issue of student learning. It appears that the coming phase must begin to focus on evidence of actual results or outcomes of the whole learning process. The university must develop effective ways to assess what students have actually learnt and what competencies they actually possess. It is important, therefore, that the university is able to show that what the students have learnt is *fit for purpose*. This will call for the establishment of performance indicators and exit measures to ensure that the stated objectives have been achieved at the desired level. This is a challenge for academics and researchers not only in Oman but also in other developing countries that seek to provide quality education in their institutions.

References

Al Barwani, T., Chapman, D. and Ameen, H. (2009) 'Strategic Brain Drain: Implications for Higher Education in Oman'. *Higher Education Policy*. 22: 415–432.

Biggs, J. (2001) 'The reflective institution: assuring and enhancing the quality of teaching and learning', *Higher Education*, 41: 221–38.

Brew, A. (2007) 'Evaluating academic development in a time of perplexity', *International Journal for Academic Development*, 12(1): 69–72.

Brunetto, Y. (2001) 'Mediating change for public-sector professionals', *The International Journal of Public Sector Management*, 14(6): 465–81.

Carroll, M., Razvi, S. and Goodliffe, T. (2009) 'Using Foundation Program Academic Standards as a Quality Enhancement Tool'. Paper, *INQAAHE 2009*, April 2009, United Arab Emirates.

Castells, M. (2001) 'Universities as dynamic systems of contradictory functions'. In J. Muller., N. Cloete and S. Badat (eds.). *Challenges of Globalization*, pp. 206–223. Cape Town, Maskew Miller Longman.

Chapman, D.W., Al Barwani, T. and Ameen, H. (2009) 'Expanding post-secondary access in Oman, and paying for it', in Jane Knight (ed.) *Financing Higher Education: Access and Equity*. Rotterdam, The Netherlands: SENSE Publishing.

Council of Higher Education (2004) *The Strategy for Education in the Sultanate of Oman, 2006–2020*. Muscat, Sultanate of Oman.

Davies, J., Douglas, A. and Douglas, J. (2007) 'The effect of academic culture on the implementation of the EFQM Excellence Model in UK universities', *Quality Assurance in Education*, 15(4): 382–401.

Ellis, R., Jarkey, N., Mahony, M., Peat, M. and Sheely, S. (2007) 'Managing quality improvement of eLearning in a large, campus-based university', *Quality Assurance in Education*, 15(1): 9–23.

Gosling, D. (2009) 'Educational development in the UK: a complex and contradictory reality', *International Journal for Academic Development*, 14(1): 5–18.

Laughton, D. (2003) 'Why was the QAA approach to teaching quality assessment rejected by academics in UK HE?', *Assessment and Evaluation in Higher Education*, 28(3): 309–21.

Ministry of Finance (2007) *The State's General Budget for the Fiscal Year 2007*. Muscat, Sultanate of Oman.

Ministry of Higher Education and the Accreditation Council (2006) *Plan for an Omani Higher Education Quality Management System (The quality plan)*. Muscat, Sultanate of Oman.

Ministry of Higher Education (2007) *Higher Education Institutions in the Sultanate of Oman*. Muscat: Sultanate of Oman.

Ministry of National Economy (2007) *Monthly Statistical Bulletin*. Muscat, Sultanate of Oman.

Oman Accreditation Council (2008) *Quality Audit Manual*. Institutional Accreditation: Stage 1. Muscat: Sultanate of Oman.

Sultanate of Oman (2004) *Oil and Gas*. Central Bank of Oman Annual Report pp. 32–38

Sultan Qaboos University (2007) *Statistical Yearbook 2007*. Muscat: Sultanate of Oman.

Sultan Qaboos University (2008) *College of Engineering, ABET Self-Study Report*. Muscat: Sultanate of Oman.

Sultan Qaboos University (2009a) *Quality Audit Portfolio*. Muscat: Sultanate of Oman.

Sultan Qaboos University (2009b) *College of Education Annual Report*. Muscat: Sultanate of Oman. Available at *http//www.sisinfo.squ.edu.om*

Taylor, L. (2009) 'Educational development practice and scholarship: an evolving discourse community', *International Journal for Academic Development*, 14(1): 1–3.

Part 6
Resources and trends in higher education quality

New directions in quality management

Hamish Coates

Abstract

The ever changing and expanding nature of quality development in recent years has placed an increased demand on undertaking continuous improvement as part of any quality cycle. As a result there is a need for the constant improvement of measures, instruments and software employed to assist the advancement of quality development. This chapter reviews: trends in the development of feedback instruments over the last few decades; tensions between the imperatives of continuous improvement, competition and quality assurance; current instruments in use by universities in Australia; and makes forecasts about future development. It will offer broad insights that assist managers and leaders to advance quality development in higher education.

Key words: changes and expansion in quality development; continuous improvement; feedback; quality enhancement tools; student-centredness; evidence-based approach; graduate skills; student engagement; Australian higher education.

Introduction

This chapter contends that quality management in higher education is moving towards being more 'evidence-based', 'student-centred' and 'outcomes-focused' in nature. This broad assertion, unpacked below, has direct implications for the focus of quality assurance activities, how they are conducted, and their impact on higher education systems and institutions. In this chapter, it is used to frame discussion of a number of new and emerging quality enhancement tools being used in Australian higher education.

The discussion in this analysis is intended to apply both to external quality regulation ('quality assurance') and internal or 'continuous' improvement activities. Occasional points of tension between these phenomena are proposed, but in line with contemporary perspectives on higher education quality it is assumed that there should be an alignment between these two activities, and that, beyond accreditation, external monitoring is a secondary process intended to ensure that continuous improvement is taking place.

As proposed by the title, the chapter outlines key resources that play a role in quality management in higher education. It does this, however, in a more conceptual manner than simply cataloguing the large and increasing number of assessments that are available to systems and institutions. Rather, it traces trends in quality management over the last few decades and reviews indicators and instruments that have been seen to play a role. In doing this, it elaborates an earlier point (Coates, 2006a) that excellent measures need to precede measures of excellence.

The current discussion does not embrace all aspects of higher education quality management. As the discussion implies, the chapter excludes analysis of the quality or impact of research, productivity considerations, institution or course accreditation, or funding. While beyond the current scope, there is value in drawing links between these considerations and the discussion in the text.

An evidence-based approach

Quality management has always played a role in Australian higher education. Since their foundation, university academic boards or senates have established and regulated 'academic standards' – an exercise which has resisted easy definition but in broad terms can be read as upholding the quality of institutional work. For most of Australia's history, the 'professoriate' (Thomson, 1934) were the managing directors of each institution's quality arrangements. The elite nature of the system meant that collegial insights and informal networks were sufficient to maintain the integrity of institutions' knowledge development activities.

The contemporary quality movement that has taken shape in the last few decades is playing an ever greater role in shaping institutional management, learning and instruction, and the impact of universities on society. As outlined below, the widespread development of performance indicator systems in the 1990s provided the conceptual substrate for a wider exchange of ideas about institutional aspirations and performance. In the last decade, this has led to the development of instruments and collection systems that generate large amounts of data on the characteristics of higher education. Such information has grown with the role played by institutions in Australia's economic and social life.

By generating increasingly transparent insights for institutions and the public, this quality-relevant information is a key driver in shifting the boundaries between institutional and national interests. Increasingly, the business of universities is becoming the business of the country, and the need for public information about performance grows accordingly (Australian Government, 2009). Detailed exploration of this trend, of its nature and 'appropriateness', lies beyond the current analysis, which instead seeks to highlight the phenomenon and explore key implications.

Most notably, the above trend gives rise to increasingly 'evidence-based' approaches to quality management. In general, 'evidence-based' implies forms of professional practice based on data collected using scientific methods. Such data provides a robust foundation for professional diagnosis, decision-making and action, when carefully designed and collected. It implies a certain way of thinking that can play out in various ways in practice. Evidence-based management can denote senior executives making decisions based on data about the quality of provision. It may also involve academic staff using locally collected data to analyse student performance and to help target teaching and support. In education it should, as advanced in this paper, involve analysis of students' learning processes and outcomes.

A shift towards students

With growing demands for information come growing calls for ensuring that data is focused on the 'right things', and that it is collected in ways that are both valid and efficient. These, of course, are contestable issues. Very few things in the diverse and complex make-up of higher education are 'right for all'. Similarly, the methods and feasibility of collection will vary with context and application. Rather than get hamstrung or sidetracked by the polyphony and even atonality of such debate, it is helpful to take a structured approach to understanding its implications for quality management in higher education.

From an analytical perspective, education is often viewed as involving inputs, processes and outcomes at a range of different levels – typically systems, institutions, teachers and students. This structure has been used in education for many decades (Bottani and Tuijnman, 1994; Astin, 1985; Ewell and Jones, 1996; Jaeger, 1978; Nuttall, 1994). Its most prominent contemporary instantiation is likely to be the Organisation for Economic Cooperation and Development (OECD)'s Indicators of Education Systems (INES) (OECD, 2008). The framework is helpful for current purposes, as it provides a means of charting how conversations about quality management have unfolded over the last few decades, and forecasting where developments may be heading.

Institutional reputation ('brand') is the oldest and still most dominant mechanism for demonstrating quality in higher education. Indeed, this take on quality management has been so much part of the woodwork that it has only recently been separated out for critical reflection. This has happened largely via the institutional rankings popularised in the last decade (Coates, 2007b; Usher and Savino, 2006). The rankings have charted various ways in which institutional brand can be assessed and reported. In many respects, these rankings might be seen as representing the culmination of this perspective. They have exposed the strengths of various approaches, the limitations of institution-level rankings, and also their value – particularly in providing information to the public.

The last few decades have seen an increasing shift towards basing quality assessments on teacher-level process factors rather than institution-level inputs. Australia has been something of a leader on this front. An instrument that measures the quality of teaching – the Course Experience Questionnaire (CEQ) – was introduced for national use in the early 1990s (Ramsden, 1991). Since that time, nearly all institutions have developed and implemented institution-wide teaching quality surveys. These teaching quality instruments (TQIs) – with labels like QOT, SET, SETL and TEVAL – have grown to play an important role in quality assurance in Australian higher education. TQIs are mandatory in around half of Australia's universities and the results are playing an increasing part in the management and promotion of teachers and their teaching (Davies et al., 2009).

For all of their limitations – and there are many – the use of such instruments has given fresh weight to the importance of teaching. Between 2005 and 2008, incorporation of the CEQ into the national learning and teaching performance fund (Nelson, 2003) prompted interest in how to enhance teaching in ways that would yield performance-based income. This prompted queries about the connection between continuous improvement and external quality regulation, and hence the links between the data used for each. It prompted questions about which indicators should be used to distribute quality-contingent funds. Importantly, it prompted debate about the kinds of indicators which might best be used to measure and report on the quality of university education.

In the last few years, these conversations have led to a growing awareness of the limitations of quality assessments that fail to take account of student learning and achievement. Good teaching is vital, yet it is the quality of student learning which is the necessary and perhaps even sufficient indicator of high-quality education. This has been recognised for many decades in school education, yet it has only very recently become manifest in a shift towards a student-centred and outcomes-focused approach in higher education. Like all large-scale social trends, this movement from teaching processes to student outcomes is underpinned by a range of complex forces. Individuals and institutions, for instance, are seeking to validate the quality of their performance (Harman, 2007). Funding agencies and regulators, at the same time, are seeking to capture such information to improve the validity of their quality allocations and assessments (Australian Government, 2009).

Within self accrediting institutions, the assessment of student competency and capability has largely been managed by teaching staff – even in highly regulated professional programmes. Teachers have had the freedom to shape content and pedagogy and assess the quality of outcomes, often using very localised materials, processes and individual frames of reference. Collaborations, compliance with accreditation requirements, outsourcing and the use of standardised materials have led to pockets of generalisability. By and large, however, the examinations and assignments that have provided the means of determining the standards of learners' attainment have been referenced to the localised frames in which the educational interactions have occurred.

This lack of generalisability, coupled with other factors such as uncertainties about the properties of the assessments and the desire to avoid grade inflation, limits the prospects of overly relying on routine student assessment data for the purposes of quality management. Such data may have a role to play, but it is likely to require reinforcement and embellishment by measures which are more generalisable in nature. This calls for the definition of such measures and of the instruments which can be used to underpin them.

Calculating what counts

Numbers can cast an allure of certainty, but the existence of data does not guarantee its veracity or relevance. As evidence-based planning, practice and quality enhancement further develop, universities and their communities are seeking more sophisticated ways of focusing, collecting and using data on education. Greater emphasis is being placed on ensuring the conceptual and empirical validity, methodological rigour, and effective use, of the information that is used to shape educational development. This underpins a need for data that measures what matters for monitoring and improving high-quality education.

There is no easy means of describing or justifying the measures or instruments that can or 'should' underpin assessments of student achievement and capability in higher education. One sign of the significance of student learning in higher education is that conversations about what to measure become very focused and complex. The current analysis does not attempt a 'grand untangling' of this matter, but the more modest task of describing a selection of the solutions that have been proposed in recent years. The discussion is mainly, although not exclusively Australian in focus, although many of the resources are international in scope. The first looks at the measurement of generic skills, the second at the measurement of student engagement, the third at employer feedback, and the fourth at various approaches to measuring academic standards. Some, all or a combination of these would seem to play a formative role in the future of quality management in higher education.

Measuring graduate skills

Generic skills assessments have the capacity to directly measure important general outcomes of university education. If administered in specific ways, they also have the capacity to produce generalisable measures of the net educational effects of university study – commonly referred to as the 'value added' (Coates, 2009).

The development of such assessments has been framed by the trends noted above and the definition of desired graduate attributes and outcomes (ACER, 2001; Barrie, 2009). Nearly every institution in Australia has developed such attribute statements. These vary according to institutional context, but also hover around the core subset of 'skills' defined in the Employability Skills Framework (ACCI and BCA, 2002) – communication, teamwork, initiative and organising, self-management, learning, and technology.

Within Australia, a number of instruments have been developed by the Australian Council for Educational Research (ACER) over the years to assess such characteristics. The Graduate Skills Assessment (GSA) (ACER, 2001), for instance, measures critical thinking, problem solving, interpersonal understanding, and written communication. Greater interest in such assessments in recent years has led to the development of assessments to measure phenomena such as work readiness, career readiness, and a range of more discipline-specific competencies. The Work Readiness Assessment Package (WRAP) developed for Victoria University (Edwards and Coates, 2007), is an example of such a resource.

Broadly, such tests are designed to gauge learners' skills in decision making and argument analysis. Within the decision making realm learners are assessed on their abilities to: make decisions about everyday situations and problems; use data to identify relationships, constraints, rules and consequences; make inferences; classify, generalise and hypothesise; and identify and evaluate explanations, hypotheses, approaches and reasoning. Within the argument analysis sphere learners are assessed on their abilities to: comprehend and interpret arguments; recognise the way arguments and evidence relate to conclusions; analyse and assess dialectical strategies; and evaluate the strength and weakness of arguments; develop and organise evidence and arguments to establish conclusions.

The Collegiate Learning Assessment (CLA), is the most well-deployed assessment of generic skills (CAE, 2009; Benjamin et al., 2009). This assessment presents an institutionally representative sample of students with realistic problems that require students to analyse complex materials. Responses are scored against rubrics designed to assess each respondent's ability to think critically, reason analytically, solve problems, and communicate clearly and cogently.

The CLA is designed to measure an institution's contribution to the development of student competencies. In so doing, the results are intended to assist teachers, leaders and managers to understand and improve the quality of teaching and learning. Institutions can benchmark their results against those from over 400 other institutions, and against results from other assessments, surveys of engagement and other locally collected variables.

Of course, such tests cannot provide a holistic or sufficient assessment of student, institutional or systemic performance. In highly diverse educational contexts, however, there is value to be gained from the provision of common data that can be used as a point of reference for tracking and improving performance. This does not happen from reporting alone, but from advising faculty members how to turn results from aggregate assessments into changes in teaching and learning. Strategies for doing this have been developed around the CLA, and through the Staff Student Engagement Survey outlined below.

Assessing student engagement

'Student engagement', defined as students' involvement with activities and conditions likely to generate high-quality learning (NSSE, 2008; Coates, 2006b), is increasingly understood to be important for higher education quality. The concept provides a practical lens for assessing and responding to the significant dynamics, constraints and opportunities facing higher education institutions. It provides key insights into what students are actually doing, a structure for framing conversations about quality, and a stimulus for guiding new thinking about best practice.

Student engagement is an idea specifically focused on learners and their interactions with the university. The idea touches on aspects of teaching, the broader student experience, learners' lives beyond university, and institutional support. The concept of student engagement is based on the premise that learning is influenced by how an individual participates in educationally purposeful activities. It operationalises research that has identified the educational practices linked empirically with high quality learning and development (see, for instance: Astin, 1979, 1985, 1993; Pace, 1979, 1995; Chickering and Gamson, 1987; Pascarella and Terenzini, 2005). While students are seen to be responsible for constructing their knowledge, learning is also seen to depend on institutions and staff generating conditions that stimulate and encourage involvement. Learners are central to the idea of student engagement, which focuses squarely on enhancing individual learning and development.

Surprisingly, given its centrality to education, information on student engagement has not been readily available to Australasian higher education institutions. The Australasian Survey of Student Engagement (AUSSE) (ACER, 2009a), conducted with 25 institutions for the first time in 2007, 29 in 2008 and 35 in 2009, provides data that Australian and New Zealand higher education institutions can use to engage students in effective educational practices. The AUSSE builds on foundations laid by the North American National Survey of Student Engagement (NSSE, 2008). By providing information that is generalisable and sensitive to institutional diversity, and with multiple points of reference, the AUSSE plays an important role in helping institutions monitor and enhance the quality of education.

Using the Student Engagement Questionnaire (SEQ), the AUSSE collects data from institutionally representative samples of first- and later-year students, and provides a foundation for analysing the engagement of first-year and near-to-graduating students and, through comparison of these, the amount of change over time. Examining change across year levels, for instance, provides insight into the extent to which people are being challenged and pushing themselves to learn. An increase in engagement in active learning practices, for instance, indicates that learners are investing more time constructing new knowledge and understanding. It also indicates that learners are intrinsically more engaged in their work, and hence more likely to be developing their knowledge and skill.

From 2008 ACER has run the Staff Student Engagement Survey (SSES) as a complement to the student data collection. The SSES is a survey of academic staff about students, which builds on the foundations set by the Faculty Survey of Student Engagement (FSSE) (FSSE, 2009). The Staff Student Engagement Questionnaire (SSEQ) measures academics' expectations for student engagement in educational practices that have been linked empirically with high quality learning and development. Data is collected from staff, but students remain the unit of analysis.

Compared with student feedback, relatively little information from academic staff has been collected in Australasian higher education. The SSES builds on processes developed in recent surveys of staff and leaders (Coates et al., 2008; Scott et al., 2008). Information from staff is important, as it can help identify relationships and gaps between student engagement and staff expectations, engage staff in discussions about student engagement and in student feedback processes. It can also provide information on staff awareness and perceptions of student learning and enable benchmarking of staff responses across institutions.

In summary, the AUSSE provides information about students' intrinsic involvement with their learning, and the extent to which they are making use of available educational opportunities. As such, it offers information on learning processes, is a reliable proxy for learning outcomes, and provides diagnostic measures for learning enhancement activities. This data can be a powerful means for driving educational change, particularly when linked with feedback from staff.

Feedback from employers

Graduate employers are important stakeholders in higher education who have the capacity to offer independent information on the quality of graduate outcomes. Surprisingly, this relevance has been generally reflected in formal quality monitoring activities. In Australia, a large amount of data is collected on learners and educational providers. Considering employers' relevance to education and the lack of available data, there would appear to be considerable value in collecting data from these stakeholders for use in quality assurance and improvement activities.

A model for collecting data from employers associated with tertiary institutions was developed in Australia in 2006 and 2007, and deployed nationally to all registered training organisations in late 2008. Three 'quality indicators' were developed to underpin a new outcomes-focused and evidence-based approach to monitoring quality in Australia's vocational education and training system (PhillipsKPA, 2006; Coates and Hillman, 2007; NQC, 2007). 'Employer satisfaction' was defined as one of the three indicators, the others being 'learner engagement' and 'competency completion'. Instruments and collection systems were developed to assist organisations collect data in each of these areas.

After design and national validation (Coates and Hillman, 2007; ACER, 2009b), the Employer Questionnaire (EQ) was developed to measure three domains (training quality, work readiness and training conditions) and the following sub-scales: trainer quality, overall satisfaction and the effectiveness of assessment, training relevance and competency development, training resources and the effectiveness of support. The EQ is designed to support training organisations to collect data from employers on the quality of education and, more generally, to enhance relationships between education providers and this key stakeholder group.

While the EQ instrument and associated collection systems were developed for use by vocational rather than higher education providers there is, as noted, an important need for such feedback in higher education. Given the increasing economic importance of higher education to the global knowledge economy, it is difficult to see why and how employer perspectives could not become more valued. Employers see graduates in context and are in a unique position to assess their capability and performance. Further, it is likely that many of the same phenomena might be measured in higher education as in more vocational types of training, including employers' perceptions of teaching quality, graduates' work readiness and educational conditions.

Measuring academic achievement

Prompted by calls from a number of directions for greater information about the academic standards of Australian higher education, Australia's higher education quality agency released a discussion paper in mid-2009 on the nature and assessment of academic standards. Following Coates (2007a), the paper identified a number of approaches that Australian institutions might use to monitor the standards of their educational provision. An eclectic selection of approaches is presented here to stimulate thinking in this area and serve as a guide to practice. Many, if not most, are already in use, although their use may not be widespread or applied in the most relevant areas.

Following the point made above, improving the tasks and processes that are used to record and inform students' learning will likely involve robust review of assessment tasks to ensure that the instruments used to assess student achievement have broadly similar measurement characteristics. Achieving consistency across tasks is vital, because variations in task severity will register as variations in student achievement, regardless of actual competence. Such review could be undertaken as an ongoing process by disciplinary groups. Disciplinary groupings may also work together to prepare exemplars, schemas and item banks to facilitate reliable assessment against specified standards.

As flagged above, supplementary data from objective assessments could be used to underpin assessments of academic achievement. Such data can provide external points of reference which help calibrate standards in a local context and validate assessment processes and outcomes. Institutions and disciplines are increasingly undertaking objective tests of student capability – either of a generic or discipline-focused nature – to inform moderation and final grading. Similar triangulation may be obtained by drawing, where appropriate, on licensing examinations, consistent feedback from graduate employers or professional bodies, or other information about the performance of graduates. Such activities would need careful definition and need to be managed as part of the wider assessment of overall achievement.

Most Australian institutions have developed general learning outcomes ('graduate attributes'), in addition to the discipline-specific ones which are used to define students' experiences, and therefore achievement, at that institution. These attributes need to be measured and graded. In the absence of a rigorous assessment approach to such tasks, they are not likely to be valued by students. Introducing standardised and understood methods of assessing and grading these attributes, at the level of difficulty appropriate to the stage of the learning process, ensures that students better understand why they must learn particular things and also provides meaningful evidence to use as part of their future career activities. An interesting approach to helping teaching staff improve practice in this area has been developed through the Valid Assessment of Learning in Undergraduate Education (VALUE) project (AAC&U, 2009). The VALUE project has developed 'metarubrics' which chart performance thresholds on various competencies, and which can be used by teachers and course coordinators to organise thinking about student performance.

A standards-referenced system of moderation could be developed in a similar way to the UK external examiner system, with appropriate revisions and enhancements. This system has been seen to provide assurance that students are performing at an appropriate level. However, ensuring the comparability of assessment processes is not sufficient to ensure the assessment of achievement against specified standards. A rigorous moderation process would need moderators within a discipline to work together and to make reference to the specified standards in addition to grading processes and outcomes. It would probably also involve benchmarking across institutions.

Setting new parameters

The current analysis has offered a contextualised perspective on the development and future directions of quality assessment in Australian higher education. It has focused in particular on detailing a series of assessment resources which institutions can use to capture feedback on the quality of learning and teaching and hence of their educational provision. Table 11.1 summarises the resources discussed in terms of their main focus. This list is indicative and forward-looking. It is designed to provide a basis for further analysis. Suggestive comments are made by way of conclusion on key relations between continuous improvement, competition and quality assurance.

As new forms of quality management take shape, it is important that external regulation is aligned with internal improvement. This has not hitherto been the case, as illustrated by the conceptual and technical differences between the national CEQ and institution-specific TQI. The AUSSE, EQ and CLA were developed with the explicit intention of bridging this divide – of providing information for internal use by institutions that can be benchmarked cross-institutionally and cross-nationally. This approach should underpin all quality management activities to ensure that detached shells are not built around the educational life of the institution. The measures used for external monitoring must also be capable of enhancing learning on the ground.

| Table 11.1 | Assessment resources reviewed |

Focus	Resource
Graduate outcomes	Graduate Destination Survey (GDS)
	Graduate Skills Assessment (GSA)
	Work Readiness Assessment Package (WRAP)
	Collegiate Learning Assessment (CLA)
	Employer Questionnaire (EQ)
Learning processes	Staff Student Engagement Questionnaire (SSEQ)
	Student Engagement Questionnaire (SEQ)
Academic achievement	VALUE metarubrics
	Validated assessments (various)
Teaching quality	Course Experience Questionnaire (CEQ)
	Teaching quality instruments (various)

It is vital that the measures developed for quality management provide information to the public. Essential asymmetries underpin the relation between potential students and universities, but in an increasingly competitive operating environment potential consumers need to be ever-more informed about the nature of the educational service in which they are considering being enrolled. With only a few exceptions (DEEWR, 2009; Hobsons, 2009), this has not typically been the case in Australia. The reports of institutional quality audits, for instance, have not been prepared in a consumer-friendly or generalisable format (see AUQA, 2009). The popularity of institution-level rankings, despite their uncertain methodological properties, is no doubt partly due to demand from the public for non-specialist information on university quality.

More specifically, the quality indicators reported publicly need to express the diversity of each institution and allow them to demonstrate their respective competitive advantages. The initiation of a multidimensional classification/ranking system by the European Commission signals a way in which this may unfold, either at the institutional or programmatic levels. Rather than stack all institutions in a single linear pile, this approach has the potential to allow them to play to their strengths, to demonstrate core quality against key measures and to spotlight their unique characteristics on more contextually specific measures.

Quality information should also play a role in shaping the aspirations and intentions of potential students, particularly those from disadvantaged backgrounds or who have not yet engaged in the system. To do this, the indicators need to be able to capture the personal and professional value that is obtained from a higher education qualification. This information needs to be reported in ways that speak to different segments of the potential student population.

The future approaches and instruments for higher education must link substantively and methodologically with those from school and vocational systems. Further, they must be international or internationalisable in character. Building substantive links may require new and flexible conceptions of university education. It may require the uptake of different methodologies, particularly as many of those used for large-scale school assessments are considerably more sophisticated than common practice in higher education.

This chapter has charted recent trends in quality management in Australian universities, and outlined instruments which have been used to operationalise key ideas. In doing this, it has highlighted a trajectory that, it is proposed, reflects a continued move towards more evidence-based, student-centred and outcomes-focused forms of quality management. Despite its critics and inherent difficulties, it seems very likely that such large-scale evaluation of university education is here to stay. Indeed, a wave of recent developments suggest that this is a fast growing area of higher education. As greater significance is placed on the outcomes of measurement, a greater significance needs to be placed on measurement itself. This shift from institutional inputs, to teaching processes, to student outcomes carries implications for the instruments and collections that are required for quality management, and the ways in which data is reported and used.

References

Association of American Colleges and Universities (AAC&U) (2009). *VALUE: Valid Assessment of Learning in Undergraduate Education*. Available at: *http://www.aacu.org/value/index.cfm* (accessed 1 March 2009).

Astin, A.W. (1985) *Achieving Educational Excellence: A Critical Analysis of Priorities and Practices in Higher Education*. San Francisco CA: Jossey Bass.

Astin, A.W. (1979) *Assessment for Excellence: The Philosophy and Practice of Assessment and Evaluation in Higher Education*. New York: Maxwell Macmillan International.

Astin, A.W. (1993) *What Matters in College: Four Critical Years Revisited*. San Francisco CA: Jossey Bass.

Australian Chamber of Commerce and Industry (ACCI) and Business Council of Australia (BCA) (2002) *Employability Skills for the Future.* Canberra: Department of Education, Science and Technology.

Australian Council for Educational Research (ACER) (2001) *Graduate Skills Assessment.* Canberra: Department of Education, Training and Youth Affairs.

Australian Council for Educational Research (ACER) (2009a) Australasian Survey of Student Engagement (AUSSE). Available at: *www.acer.edu.au/ausse/* (accessed 1 February 2009).

Australian Council for Educational Research (ACER) (2009b) Employer Questionnaire (EQ). Available at: *http://www.acer.edu.au/aqtf/employerqi. html* (accessed 1 March 2009).

Australian Government (2009) *Transforming Australia's Higher Education System.* Canberra: Commonwealth of Australia.

Australian Universities Quality Agency (AUQA) (2009) *Audits: Universities.* Available at: *http://www.auqa.edu.au/qualityaudit/universities/* (accessed 1 March 2009).

Barrie, S. (2009) *The National Graduate Attributes Project.* Sydney: Australian Learning and Teaching Council.

Benjamin, R., Chun, M., Hardison, C., Hong, E., Jackson, C., Kugelmass, H., Nemeth, A. and Shavelson, R. (2009) *Returning to Learning in an Age of Assessment: Introducing the Rationale of the Collegiate Learning Assessment.* New York: Council for Aid to Education.

Bottani, N. and Tuijnman, A. (1994) 'International Education Indicators: Framework, development and interpretation', in A. Tuijnman and N. Bottani (eds) *Making Education Count: Developing and Using International Indicators.* Paris: OECD.

Chickering, A.W. and Gamson, Z.F. (1987) 'Seven principles for good practice in undergraduate education', *AAHE Bulletin*, 39(7): 3–7.

Coates, H. (2006a) 'Excellent measures precede measures of excellence', *Proceedings of AUQF2006 Conference.* Melbourne: Australian Universities Quality Agency.

Coates, H. (2006b) *Student Engagement in Campus-based and Online Education: University Connections.* London: Routledge.

Coates, H. (2007a) 'Developing generalisable measures of knowledge and skill outcomes in higher education', *Proceedings of AUQF2007 Conference.* Melbourne: Australian Universities Quality Agency.

Coates, H. (2007b) 'Universities on the Catwalk: Models for performance ranking in Australia', *Higher Education Management and Policy*, 19(2), 1–17.

Coates, H. (2009) 'What's the difference? A model for measuring the value added by higher education in Australia', *Higher Education Management and Policy*, 21(1), 69–88.

Coates, H. and Hillman, K. (2007) *Development of Instruments and Collections for the AQTF 2007 Quality Indicators.* Canberra: Department of Education, Employment and Workplace Relations.

Coates, H., Goedegebuure, L., van der Lee, J. and Meek, L. (2008) *The Australian Academic Profession: A First Overview.* Armidale, Australia: Centre for Higher Education Management and Policy.

Council for Aid to Education (CAE) (2009) *Collegiate Learning Assessment.* Available at: *http://www.cae.org/content/pro_collegiate.html/* (accessed 1 February 2009).

Davies, W. M., Hirschberg, J., Johnston, C. and Lye, J. (2010) 'Transforming student evaluation of teaching surveys to quality improvement indices', *Assessment and Evaluation in Higher Education,* 35(1): 83–96.

Department of Education, Employment and Workplace Relations (DEEWR) (2009) *Going to Uni: Higher Education for Students in Australia.* Available at: *http://www.goingtouni.gov.au/* (accessed 1 March 2009).

Edwards, D. and Coates, H. (2007) *Development and Piloting of the Victoria University Student Dividend.* Footscray, Victoria: Victoria University.

Ewell, P.T. and Jones, D.P. (1996) *Indicators of 'Good Practice' in Undergraduate Education: A Handbook for Development and Implementation.* Colorado, USA: National Center for Higher Education Management Systems.

Faculty Survey of Student Engagement (FSSE) (2009) *Faculty Survey of Student Engagement (FSSE).* Available at: *http://nsse.iub.edu/* (accessed 1 February 2008).

Harman, E. (2007) *Raised Voices or Raising Voices? Taking Business at its Word in the New VU.* Paper presented at the Australian Financial Review Higher Education Summit. Melbourne: Victoria University.

Hobsons Australia (2009) *The Good Universities Guide 2009.* Melbourne: Hobsons Australia.

Jaeger, R.M. (1978) 'About educational indicators: statistics on the conditions and trends in education', *Review of Research in Education,* 6: 276–315.

National Quality Council (NQC) (2007) *Australian Quality Training Framework (AQTF) 2007.* Canberra: NQC.

National Survey of Student Engagement (NSSE) (2008) *Promoting Engagement for All Students: The Imperative to Look Within – 2008 Results.* Indiana University, USA: Center for Postsecondary Research.

Nelson, B. (2003) *Our Universities: Backing Australia's Future.* Canberra: Department of Education, Science and Training.

Nuttall, D.L. (1994) 'Choosing indicators', in K.A. Riley and D.L. Nuttall (eds) *Measuring Quality: Education Indicators: United Kingdom and International Perspectives.* London: Falmer Press.

Organisation for Economic Cooperation and Development (OECD) (2008) *Education at a Glance 2008: OECD indicators.* Paris: OECD.

Pace, C.R. (1979) *Measuring Outcomes of College: Fifty Years of Findings and Recommendations for the Future.* San Francisco: Jossey Bass.

Pace, C.R. (1995) *From Good Practices to Good Products: Relating Good Practices in Undergraduate Education to Student Achievement.* Paper presented at the Association for Institutional Research, Boston.

Pascarella, E.T. and Terenzini, P.T. (2005) *How College Affects Students: A Third Decade of Research.* San Francisco: Jossey Bass.

PhillipsKPA (2006) *Investigation of Outcomes-based Auditing.* Melbourne: Victorian Qualifications Authority.

Ramsden, P. (1991) 'A performance indicator of teaching quality in higher education: The Course Experience Questionnaire', *Studies in Higher Education,* 16(2), 129–50.

Scott, G., Coates, H. and Anderson, M. (2008) *Academic Leadership Capabilities for Australian Higher Education*. Sydney: Australian Learning and Teaching Council.

Thomson, H. (1934) 'The Australian University', *The Australian Rhodes Review*, March, 103–9.

Usher, A. and Savino, M. (2006) *A World of Difference: A Global Survey of University League Tables*. Toronto: Educational Policy Institute.

Dubai's Free Zone model for leadership in the external quality assurance of higher education

Martin Carroll

Abstract

Higher education is not value free. Notions of what is optimal or ideal are locally contextualised by such factors as the predominant religion, political system, language, the local employment market and the quality of local secondary schooling. As such, the external quality assurance of higher education must also be contextualised if it is to be effective. In the case of Dubai, the task of designing a contextualised quality assurance system is quite particular. Like many developing higher education sectors, Dubai is heavily reliant upon imported higher education; but unlike most of its peer states, Dubai, through targeted Free Zones, is specifically seeking to maintain the international nature of the imported programmes rather than customise them through the application of localised accreditation standards. It has developed a method of institutional and programme validation that requires initial selection of institutions based upon credible approvals from the place of origin, complemented with evidence of effective transnational quality assurance processes. Alongside the federal accreditation process and institutions established by Royal Decree, this has resulted in a pluralistic framework that enables a variety of models of quality higher education to be available within the United Arab Emirates.

Key words: contextualised quality assurance; values-based quality assurance; higher education system in Dubai; imported higher education; pluralistic framework of higher education models; transnational quality assurance processes.

Higher education is culturally relative

National leadership is, in part, about the values that underpin choices governments make when setting public policy. This is especially so in the case of higher education, not only because of the vital role it plays in the development of national economies but also because of its role in social development. Throughout history, this role has alternated between the maintenance of social values and traditions on the one hand, and the generation of new ideas and being an instrument for social change on the other (Bowen, 1972). To a large extent, the choice of which role is emphasised at any given time has depended upon the political leadership. This chapter provides the case study of Dubai, and shows how political leadership can have a direct emphasis on quality assurance systems which, in turn, can impact upon the role that higher education plays in society.

Central to the case study is the phenomenon of internationalisation. Higher education has ever been international in its orientation as professors and students have been drawn to universities in foreign lands since the ancient library (or perhaps now *university* – see Kamil, 2005) of Alexandria. However, over the past two or three decades, internationalisation has taken on a new prominence. For the more developed higher education sectors in the English speaking world (such as the United States, the United Kingdom and Australia) a shift away from higher education being the domain of the elite to being more broadly accessible, combined with limitations to government funding of universities, have created an economic imperative forcing universities to diversify their revenue streams. One of the main government-independent streams is fee-paying international students. Advances over the past two decades in transportation services and communication technologies make internationalisation more achievable *en masse*. Combined with new political and economic international relations (such as Free Trade Agreements), this has meant that staff and students are not only going to universities, but vice-versa as well.

The advantages to universities are not only financial. An increase in public accountability of higher education, combined with global networking (of institutions, external quality agencies, governments and graduates) has meant that an institution's reputation is increasingly linked to the success of its internationalisation endeavours.

Governments, which typically focus their higher education attentions domestically, are now having to confront the reality that much of the higher education activity ostensibly occurring within their political remit has aspects which challenge or even exceed this remit. 'National governments or agencies have difficulty defining their position and role towards quality assurance of international(ised) higher education. This may well be related to the fact that internationalisation is affecting the relationship between higher education and the national government' (Van der Wendt, 1999, p. 233).

Since that shrewd analysis, there have been several strategies designed to align external quality assurance systems with growth of the internationalisation of higher education – and the various forms it takes. These strategies have taken place at institutional, agency and multinational levels. For example, some institutions – and particularly in countries with developing higher education sectors where the external quality assurance system is not yet fully established – have turned to accrediting bodies from countries such as the United States of America for accreditation services. Some external quality assurance agencies (EQAAs), such as the Australian Universities Quality Agency and the Quality Assurance Agency have – for several years now – incorporated an institution's cross-border activities within the scope of their quality audits (AUQA, 2009, p. 40). At the multi-national level, governments and EQAAs are variously collaborating towards mutual recognition of credit, qualifications and accreditation results. The most notable examples are perhaps the European Higher Education Area's 'Bologna Process' and the Washington Accord (International Engineering Alliance, 1989).

Notwithstanding these strategies, challenges in maintaining the quality of programmes offered in multiple countries continue. One of the prevailing reasons is cultural context. It has long been understood, though not always explicitly addressed, that higher education is a culturally contextualised phenomenon. The quality assurance of higher education is equally culturally contextual. Quality assurance is a value-laden activity, and the values that are embedded within the quality assurance system are culturally relative rather than universal. One frequently hears the term 'international standards' used as if there was a common global curriculum for every field of study, or universal accreditation standards. There is not. The reasons for this are not only logistical – they are socio-political. Even in this climate of increased internationalisation of higher education, governments are reserving the right to prioritise certain higher education issues taking place within their borders. Sometimes these issues will be based on explicit values or religious beliefs. For example, the Kingdom of Saudi Arabia requires that all graduates should 'behave in ways that are consistent with Islamic values and beliefs, and reflect loyalty, responsibility, and commitment to service to society' (NCAAA, 2006, p. 16). At other times, these priorities will be based upon an assessment of what programmes a country requires (typically enforced through targeted public funding or licensure decisions) or even whether the specific curriculum detail aligns with the resources of a country. For example, the Sultanate of Oman may choose to have architecture and civil engineering programmes, but with an emphasis on concrete rather than timber owing to the lack of timber resources.

One government that has explicitly factored an awareness of this cultural relativism into its quality assurance system for transnational education is that of Dubai. Unlike other governments which have (internationally or otherwise) embedded local values into imported curricula through the application of local accreditation systems, Dubai has explicitly designed a quality assurance system that will embrace and maintain international standards in the truest sense.

In this chapter the term 'transnational' is used to refer to a form of education whereby the curriculum is sourced from one country (not only originally, but also in its continuing form) and offered in another (in this case, Dubai). This is a specific component of 'international(ised) higher education', which is a broader concept. However, this definition of transnational higher education ought not to be interpreted as limiting any other variables. As examples, the students taking a programme (and, for that matter, the staff teaching the programme) in Dubai may be Emirati, or from some other country including the country from which the programme originates; the programmes may be offered via a fully internal mode or, as is increasingly the case, offered in a blended mode (i.e. using a mix of physically-present learning methods and distance learning technologies such as online learning or videoconferencing).

The term 'transnational' may be used interchangeably with 'cross-border', but not synonymously. 'Cross-border' seems to imply an emphasis on the *boundaries* of legal jurisdiction as if that should be the dominant consideration; 'transnational' implies multiple national *contexts*. This chapter is based on the premise that the latter, more inclusive, term is the more potent influence on the efficacy of higher education and therefore ought to be the dominant consideration.

The United Arab Emirates

The United Arab Emirates (UAE) is a young country founded in 1971 and comprising seven Emirates – Abu Dhabi, Dubai, Sharjah, Ajman, Fujairah, Umm al-Quwain and Ras Al Khaimah. In the years that followed, higher education in the UAE was guided by four key policy decisions (MOHESR, 2007, p. 11). The UAE would:

- build and operate its own universities;
- employ faculty qualified to international standards;
- teach – predominantly – in the English language; and
- provide education to all qualified Emiratis – including women.

From the outset it can be seen that these were 'policy choices based on cultural values and social expectations of the county' (Fox, 2008, p. 114). The first and fourth decisions emphasised local control and a nationalisation focus, while the second and third demonstrated a desire to build a nation capable of operating internationally. Progress against these decisions has been strong although, as will be shown here, in the case of a rapidly developing nation, values-based decisions need to be revisited.

Since these decisions were made, the UAE has taken a federal approach to the provision of higher education. It established three public institutions to attend to the higher education needs of Emiratis:

- UAE University, founded in 1976;
- Higher Colleges of Technology, founded in 1989 (a network of technical-vocational colleges); and
- Zayed University, founded in 1998.

These institutions were established by Royal Decree, which 'ensures that appropriate due diligence took place to serve national interest and to safeguard the use of Government money. However, it does not provide for recurring independent quality assurance activities; these institutions are subject to their own quality assurance mechanisms' (Rawazik and Carroll, 2009, p. 80).

Today these three institutions cater for around 35,000 students (ibid.). Yet, in a report entitled *Funding Students First: Access to Quality Higher Education in the United Arab Emirates* (MOHESR, 2004), the Ministry noted that the public system was not able to cope with the demand from qualified Emiratis for access to higher education places. One must add to that consideration the increasing demand from the expatriate population, which is currently over 80 per cent of the total population.

This has given rise to a number of private higher education institutions. In 2000, the Minister of Higher Education and Scientific Research formed the Commission for Academic Accreditation (CAA), as a part of the Ministry, to provide quality assurance to all non-federal institutions of higher education in the UAE. This development was in keeping with the international trend towards having external quality assurance of higher education based upon peer review and explicit and internationally-benchmarked standards. Subsequent to international benchmarking, the CAA developed a set of standards for institutional licensure and programme accreditation based on those of the Southern Association of Colleges and Schools (USA). The CAA has subsequently reviewed these standards every two years (the current standards were issued in 2007). As of July 2008, the CAA had licensed 55 institutions and accredited over 350 programmes. Only degree programmes that are accredited by the CAA or provided by one of the three public institutions are recognised by the Civil Service for employment and promotion purposes.

The CAA's approach requires all institutions and programmes to conform to local standards. This has the advantage of allowing the Federal Government to exercise control over key aspects of higher education; it has the disadvantage of potentially undermining programmes imported from other countries by requiring them to change in manners that may or may not result in a superior learning outcome from an international perspective, even though it may result in a learning outcome desired by the UAE Government.

An example of this was the case of the University of Wollongong. Based in New South Wales, Australia, this university established a branch campus in Dubai to offer Australian degrees. Upon being accredited by the CAA, the branch became an Emirate institution and the degree programmes became Emirate degree programmes (AUQA, 2006, pp. 52–6). The institution in Dubai changed its name to University of Wollongong Dubai (UOWD). The programmes were no longer the same as those offered in Australia because they complied with different standards and were accredited through a different process and by a different body (i.e. the CAA). This is not to conclude the UOWD degree was better or worse than the UOW degree – only different. The precise range of differences is almost impossible to know: some are dramatic (the most obvious example being the number of years of study: 3 years in Australia; 4 years in Dubai); others more subtle. Some will be directly attributable to the application of CAA standards; others will be a consequence of transnational contextual differences. The key issue is this: graduates of UOWD could no longer say they had an Australian degree from an Australian university. This meant that separate equivalency arrangements needed to be made between UOW and UOWD for those students who specifically wished to receive the Australian degree.

There are other key issues in addition to equivalency. Studies of programmes run in multiple countries with students from diverse cultural backgrounds have shown that the cultural alignment of curriculum has an impact on the *perceived value* of the programme. One study of faculty involved in transnational programmes found that 'when values coincided interviewees tended to make more positive statements about the overall benefits of the programme; when they did not, interviewees tended to be more negative about the quality of the programme and its value to their institution' (Dunworth, 2008, p. 104). That particular study concluded that 'good practice demand that both the home and overseas partners familiarize themselves with the cultural and educational milieu in which the education takes place and can provide a rationale for the delivery of that particular programme in that particular location' (ibid, p. 106).

It would be a tempting oversimplification to use the above as an argument in favour of nationalising standards. One must first consider what are the values of the nation and its populations: these may not necessarily be the same. The case of the UAE requires particular attention.

In 2007, the UAE issued *Educating the Next Generation of Emiratis: a Master Plan for UAE Higher Education*. This *Master Plan* states that 'almost all elements of UAE society are becoming part of a global economy and global network. It is important for the higher education system to reflect this new reality in many of the activities it undertakes and in the kinds of educational experiences it offers its students' (MOHESR, 2007, p. 35).

Bearing in mind that over 80 per cent of the UAE population are expatriates, and considering the growth of private higher education and the increasing globalisation of the UAE economy, it is perhaps surprising that expatriates were ignored in the *Master Plan*, except that the potential to admit them into national colleges and universities on a fee-paying basis was floated as a potential strategy for relieving the higher education funding crisis (p. 31). Unlike policies in some other countries where there is a clear desire to nationalise immigrants as a means for developing an appropriately skilled and diverse population, the UAE's emphasis is on strengthening the position of Emiratis (which is understandable, given the extent to which Emiratis have become a minority in their own country). One strategy for achieving this is to maintain the status of expatriates as expatriates. As such, although expatriates are in the UAE at the behest of the Emiratis, they do not necessarily have a voice in the formulation and/or maintenance of the UAE's cultural values. Nor may they necessarily share in the same strong sense of commitment to those values and the long term future of the UAE.

The dilemma is this – many of these expatriates are medium or long-term residents with daughters and sons seeking higher education. The public institutions are, for the most part, not available to them although they may access the private institutions. In any event, expatriates may be more interested in foreign higher education than UAE higher education. Foreign degrees are perceived as being of better quality, and expatriates are not as concerned as Emiratis about whether their degrees will be recognised by the UAE Civil Service, because they are more likely to be employed in the private sector and in any event may not remain long in the UAE. As such, the international value of the degree is more important than the UAE recognition. More implicitly, expatriates may have greater affinity with the cultural values embedded in the provider institutions, the curriculum and the teaching methods.

The UAE has recognised and responded to this in a manner that augments rather than changes its *Master Plan*. Over the past few years, Emirate-specific strategies have emerged to complement the national strategies. The governments of Dubai, Abu Dhabi and Sharjah have, through their Education Councils, sought to develop their own quality assurance processes to manage the quality of imported higher education being provided from within their Free Zones (specifically defined locations designed to provide economic and regulatory incentives for targeted foreign investment).

This has created what Warren Fox, Director of Higher Education Dubai, described as 'a more crowded policy environment that makes national policy more difficult to plan and implement' (Fox, 2008, p. 119). The higher education policy environment within the UAE now comprises at least three parallel quality assurance systems:

- royal decrees (for the public institutions);
- accreditation by the CAA; and
- quality assurance undertaken by individual Emirate governments in their Free Zones.

The remainder of this chapter will focus on one of these strategies: the provision and quality assurance of foreign higher education provided in Dubai's Free Zones.

The Dubai Free Zone model of higher education provision

Dubai's strategic vision is to become a truly international city; a commercial hub for the Arab region. With over 80 per cent of the population being expatriate, demographic internationalisation is already a reality. Whereas in the early years of national development (1970s and 1980s) the expatriates were imported work-ready, the nature of the expatriate population is changing both as a consequence of the long-term nature of some expatriates' length of residence and the changing nature of the industries that expatriates serve. As construction projects are being completed, the workforce emphasis is shifting towards the growth of professional service industries that will utilise these buildings.

There have been fears that the current global financial crisis would bleed Dubai of its expatriate workforce (given that, unlike Abu Dhabi, Dubai does not have its own oil resources and is reliant on construction, commerce and tourism). Indeed, these fears have been fuelled by reports of rising vacancies in the housing market (FATTAH, 2009) and a cessation of work on capital projects resulting in a slowdown in construction growth rates from 20 per cent to 13 per cent (Reuters (1)) and the loss of thousands of jobs (Reuters (2)). However, population statistics reveal that the UAE – and Dubai in particular – continue to experience strong growth rates of about 3.4 per cent for Emiratis and 6.9 per cent for expatriates (UAE Interact, 2009).

All of this has led to an increased demand for expatriates to be able to access international higher education in Dubai, rather than having to leave the UAE to pursue their studies elsewhere. Dubai responded to this by establishing two Free Zones dedicated to branches of foreign Higher Education Providers (HEPs): Knowledge Village (established in 2003) and Academic City (established in 2006).

The Dubai Free Zones provide a location exempt from the jurisdiction of the CAA, where selected foreign HEPs can set up branch campuses and offer their degree programmes in their original form, unmodified by a requirement to meet UAE standards.

These Free Zones:

> thus provide a mechanism for bringing international higher education providers and programmes to Dubai in a manner that protects and assures the integrity of their academic activities and outcomes. This creates attractive international higher education opportunities for Dubai residents, without them having to study abroad. Moreover, it means that the programmes, while retaining their international curriculum, can be studied and applied in the local context, helping ensure graduates will be able to contribute effectively to the ongoing economic and cultural development of the UAE. (Rawazik and Carroll, 2009, p. 81)

There are currently 35 international HEPs in the Dubai Free Zones, teaching nearly 17,000 students – interestingly, including expatriates and Emiratis (Rawazik and Carroll, 2009). These HEPs come from twelve different countries including the United Kingdom, United States of America, Australia, France, Lebanon and Iran. Some of the HEPs are Michigan State University, Heriot Watt University and Middlesex University.

Given that these HEPs are neither licensed by the CAA nor have their programmes accredited by the CAA (although there are some exceptions), the UAE's Civil Service does not yet recognise their qualifications for the purposes of employment or promotion decisions. The increasing trend in enrolments shows that this is not a deterrent for many students, supporting the analysis that limiting higher education quality assurance to the application of nationalised standards is not necessarily the only appropriate strategy.

Nonetheless, there are quality assurance challenges. Experience with transnational higher education has shown that there are many issues to consider in maintaining equivalent student learning outcomes, and that

> a number of particular issues have emerged which suggest that, generally, a university's usual quality assurance systems designed for domestic operations require modification in order to effectively encompass transnational operations. In other words, quality assurance systems for higher education are not necessarily universal, but rather, are developed to address particular situations. (Carroll and Woodhouse, 2006, p. 87)

The creation of deregulated Free Zones and the invitation to HEPs from many different countries to come to Dubai has resulted in a plethora of higher education provision and their concomitant quality standards. This raises, at the very least, a need to ensure that the programmes are of acceptable quality, and that students and subsequent employers of graduates are very clear about the status of the programmes. This has given rise to an innovative approach to higher education quality assurance.

The Dubai Free Zone model of higher education quality assurance

The Dubai Government has established the Knowledge and Human Development Authority (KHDA). This authority has, *inter alia*, responsibility for the quality assurance of all education in the Free Zones. It exercises this responsibility through licensure of institutions and validation of their programmes. This chapter will not discuss the fine detail of those processes (which will be available in a manual to be published soon by KHDA) but rather will consider the underpinning philosophy.

Conventional wisdom suggests that while external quality assurance is essential for public accountability purposes and vital for independent assessment of improvement opportunities, it remains the case that institutions themselves bear the primary responsibility for the quality of the education they provide. After all, it is the institutions that provide the environment, hire the faculty, design (or select) the curriculum, teach the students and mark the work. Indeed, this wisdom is enshrined in the INQAAHE *Guidelines for Good Practice*, which state:

> The EQAA:
>
> - recognises that institutional and programmatic quality and quality assurance are primarily the responsibility of the higher education institutions themselves;
>
> - respects the academic autonomy, identity and integrity of the institutions or programmes. (INQAAHE, 2007, p. 7)

KHDA's model puts this recognition and respect to the forefront of its quality assurance processes, rather than its own EQAA set of standards. It has designed a process whereby the HEP must demonstrate its worth according to its own character and foreign credentials, rather than according to conformity with UAE standards. At its most rudimentary level, the KHDA model seeks to ensure (a) that each HEP Branch is a branch of a reputable and appropriately approved HEP Home and (b) that there are effective processes in place for maintaining the quality of the HEP's Home programmes at the HEP Branch. In the end, the degree earned by the student will be the degree of the HEP Home and not a UAE degree.

To meet these criteria, HEPs are required to periodically furnish KHDA with current evidence that the HEP Home is a *bona fide* institution appropriately authorised in the home jurisdiction. Some of these evidences include copies of the HEP Home accreditation (or equivalent) and the latest quality audit report or equivalent from the HEP Home EQAA.

The HEP must also prove that effective quality assurance processes are in place for ensuring that the student learning outcomes achieved at the HEP Branch in Dubai are equivalent to those achieved in the HEP Home.

One of the most significant items of evidence is a guarantee from the HEP Home, signed by two senior officers and bearing its common seal, testifying to the following:

- that it fully financially underwrites the HEP Branch;
- that all the programmes at the HEP Branch are equivalent to the programmes at the HEP Home;
- that all students of the HEP Branch are enrolled students of the HEP Home;
- that all students of the HEP Branch will receive their qualification from the HEP Home;
- that the HEP Home bears the same legal and financial liabilities towards the HEP Branch students as towards the HEP Home students;
- that, in the event of an academic programme or the entire HEP Branch being closed, the HEP Home will take full responsibility for ensuring the students have reasonable opportunities to complete their academic programme without suffering undue disadvantage;
- that no investor, academic infrastructure provider or other venture partner will be permitted to interfere in the academic decision-making of the HEP Branch.

Items of evidence required for programme validation include (but are not limited to) the following:

- side-by-side comparisons of the programme prospecti for the HEP Home and HEP Branch iterations;
- moderator and/or external examiner reports; and
- comparative analysis of student results for the HEP Home and HEP Branch.

KHDA established a Universities Quality Assurance International Board (UQAIB) comprised of leading experts in higher education quality assurance. The members have been drawn from nine countries – particularly from major exporters of higher education (such as the USA, UK, Australia, New Zealand and India). Members are typically vice-chancellors and/or highly experienced quality assurance professionals and external reviewers.

UQAIB is charged with the policy issue of determining what evidence would satisfy the validation criteria (as mentioned above), and for the operational issue of subsequently considering the submissions from HEPs. This blend of policy and operational input by UQAIB is unusual. Boards of EQAAs are typically focused on policy matters, with a competent technical secretariat handling the operational issues – often in conjunction with panels of external reviewers. However, in the case of the KHDA model, considerable emphasis is placed on what the HEP can already provide rather than the HEP preparing new information conforming to UQAIB requirements. Many (perhaps most) of the items of evidence called for are not common internationally and therefore equivalent items may be submitted. This reliance on a diverse range of evidence requires a particularly high level of experience and expertise to interpret and analyse. As such, UQAIB provides a very engaged model of leadership in higher education quality assurance.

The result of UQAIB deliberations are recommendations to KHDA as to whether a HEP Branch ought to be approved for academic licensure (in effect permission to operate in the Free Zone as an HEP) and validation of their programmes. UQAIB was established in 2008 and although still in its early stages it has already demonstrated its effectiveness as a model of quality assurance. One HEP has been closed down in the Free Zones for failing to meet the criteria. Others have had to implement improvement plans to prove their status as HEP Branches of credible HEP Homes.

Conclusions

Dubai's higher education trajectory can be seen as following a familiar pattern in the newer countries in the GCC (such as Oman – see Carroll et al., 2009), namely:

- establishment of a public higher education sector targeting local students;
- rapid expansion, through the import of higher education providers and programmes, to meet with growth in demand for places; and then
- consolidation of a diverse sector and increasingly systematic attention to quality.

Models of quality assurance are not value-free variations on a common process. Rather, each model can have a distinct and profound impact on social development. It behoves governments and higher education sectors to work together towards agreeing upon a cohesive vision of national development, determining the role of higher education in achieving that vision, and designing an appropriately aligned quality assurance system.

The case of Dubai is perhaps unique at this point in time. Nested within a strong federal framework for higher education, it has established a system that allows genuinely international higher education to be provided to expatriates and Emiratis without being altered to local context in a manner that may undermine its international character. Through usage of the Free Zone structure, the UAE has created a pluralistic framework without compromising the nationalisation strategy. The Federal Government is still able to target its limited higher education resources in the interests of Emiratisation.

Implementation of this model required use of meta-level standards, or criteria. Because of the greater difficulty in assessing compliance with transnational criteria than with more precise localised standards, greater reliance is placed upon professional judgement. To that end, a highly credible and engaged board has been established.

It may not be appropriate for every country to consider a pluralistic framework for higher education quality assurance. The UAE's international focus, large expatriate population, recent increase in imported education and limited public provision has led to circumstances in which a pluralistic framework was appropriate. Progress to date has suggested that this framework is appropriate and effective. This may change prevailing notions about insisting upon national standards in an increasingly international world.

References

Australian Universities Quality Agency (AUQA) (2006) *Report of an Audit of University of Wollongong*. Melbourne, Australia, AUQA.

Australian Universities Quality Agency (AUQA) (2009) *Audit Manual version 6.0*. Melbourne, Australia, AUQA.

Bowen, J. (1972) *A History of Western Education, Vol. 1: The Ancient World: Orient and Mediterranean*. London, UK: Methuen & Co, p. 38.

Carroll, M.I. and Woodhouse, D. (2006) 'Quality assurance issues in transnational higher education – developing theory by reflecting on thematic findings from AUQA audits', in J. Baird (ed.) *Quality Audit and Assurance for Transnational Higher Education*, Occasional Publication Series No. 10, Australia, AUQA.

Carroll, M.I., Razvi, S., Goodliffe, T. and Al-Habs, F. (2009) 'Progress in developing a national quality management system for higher education in Oman', *Quality in Higher Education*, 15(1): 17–28.

Dunworth, K. (2008) 'Ideas and realities: investigating good practice in the management of transnational English language programmes for the higher education sector', *Quality in Higher Education*, 14(2): 95–107.

European Higher Education Area. *The Bologna Process 2007–2020* Available online at *http://www.ond.vlaanderen.be/hogeronderwijs/bologna/* (accessed 17 July 2009).

Fattah, Z. *Dubai's Empty Homes May Double to a Third Next Year.* Bloomberg. com. Available online at: *http://www.bloomberg.com/apps/news?pid=206011 04&sid=ajPfdg1UZWRA* (accessed 21 June 2009).

Fox, W. (2008) 'The United Arab Emirates and policy priorities for higher education', in C. Davidson and P. Mackenzie Smith (eds) *Higher Education in the Gulf States: Shaping Economies, Politics and Culture*, pp. 110–25, The London Middle East Institute.

International Engineering Alliance (1989) *Washington Accord.* Available online at: *http://www.washingtonaccord.org/* (accessed 17 July 2009).

International Network of Quality Assurance Agencies in Higher Education (INQAAHE) (2007) *Guidelines of Good Practice.* Available online at *http://www.inqaahe.org/* (accessed 17 August 2008).

Kamil, J. (2005) 'Intellectual life in Roman Alexandria', in *Al-Ahram*, No. 726. Available online at: *http://weekly.ahram.org.eg/2005/726/heritage.htm* (accessed 28 July 2009).

Ministry of Higher Education and Scientific Research (MOHESR) (2007) *Funding Students First: Access to Higher Education in the United Arab Emirates.* United Arab Emirates.

Ministry of Higher Education and Scientific Research (MOHESR) (2007) *Educating the Next Generation of Emiratis: A Master Plan for UAE Higher Education.* United Arab Emirates.

National Commission for Academic Accreditation and Assessment (NCAAA) (April 2006) *National Qualifications Framework for Higher Education in the Kingdom of Saudi Arabia.* Kingdom of Saudi Arabia.

Rawazik, W. and Carroll, M.I. (2009) 'Complexity in quality assurance in a rapidly growing free economic environment: a UAE case study', *Quality in Higher Education*, 15(1): 79–83.

Reuters (1). *UAE Construction Growth Seen Slowing to 13% in '10.* Available online at: *http://www.arabianbusiness.com/539522-uae-construction-growth-seen-slowing-to-13-in-10* (accessed 21 June 2009).

Reuters (2). *Drake & Scull to Continue Dubai Projects.* Available online at *http://www.business24-7.ae/Articles/2009/4/Pages/DrakeSculltocontinue Dubaiprojects.aspx* (accessed 21 June 2009).

UAE Interact. 'UAE Population to Grow 6% in 2009'. Available online at *http:// uaeinteract.com/docs/UAE_population_to_grow_6_in_2009_/35846.htm* (accessed 20 June 2009).

Van der Wendt, M. (1999) 'Quality assurance of internationalisation and internationalisation of quality assurance', in IMHE *Quality and Internationalisation in Higher Education*, France: OECD.

Trends in quality development

Robyn Harris and Graham Webb

Abstract

This chapter outlines directions in the development of a more systematic approach to the management of quality assurance and improvement especially with regard to teaching and learning. It suggests that as quality assurance and improvement continues to grow in importance a new emphasis on management at the institutional level is emerging, reducing the over-reliance there was in the past for responsibility being assumed at the level of the individual and/or professional association. New data capacity through business intelligence systems is driving the ability to provide institutional accountability in all areas including teaching and learning, and this is leading to the articulation of an agreed institutional approach to quality, performance indicators, targets, recognition of excellence, uptake of good practice and remediation. External quality assurance agencies are yet to reflect this changed institutional context in their approach to quality review.

Key words: quality; assurance; improvement; management; business intelligence; accountability; professionalisation; teaching; learning.

Introduction

The management of academic quality assurance and improvement at the institutional level is where much current work is taking place and is the focus of this chapter. The emergence of measurement towards institutional objectives through designated key performance indicators is considered and the manner in which business intelligence tools are heightening the degree to which university decision-making is evidence-based and for the development of data-driven reward and remediation strategies. Traditional academic peer review as the core of the institutional quality system has been supplanted by these more effective monitoring tools. This shift has profound implications for external quality assurance agencies whose methods are yet to adapt to reflect changed institutional practice.

The importance of quality

Factors leading to the increased importance of quality assurance have been well documented over the past 20 years and include the following.

- The large increase in student numbers (massification) associated with national agendas for extending participation driven by new expectations in terms of qualifications for subsequent employment (OECD, 2008).

- Associated with greater participation and larger student numbers has been growth in the diversity of people enrolling for higher education (OECD, 2008).

- Internationalisation, especially in terms of international students attending domestic campuses (OECD, 2008) and universities opening off-shore campuses and engaging in transnational education.

- The entry of new higher education providers into the market including private, single-purpose and corporate universities (Morey, 2004).

- The transformational effect of information technology in all areas of higher education including teaching and learning, research and research training, and new and increased opportunities for student contact and support (Murphy et al., 2001; Crosling and Webb, 2002).

- Requirements for effective and efficient management and accountability given that universities are now multi-million or billion dollar enterprises (King, 2007).

There have also been associated societal trends towards greater competition, spread of the market economy, user (student) pays, increased consumer (student) choice and sovereignty, protection and increased opportunities for litigation.

The location of quality

As the importance of quality has grown, sites for ensuring quality have changed and continue to change. Quality assurance and improvement can be located at many levels, such as the individual, department/school, faculty/division, campus, institution, professional association, national or regional quality agency and international quality organisation. In the past, there was probably an over-reliance on the individual and professional association. Where previously this may have worked when individuals were spontaneously interested in improving their knowledge of the discourse of teaching and learning in higher education together with their practice, systems to ensure that all were thus informed, skilled and impelled to action were often ineffective or missing. Similarly, the problems associated with a reliance on professional associations for quality include the fact that:

- many areas taught in universities are not subject to accreditation by professional bodies;
- accreditation bodies are naturally concerned with accreditation rather than quality as continuous improvement;
- their focus is on the discipline rather than other levels such as the institutional perspective and/or inter-disciplinarity.

Where there has been over-reliance on quality at the level of the individual and discipline, there has also been under-reliance at the level of the department/school, faculty/division, campus and institution. These can be thought of together as the institution because if evaluative instruments, improvement processes and quality management are properly developed, they will allow comparisons at all levels, including departments/schools, faculties/divisions, campuses, partnerships and modes of the institution. The management of academic quality assurance and improvement at the institutional level is where much current work is taking place and is the focus of this chapter. It is also worth noting, however, that virtually all 'first-world' countries have developed national quality agencies and that many countries in the developing world are now following suit. This offers new opportunities for international groupings of quality agencies based on the establishment of common standards, a matter that will be considered in more detail later in this chapter.

An institutional level of quality

If quality is increasingly to be assured and improved at the institutional level there is need for an agreed, institutional approach to quality. Some in leadership positions in universities are deeply sceptical of a whole-of-organisation system, but the experience of external quality audits illustrates that without an organising concept, those interviewed during audit interviews often fail to put together all the elements and properly conceive of the institution's approach, policies, procedures and practices as a system. Whereas a number of national quality agencies have used the 'Approach, Deployment, Results, Improvement' (ADRI) scheme for auditing purposes, a more popular model used within universities and designed for institutional action and change is that of the quality cycle. Originating from the action research literature but slightly modified to discriminate between monitoring and review, the cycle may appear as shown in Figure 13.1.

In the area of teaching and learning the institution, faculty, school, course (programme), unit (subject) or individual teacher would be able to conceive of and demonstrate that planning of teaching and learning takes place, plans are translated into action, there is evaluation in terms of shorter term monitoring and longer term review of teaching and learning and that improvement occurs as a consequence of this process.

An institutional approach to key performance indicators

The Vice-Chancellor or President of many universities today can present to her or his governing body a one-page summary of key performance indicators (KPIs) demonstrating and tracking the university's performance. Typical categories may include reputation (rankings), teaching and learning, research and research training, engagement, equity, sustainability (environment) and financial performance. Each of these categories

Figure 13.1 Quality cycle

may have up to half a dozen variables and each variable will have an actual performance number, time series of performance usually measured over the last five years and targets often set to position the university with a comparable group of organisations, with 'traffic light' indicators (red being 'poor', amber 'average' and green 'good') providing an immediate visual representation of performance against targets.

Within the teaching and learning category typical variables will be student recruitment in terms of effective full-time students, retention, progression, graduate employment, graduate salary levels, students pursuing further study on graduation, student satisfaction metrics on the quality of teaching, development of graduate attributes and overall course satisfaction. Behind the institutional level of reporting are more extensive data held either in a data warehouse (currently in development by many institutions) or still in separate databases such as the student administrative system, teaching and learning evaluation system, planning area and so on. In either case, modern business reporting software such as Cognos allows information from the database (or databases) to be automatically extracted and drawn into reports, which may be viewed onscreen at the level of the entire institution, faculty/division, school/ department, campus, partnership, mode, course (programme) and unit (subject). Commonly termed 'business intelligence', this new capacity to produce systematic data on teaching and learning, capable of disaggregation and reporting at every level down to the individual unit and beyond, allows an unprecedented opportunity for the systematic implementation of the quality cycle across an institution.

Systematic data moves quality from review to monitoring

Under the category of 'evaluation' in the quality cycle there is an important change currently in progress. Universities that have made the investment necessary to establish a business intelligence capacity are reducing the reliance traditionally placed on 'reviews' and instead are moving towards 'monitoring'. Reviews usually only happen every five years or so and tend to be 'set pieces' which stand outside of and often disrupt normal operations. They are typically dominated by external discipline experts with limited knowledge of the institutional strategic context, and inadequate grasp of the discourses of quality assurance and improvement and teaching and learning beyond a specific discipline. With the new data capacity, 'monitoring' is assuming a greater role as institutional, faculty, school, course and unit KPIs are clearly defined and instantly available through the business intelligence system. The implications of this change are elaborated below in terms of the management of quality within institutions. It is also worth noting, however, that national quality agencies have thus far shown little willingness to move away from the 'set piece' five-yearly or so audit process that has been the norm. It will be interesting to judge the capacity of such agencies to engage in their own continuous improvement if they are to keep pace with the changes happening on the monitoring side of quality management within universities.

Using systematic data for reward and remediation

The new data capability allows each unit (subject) and course (programme) to be evaluated across a number of KPIs, each with target ranges and time series data. A routine report therefore allows the unit or course manager to see where the unit or course lies in relation to others. 'Others' can be defined variously, for example, as all other units in the university, those in the faculty, those on a particular campus or of a particular mode. As well as this kind of normative evaluation it is also possible to nominate a criterion value for each variable – for example on a five-point Likert scale, any unit with an 'overall quality' unit evaluation score of three or lower will be investigated. It is possible therefore to indentify units and courses which are performing very well on a number of variables and use this information to celebrate their success (perhaps with a letter from the Vice-Chancellor or nomination for a Vice-Chancellor's award), reward the teaching team, investigate what is making the unit or course a success and use this information to inform the development of best practice elsewhere. Similarly, it is possible to identify units and courses that are performing poorly on a number of variables, including student evaluation.

Most universities invest in academic/staff development with the total investment sometimes amounting to millions of dollars expended centrally, at faculty, school and/or departmental levels. Academic development centres have not, as a rule, deployed this resource particularly strategically in terms of expending the largest part of this resource in areas of most need, as evidenced by student feedback on poor experiences. Nor have the improved results of their work been particularly easy to demonstrate. A common criticism of such centres is that as they generally work with staff on a voluntary basis, much of their energy is expended in working with already enthusiastic and good teachers, whereas those who need their attention most are the least likely ever to come into contact with staff from an academic development centre. It has been a failure of university management as well as of academic development centres themselves that the sometimes considerable resource spent on academic development has not been deployed towards the worst cases of student experience, and that accountability in terms of being able to demonstrate improvement has not been required. However, with the new data capacity it has become much easier to identify poorly performing units and courses and for academic management and staff development management to ensure that resources are used to support remediation.

The remediation process requires clear protocols to be established and followed. For example, in an annual or bi-annual monitoring process, a unit may be identified as performing poorly and therefore requiring an investigation. Usually this will be established at the school or faculty level but if not, both are accountable to a central university officer such as a Pro Vice-Chancellor (Academic). Working through the dean to head of school, the course or unit convenor will be required to undertake an investigation in concert with academic or staff development personnel. The quantitative data already available is supplemented by qualitative data, which often gives an immediate and very good indication of problems, and other data may also be available especially from the teaching staff. While information from teaching staff can be useful, it also needs to be carefully assessed as the experience reported by students and the perceptions of the teaching staff can vary. The problem may come from any part of the learning process, for example poor equipment in a lab or texts not being available. It is common, however, for problems to be associated with poor educational design (e.g. poorly conceived assessment tasks), poor course management (e.g. assignments not providing useful or timely feedback) or poor teaching. In such cases the academic development centre personnel work with the unit teaching team for a set period – perhaps six weeks – after which the results of the improvement initiative can be judged at the next monitoring process. In this way the effectiveness of the academic development process can be clearly demonstrated. It should also be said that when a systematic data capacity and monitoring process is established, units that have been performing poorly and perhaps have been doing so for many years, may be withdrawn, as part of the academic renewal process.

The key is accountability

The kind of process outlined above can develop systematic quality assurance and improvement across the institution. The key is accountability with individuals identified as having responsibility to ensure that it works. Such responsibility starts with the Vice-Chancellor and her or his briefing of the Deputy or Pro Vice-Chancellor (Academic) to ensure that the Vice-Chancellor's reports to the governing body are complete and accurate. Accountability then moves down the management line to the dean of faculty, head of school, course and unit coordinator, and to individual staff. The director of academic development and her or his staff also have defined responsibilities with regard to working with identified units, either for the purpose of award/citation/reward/celebration or for remediation, as outlined above.

Given this action and management-orientated agenda, what then of the committee system which sits alongside line management? School and faculty level education or teaching and learning committees, and the university level education committee and academic board, should receive summary reports of the monitoring data and actions taken which are relevant to their level – in other words the amount of detail will diminish for each organisational unit at each level. By this mechanism all teachers within the organisational unit are kept informed and the process is transparent. This is a worthy role for the committee system. However, the locus for action should be clearly in the hands of line management, thus avoiding any obscuring or weakening of accountability that may result when responsibility for action lies with a committee, and especially one normally comprised of peers.

Lack of professionalisation remains an inhibitor

The lack of professionalisation of teaching in higher education remains an inhibitor in terms of improving teaching and learning even when a systematic quality assurance and improvement system, based on new data capabilities, has been developed (Webb, 2003). This is because there is no systematic way for teachers to develop a common understanding regarding the discursive practice of teaching and learning in higher education. It cannot be taken for granted, for example, that teachers understand the definition and importance of teaching and learning KPIs, the literature on student evaluation of teaching, the basic skills of curriculum formation such as developing learning outcomes, embedding graduate attributes, creating authentic assessment tasks, a student community of practice, theories of teaching and learning, regressive and progressive uses of technology and so on. While universities are in the business of equipping our students to gain qualifications that allow them to join the workforce and contribute in professional contexts, teaching in higher education remains the only teaching activity and one of very few professions that has not been professionalised. Virtually all professions regard it a necessity to gain a formal professional qualification, followed by registration to a professional organisation and a requirement for formal continuing professional development for continued registration. Were there a common expectation for higher education teachers to demonstrate performance in attaining knowledge and skills in teaching and learning through a professional process, the continuous improvement opportunities presented by modern data and monitoring systems and remediation in poorly performing areas would be easier to implement, and improvements in the student experience would be delivered more swiftly.

The future of external quality assurance

Earlier in this chapter the rise of national external quality agencies in the developed and across much of the developing world was noted. The establishment of these agencies has been followed by the formation also of international groupings of quality agencies, aimed at facilitating the sharing of information and establishing common standards. The International Network for Quality Assurance Agencies in Higher Education (INQAAHE) was established in 1991 and exists to collect and disseminate information on current and developing theory and practice in the assessment, improvement and maintenance of quality in higher education and 'to assist members to determine the standards of institutions operating across national borders and facilitate better-informed international recognition of qualifications' (INQAAHE, 2008). There exist at least 10 regional quality agencies worldwide, six of which since May 2008 have signed a Memorandum of Cooperation with INQAAHE to support the overall goal of enhanced global understanding and practice in the field of quality assurance in higher education.

While this network of external quality agencies is very active, it is not well connected with the changing trends in institutional quality systems described in this chapter and agencies are yet to amend their methods for external quality oversight to take account of these new approaches. The 'Guidelines of Good Practice in Quality Assurance' (INQAAHE, 2006) presuppose a method for external quality assurance that is the current dominant methodology of self-review, peer visit and documentary (or statistical) evidence followed by presentation of a public report. This method will become less well suited as the level of sophistication in quality monitoring and evaluation in evidence within higher education institutions continues to develop. To remain relevant and expend tax payer funding in the most effective and efficient manner, external agencies have an obligation to ensure that their approach to assessing the quality systems of individual institutions is 'fit for purpose' and tailored flexibly to match the approach being taken by the university under consideration. Where an institution's quality system is based upon comprehensive business intelligence to drive planning and action, with the effects of that action captured and demonstrable also through business intelligence reporting, the traditional quality audit model of a many day site visit to conduct interviews with upwards of several hundred participants is no longer necessary nor warranted. Instead, the quality agency might call from time to time for reports from the institution's integrated data repositories to observe the extent to which it is progressing the achievement of its own objectives and taking responsibility for quality, which ultimately must rest with the institution itself.

References

Crosling, G. and Webb, G. (eds) (2002) *Supporting Student Learning: Case Studies, Experience and Practice from Higher Education.* London, UK and Sterling: Kogan Page.

International Network for Quality Assurance Agencies in Higher Education (INQAAHE) (2006) 'Guidelines of Good Practice in Quality Assurance', INQAAHE. Available at: *http://www.inqaahe.org/main/capacity-building-39/guidelines-of-good-practice-51* (accessed 8 June 2009).

International Network for Quality Assurance Agencies in Higher Education (INQAAHE) (2008) *Constitution.* Buenos Aires, INQAAHE. Available at: *http://www.inqaahe.org/main/about-inqaahe-1/constitution* (accessed 24 May 2009).

King, A.F. (2007) 'The changing face of accountability', *Journal of Higher Education,* 71(4): 411–31.

Morey, A.I. (2004) 'Globalisation and the emergence of for-profit higher education', *Higher Education,* 48: 131–50.

Murphy, D., Walker, R. and Webb, G. (eds) (2001) *Online Learning and Teaching with Technology: Case Studies, Experience and Practice.* London and Sterling: Kogan Page.

Organisation for Economic Cooperation and Development (OECD) (2008) *Education at a Glance: OECD Indicators*. Paris: OECD.

Webb, G. (2003) 'Management of academic development', in S. Panda (ed.) *Planning and Management in Distance Education*, pp. 87–97. London, UK and Sterling: Kogan Page.

Index